Politics, Plague, and Shakespeare's Theater

THE STUART YEARS

Leeds Barroll

CORNELL UNIVERSITY PRESS

Ithaca and London

Copyright © 1991 by Cornell University

All rights reserved. Except for brief quotations in a review, this book, or parts thereof, must not be reproduced in any form without permission in writing from the publisher. For information address Cornell University Press, Sage House, 512 East State Street, Ithaca, New York 14850.

First published 1991 by Cornell University Press.
First printing, Cornell Paperbacks, 1995.

International Standard Book Number 0-8014-2479-8 (cloth)
International Standard Book Number 0-8014-8275-5 (paper)
Library of Congress Catalog Card Number 91-55238

Printed in the United States of America

*Librarians: Library of Congress cataloging information
appears on the last page of the book.*

⊛ The paper in this book meets the minimum requirements
of the American National Standard for Information Sciences—
Permanence of Paper for Printed Library Materials, ANSI Z39.48-1984.

For Susan

Contents

Preface ix

Abbreviations xiii

1. Privileged Biographies, Marginal Shakespeare 1

2. Shakespeare without King James 23

3. Pestilence and the Players 70

4. Shakespeare after the First Stuart Plague: 1604–1606 117

5. 1606: Social Confusion and Creative Concentration 153

6. The Problem of the Later Shakespeare 172

Appendix 1. Playing in Lent: 1580–1613 211

Appendix 2. Plague Figures for Shakespeare's Stuart
Period: 1603–1610 217

Appendix 3. The Playing Season at the London Theaters 227

Appendix 4. The Difficulty of Dating Shakespeare's Plays
through Internal Evidence 233

Appendix 5. The Date of *Coriolanus* 240

Index 243

Preface

This book originally began with my curiosity about the effect of bubonic plague on the commerce of Shakespeare's playhouse. Although theater closings from plague had been generally understood to prevail in times of epidemic (1592–93, 1603), no one had closely examined "plague-free" times. I published a preliminary essay on the subject some years ago, and as a result the occurrence of theater closings because of plague between 1604 and 1610 may no longer seem unfamiliar. But in that essay I also observed that an awareness of plague restrictions might alter our notions of when several Shakespeare plays were first presented on the London stage. Since then I have learned that London playhouse closings might have had not only larger social causes, but also wider individual consequences for a playwright such as Shakespeare. This view in turn raised the question of the rate of Shakespeare's artistic production as a whole, the more general issue of Shakespearean biography, and, finally, the implications of this issue for historical method in the study of the Stuart social milieu.

Having wandered ever more deeply into this conceptual labyrinth, I have had to spin the thread of a larger narrative that would help me return from this maze. The result has been an approach that, redefining a number of "events" from known documents of the time, offers a narrative of Shakespeare's Stuart career as both shaped and impeded by his working environment—not only by plague, but by other pressures of the time as well.

In retrospect—a time in which all prefaces are inevitably written—it seems to me that an exclusive focus on Shakespeare, necessary if only to delimit a field of inquiry, may have blurred a wider panorama. Shakespeare was not the only dramatist implicated in those difficulties of artistic biography raised by the social forces that surrounded the Stuart playwrights. Nor was the early reign of James I the only period in which Shakespeare lived and worked. Thus perhaps the most useful directions to which this book might point is the reconsideration of Shakespeare's Elizabethan career (a subject on which I am presently writing), and, more important, of the dramatic careers of those writers aside from Shakespeare who produced the corpus of Elizabethan and Stuart drama and whose work was subject to the social vicissitudes that governed playhouse performance. Only then, I think, can a new history of Renaissance English drama begin, for history, whatever its many narratives, continues to insist on chronicle (however defined) as the soul of its endeavor.

Any book, whenever written, inevitably emerges as the product not only of its author but of the intellectual support it has received. The present work is no exception. Different sections of it were read by David M. Bevington of the University of Chicago, Sheila Cavanagh of Emory University, Jean E. Howard of Columbia University, Jill L. Levenson of the University of Toronto, Barbara A. Mowat and Lena Cowen Orlin of the Folger Shakespeare Library, J. G. A. Pocock of Johns Hopkins University, James S. Shapiro of Columbia University, James R. Siemon of Boston University, and Susan Zimmerman of Queens College (CUNY). Herbert Berry of the University of Saskatchewan, Michael D. Bristol of McGill University, Susan P. Cerasano of Colgate University, Scott McMillin of Cornell University, Gordon J. Schochet of Rutgers University, and E. Paul Werstine of King's College, University of Western Ontario, helped me greatly in correspondence and conversation. Laetitia Yeandle, curator of manuscripts of the Folger Shakespeare Library, has always been generous with her knowledge, expertise, aud time. I thank all for their collective wisdom and dissociate them from my inability fully to exploit it.

The Folger Shakespeare Library, where most of this work was pursued, has been most hospitable, especially the staff of the reading room, under the guidance of Betsy Walsh. Unfailingly supportive, she, Rosalind Larry, LuEllen DeHaven, Harold Batie, and Camille Seerattan have now endured several book projects with great kindness.

William Ingram of the University of Michigan and Rebecca Weld Bushnell of the University of Pennsylvania were enormously helpful with their knowledgeable and careful readings for Cornell University Press, saving me from many absurdities and failures of conception; I retain the credit for those that have remained. Finally, I express my special gratitude to Bernhard Kendler of the Press for both his encouraging support and his kind patience throughout.

LEEDS BARROLL

Washington, D.C.

Abbreviations

Texts used frequently throughout this book are identified by the following abbreviations.

Acts   J. R. Dasent, ed., *Acts of the Privy Council of England* (1542–1604). 35 volumes. London, 1890–1907.

Annals   John Stow and Edmond Howes, *Annals*. London, 1615.

Carleton   *Dudley Carleton to John Chamberlain (1603–24)*. Edited by Maurice Lee, Jr. New Brunswick: Rutgers University Press, 1972.

Chamberlain   *John Chamberlain, Letters*. 2 volumes. Edited by N. E. McClure. Philadelphia: American Philosophical Society, 1939.

Diary   *Henslowe's Diary*. Edited by R. A. Foakes and R. T. Rickert. Cambridge: Cambridge University Press, 1961.

DNB   *Dictionary of National Biography*. 66 volumes. Edited by Leslie Stephens and Sidney Lee. Oxford: Oxford University Press, 1885–1901.

Hatfield   *Calendar of the MSS of the Marquess of Salisbury Preserved at Hatfield House*. 23 volumes. Edited by M. S. Giuseppi. London: Historical Manuscripts Commission, 1883–1976.

L'Isle   *Manuscripts of the Lord de L'Isle and Dudley Preserved at Penshurst Place*. 6 volumes. Edited by C. L. Kingsford and William A. Shaw. London: Historical Manuscripts Commission, 1936.

MSC　　　　　　*Malone Society Collections.* 14 volumes. Oxford: Malone
　　　　　　　　　Society, 1907–1991.

Proclamations　J. F. Larkin and P. L. Hughes, eds., *Stuart Royal Procla-*
　　　　　　　　　mations. 2 volumes. Oxford: Clarendon Press, 1973.

SPD　　　　　　*Calendar of State Papers: Domestic Series, of the Reigns*
　　　　　　　　　of Edward VI, Mary, Elizabeth, and James I (1547–1625).
　　　　　　　　　Edited by Robert Lemon and M. A. E. Green. 12 volumes.
　　　　　　　　　London: Historical Manuscripts Commission, 1856–72.

SPV　　　　　　*Calendar of State Papers and Manuscripts Relating to En-*
　　　　　　　　　glish Affairs, Existing in the Archives and Collections
　　　　　　　　　of Venice and in other Libraries of North Italy. 35 vol-
　　　　　　　　　umes. Edited by R. Brown et al. London: Historical
　　　　　　　　　Manuscripts Commission, 1864– .

STC　　　　　　*A Short-Title Catalogue of Books Printed in England, Scot-*
　　　　　　　　　land, and Ireland: 1475–1640, 2d ed. 2 volumes. Edited
　　　　　　　　　by Katherine F. Pantzer et al. London: Bibliographical
　　　　　　　　　Society, 1976–86.

I

Privileged Biographies, Marginal Shakespeare

Biography is a difficult art because a "life" cannot be a mere chronology of records. Instead the biographer must reach delicately back through time—in Shakespeare's case, four hundred years—and through surviving texts to some notion of the reality of the historical personage. And because the number of conscious or unconscious reasons behind any of the subject's behavior may be myriad, the hope of accounting for all that happened (and did not happen) in a year or in a decade, let alone in the entirety of a life, is the height of optimism. In the end, any arrangement of the texts, in the widest sense, that underlie such a new "life" will fall along the lines inscribed by a psychological paradigm that seems obvious only to the biographer.

A historical "life" is all the more difficult when it attempts to display the career of a figure such as William Shakespeare, who seems in traditional biography to have participated in a psychological journey allegorically expressed by his work. The currently privileged "lives" of the dramatist have him leaving Stratford-upon-Avon as a youth, writing comedies in London, gaining status and growing in maturity and dramatic craftsmanship to arrive at the period of the major tragedies. These periods are followed by thoughts of retirement, the final "tragicomedies," and then Stratford again, with relaxation and death. It is often as if the plays inform Shakespeare as much as Shakespeare informs the plays. Or, in terms of a theory of "progress," the order of the plays determines Shakespeare's spiritual odyssey just as Shakespeare's spiritual journey—youth, maturation, and death—determines the order of the plays.

Some of the details of such traditional narrative, fleshed out, reveal the unnatural symmetry effected by this circular approach. Led by it, one observes the dramatist "in the period of his success" buying and selling houses, making money, becoming well known among drama devotees and being honored by the crown. Prosperously and peacefully plying his capitalist trade, the traditionally fabricated middle-aged Shakespeare emerges as somehow apart from the political and psychological configurations of his culture—the only tidy corner in a cluttered epoch.[1]

But the records of the poet's life do not force this kind of tale, which, in its emphasis on worldly success, lends itself not to what is known of William Shakespeare but to what is known of a contemporary who poses a suggestive contrast, Edward Alleyn. This famous Marlovian actor, later an entrepreneur, married the stepdaughter of his older business partner, Philip Henslowe (financier of the Rose and Fortune playhouses), bought and sold much property, took a percentage of all performance profits made by the Lord Admiral's Servants and some from other playing companies, attained the monopoly on bringing bear-baiting to court several times a year, and made a real fortune in the theater, founding the College of God's Gift at Dulwich. Shakespeare did not have this wholly entrepreneurial life, so the traditional tale of his commercial success in the theater cannot show the whole way to the profusion of such texts as *Othello* and *King Lear*.

Many business documents do survive which bear Shakespeare's name, but it is important to avoid that notion of the intrinsic which makes texts and documents signs rather than symbols in history. When time has left us a text—an executed lease, a published play, an absence from a list, or a presence at a judicial hearing—such a text becomes a locus, but not one with intrinsically real implications; these have already been defined and shaped to suit the program of the historian-narrator.[2] Like Proteus, the "event" changes as it is

---

1. As examples of this tradition, see S. Schoenbaum, *William Shakespeare: A Compact Documentary Life* (New York: Oxford University Press, 1977), pp. 237–238, or Russell Fraser, *Young Shakespeare* (New York: Columbia University Press, 1988), pp. 24, 28.

2. "Locus" is used throughout this book for that portion of a surviving text from which an interpreter creates fact and derives narrative. In this sense, the locus be-

handled. If Shakespeare signed a business document purchasing New Place in 1597, what are we to think? A current assumption might view this purchase as a desire for respectability or even gentility, but Shakespeare could have bought the large house in Stratford-upon-Avon for any number of other reasons. He may have wished to compensate his wife for his absences. The purchase of New Place on the other hand, could have been the least important thing, emotionally, ever to have happened to Shakespeare and Anne Hathaway. The size, concreteness, or expense of New Place as a physical building does not qualify it as the avatar of an equally massive psychic event. Buying things, receiving things, signing things, all transactions that generate physical records, are no more (or less) accurate indices of the emotional life than the (undocumented) forgetting, or losing, or stealing, or relinquishing of things. Domestic and business records need not inevitably melt together to refreeze into one canonical account of peace and prosperity.

Indeed, recent countermovements in the literary study of early modern English society—cultural materialism in England, cultural poetics in the United States, as well as the historical revisionism that many historians have described as "the new history"—have challenged traditional biography to bring into focus less comfortable elements of Shakespeare's English scene.[3] These writings have

---

comes epistemologically interesting because it serves as a differentia of various approaches to history. Any operation with the locus inevitably generates from it a historical "event" already implicit in the terms that formulated the operation. A locus becomes an event.

3. Jean E. Howard, "The New Historicism in Renaissance Studies," *ELR* 16 (1986), 13–43, is an important analysis. It should be supplemented with Louis A. Montrose, "Professing the Renaissance: The Poetics and Politics of Culture," in *The New Historicism*, ed. H. Aram Veeser (New York: Routledge, Chapman, and Hall, 1989), pp. 17–18, which notes the term "cultural poetics" as a replacement for "the New Historicism" as does Stephen Greenblatt, *Shakespearean Negotiations: The Circulation of Social Energy in Renaissance England* (Berkeley: University of California Press, 1988), chap. 1. For a distinction among positions within the study of "cultural poetics" regarding the role of history itself, see Montrose, n. 7. "Cultural materialism" has been defined by Raymond Williams in "Crisis in English Studies," *New Left Review* 129 (1981), 51–66, and specified for Renaissance studies by Jonathan Dollimore in *Radical Tragedy* (Brighton: Harvester Press, 1984), esp. pp. 153–181, 269–271, and most lately in the introduction to the second edition of *Radical Tragedy* pp. xxi-xlv, sent to me by the author in page proof. Cf. Marvin Harris, *Cultural Materialism* (New York: Vintage, 1980), esp. chap. 3: "Theoretical Principles of Cultural Materialism" differs from Dollimore in important respects. The concept of the "new history" moves in a different context from that established by the literary study of "new historicism" and is used by historians to indicate a questioning of both the

sketched the lineaments of a culture in which such phenomena as patriarchalism, mass psychic repression, subversive resistance to the containment efforts of the state, and other social stresses violently bent the gracious lines of traditional Renaissance vistas.[4] Current viewers have begun to make out a turbulent social and psychological atmosphere in that past time which not only generated mutterings, winds, and storms as charged as those today but from which Shakespeare's own dramas emerged as crucial signifiers of cultural trauma.

Yet, oddly, the illumination cast on the early modern English scene by such recent studies of Shakespeare's plays and poems has left their author himself in shadow. Though his works are now seen as centered in the dynamism of a strange new landscape, Shakespeare himself remains curiously static. His professional existence intimately involved him in the cultural tensions under current critical scrutiny, and he lived in the midst of those social storm systems now being traced. But, though this is obviously so, the same perceptions that are conceiving anew the difficulties of a Renaissance historiography problematize only the plays and sonnets, not the life and career of its most prominent figure. It is as if there were two separate conceptual entities: the dramatist, and his plays. The plays bob and twist in the currents of the time; Shakespeare himself seems to rest in changeless levitation just above these waters.

The reason is somewhat paradoxical. Many critics urging a twenty-first-century sense of Shakespeare's texts as interrelated with his culture continue to privilege a nineteenth-century daguerreotype of Shakespeare the dramatist and even to build on its colorless angles and lines. Traditional historical texts, with the old narratives still regarded as inseparable from them, continue to inform currently received biography.

Some recent approaches, for example, in order to implicate Shakespeare's plays in the stresses of his time, have nonetheless positioned Shakespeare himself traditionally—as in still-maintained views of his political relationship with James I. Very early in the Stuart reign, long-known documents indicate, the poet and his fellows were cre-

---

philosophical and methodological bases of history in general. See, for example, *The New History: The 1980's and Beyond*, ed. Theodore K. Rabb and Robert I. Rotberg (Princeton: Princeton University Press, 1982), and, for later references, L. Barroll, "A New History for Shakespeare and His Time," *Shakespeare Quarterly* (1988), 441–464, esp. pp. 461–464.

4. For a representative list of such works, see Montrose, "Professing the Renaissance," p. 36 n. 19.

ated by patent "Servants of the King," and some revisionist criticism, projecting Shakespeare into the larger social colloquies of the time, has depended on traditional interpretations of this event. The poet's dramatic writing, in his role as one of the "king's men," now seems to play out significant political roles—either through some dialogue between playwright and king or as part of propagandistic efforts in the policy programs of the Stuart crown.[5] "When King James came to the throne," writes one commentator, invoking a traditional story, "his first act in the literary realm was to take the theaters under his patronage." For "as part of his entertainment, James demanded court performance of plays." Indeed, observes another critic, "King James wanted the theatrical companies under royal patronage because he believed in the offering of theater as an attribute of royal authority." Players, by this token, "were the "outward and visible signs of James's sense of his office."[6]

It is immediately bewildering that the prospect of directly commanding a troupe of players could increase the self-esteem of an early modern English monarch such as James I—if that were the motive for repatenting an acting company under the name of the king. James had literally hundreds of household servants. Men of noble birth vied to be grooms of the stool—honored to be present at his defecations. In public ceremonies, the king was waited on at table by earls—one who proffered him the silver bowl in which he washed his hands before dining, another who offered him the towel

5. See Jonathan Goldberg, *James I and the Politics of Literature* (Baltimore: Johns Hopkins University Press, 1983), pp. 231–239. The matter was argued over thirty years ago by Glynne Wickham, who wrote that at James's accession "almost at a single stroke, the leading actors of the day were snatched out of the hands of their enemies into the sanctuary of the sovereign's personal protection or that of his family"; see G. W. Wickham, *Early English Stages: 1300–1600*, 3 vols. (New York: Columbia University Press, 1959–), 2.1:90–91. For more recent expressions of this assumption about James and the drama, see David Mathew, *James I* (London: Eyre and Spottiswoode, 1967), p. 234; Margot Heinemann, *Puritanism and Theater* (Cambridge: Cambridge University Press, 1980), pp. 36–37; Ronald D. S. Jack, "James VI and I as Patron," in *Europäische Hofkultur im 16. und 17. Jahrhundert*, 3 vols., ed. August Buck et al. (Hamburg: Kongress des Wolfenbutteler Arbeitskreises für Renaissanceforschung, 1981), 2:179–185; and Leonard Tennenhouse, "Strategies of State and Political Plays," in *Political Shakespeare*, eds. Jonathan Dollimore and Alan Sinfield (Ithaca, N.Y.: Cornell University Press, 1985), p. 116.

6. See Jonathan Goldberg, *James I and the Politics of Literature* (Baltimore: Johns Hopkins University Press, 1983), p. 231, and Stephen Orgel, "Making Greatness Familiar," in *Pageantry in the Shakespearean Theater*, ed. David. M. Bergeron (Athens: University of Georgia Press, 1985), pp. 22–23. See also Leonard Tennenhouse, *Power on Display* (New York: Methuen, 1986), pp. 159–160.

with which he wiped them, two others who performed similar services at the end of the meal.[7] In this context, the fact that Shakespeare and his fellows were created Servants of the King in a patent does not seem to elevate them as serious competitors for royal attention.

But for any historical narrative about Shakespeare's professional life, the issue reaches beyond such immediacies. To assume the centrality of Shakespeare and his theater to the Stuart court or to seventeenth-century London—perhaps the most enduring of traditional legacies about Shakespeare—and from these assumptions to fashion new approaches to Shakespeare and his time is finally to attach them to a secondary order of hermeneutics. One newly interprets received *readings* of historical documents rather than the documents themselves. And the very privileging of such received readings is what foregrounds the (traditional) theme of a close relationship between Shakespeare's acting company and the king of England.

Nevertheless, current historical thinking—cultural poetics, cultural materialism, and the "new history"—itself recognizes that the physically recorded signs of past human activity are not in themselves univocal. They are inevitably appropriated by a history into some ideology, and, as J. G. Droysen long ago suggested, the use of any text to establish the immutability of a fact is merely redundant.[8] A grouping of records can produce narrative to be taken as "the basic event," but the historical "fact" so assembled is no more real than are the structural principles that inform its production. The crucial point—that at issue, for example, between J. L. Gorman and Paul Veyne—is the problem of the very nature of the material that can be taken, or defined, as history.[9] Such material, often preserved

7. See, for example, the account of the Venetian ambassador in *Calendar of State Papers and Manuscripts relating to English Affairs, exisiting in the Archives and Collections of Venice and in other Libraries of North Italy*, 35 vols, ed. R. Brown et al. London: HMSO, (1864–), 10:121–122 (hereafter cited as *SPV*). When adducing such documents throughout, I quote the calendared summaries; in the case of *SPV* such summaries are from records written in Italian. Unless otherwise noted, year dates are English New Style.

8. See J. G. Droysen, *Historik*, ed. Rudolf Hubner (Munich: R. Oldenbourg, 1967), pp. 133, 167. Claude Lévi-Strauss expands on the concept in *The Savage Mind* (Chicago: University of Chicago Press, 1966), pp. 257–262, as does Paul Ricoeur in "Objectivity and Subjectivity in History," in *History and Truth*, trans. Charles A. Kelbley (Evanston: Northwestern University Press, 1965), pp. 21–40.

9. See Gorman's review of Paul Veyne's *Writing History*, trans. Mina Moore-Rinvolucri (Middletown: Wesleyan University Press, 1984) in *History and Theory* 26

merely by the predispositions of those who created it and culled by critics according to their own story-making propensities, inevitably brings instability to the basis of any historicism, no matter what narrative form it takes.

For such reasons, therefore, any approach to Shakespeare's career which seeks to accord epistemologically with the more theoretical aims of modern literary study must deal with records as offering not single but multiple interpretive possibilities.[10] Otherwise, the canonization of certain traditional accounts of Shakespeare's career finally moves counter to the aims of any revisionist approach to Shakespeare. Such privileging of supposed events as basic facts has the effect of grammatically (in Wittgenstein's sense) reifying what have only been presuppositions about historical causation.[11] And the result, at least as far as the study of Shakespeare is concerned, is not the expansion but the freezing of the number of available viewpoints that might otherwise be brought to bear.

As this difficulty applies to Shakespeare, new narratives from both old and new documents must deconstruct the traditionally privileged descriptions of the poet's life if we are to envision this life as consonant with an early modern England so arrestingly refashioned in recent criticism. And even though no single narration can rise above the theoretical problems inherent in the structuring of narrative itself, in the question of Shakespeare's life it is procedurally important to break the traditional stories of his career out of their amber, to deossify this old history before it is ironically reossified in the very effort to develop a new historical dynamics.

I

The approach offered in this book invokes the foregoing considerations to encounter once again the historical problem of Shake-

---

(1987), 99–114. Gorman's own views of the nature of historical accounts are to be found in J. L. Gorman, *The Expression of Historical Knowledge* (Edinburgh: Edinburgh University Press, 1982), chaps. 3–6.

10. For such aims, see Michel Foucault, *The Archaeology of Knowledge*, trans. A. M. Sheridan Smith (New York: Pantheon, 1972), esp. pp. 202–204, where Foucault succinctly summarizes his aim of allowing history "to be deployed in an anonymity on which no transcendental constitution would impose the form of the subject."

11. For Wittgenstein's use of "grammatical" as a description of a certain kind of philosophical confusion, see Ludwig Wittgenstein, *Philosophical Investigations*, tr. G. E. M. Anscombe (New York: Macmillan, 1953), pt. 1, § 251.

speare's "life." Even so, space and time allow an approach only to
a particular aspect of his biography. Thus I consider only the effects
of Shakespeare's society and culture on the manner in which the
poet was trying to forge a creative career, to wrest a living from a
largely untried and new focus of public expression. This focus was
the London playhouse, an institution only fourteen years old in 1590.
Modern enough to be resisted or espoused by state censorship, repression, or appropriation, the public playhouses and their professional
acting companies were phenomena so turbulently new to London
that no comfortable conceptual models had yet accommodated
them. Further, no one had ever been a city *playhouse* dramatist
before 1576, when the Theater (the first known London playhouse)
was built outside the city limits of northern London. Thus William
Shakespeare cannot necessarily have been able to envision how his
life as a professional dramatist would shape itself. One must therefore wonder whether his creative experience remained as serenely
Virgilian as biographies intimate, or proved, instead, a series of en-
counters with the unexpected.

But no single book can deal with such a broad question: the imag-
ining of Shakespeare's whole creative life. One limited study can
problematize only some constituent topics and this work considers
only one: the consequences for Shakespeare's career of his social
status. Even this topic is still too broad, however, and the question
must be limited to the matter of social status as it affected Shakespeare's professional career in the theater: his ability to practise as
a dramatist.

What problematizes social status in this regard? When Shakespeare, even after the success of *Venus and Adonis* and *Lucrece*,
persisted in writing drama for the public stage, he was, in effect,
deciding to remain in a particular social category. It is easy even
now to forget the position of actors in late sixteenth-century England. Players lacked the tradition of respectability possessed by
trades such as that of the merchant tailors, which had accumulated
wealth, an imposing guild hall, and over several centuries a good
representation of members serving as lords mayor of London. Those
playing for money had no guild. They had always been at the margins
of society.

Moreover, if players were thus unprivileged, marginalized as a
class, their activities were also suspect: they hinted social menace.
Since the 1570s when John Brayne or James Burbage had built the
first playhouses in London, playing had come to depend for its profits

on the presence of crowds large enough to repay investment in build-ings and leases.[12] But unless they gathered in churches, at executions for treason, along the streets for the ancient accession ceremonies of the London lords mayor, or for the very occasional coronation procession, crowds disturbed the authorities. Viewed as the essence of those subversive forces that the Tudor and Stuart crown meant to hold in careful containment, they represented a continual poten-tial for dangerous riot, and riot for insurrection. A melee of London apprentices in Southwark and around the Tower of London as re-cently as May 1595 had been so difficult to suppress that it even threatened the person and authority of the lord mayor, required a special proclamation and curfew, and culminated in the hanging, drawing, and quartering of four of the rioters for treason (see Ap-pendix 3). Playing, the very purpose of which was to draw crowds, had therefore to be immediately supervised by the authorities as goldsmithing and carpentering seldom were. To be a player was continually to be policed.

Players were also at the margins of society because they had no formal accountability to the authorities through the guild system, and thus (even though many in their number belonged to various legitimate craft guilds) they were in effect behaving as "masterless men" classed with vagrants, tinkers, and peddlers. The actors, merely to keep working at their plays, had somehow to evade this vagabond classification. So, long before the invention of the London playhouse, they had positioned themselves via a quasi-feudal social form into an imitation of the status of men with masters, attaching themselves *en compagnie* to barons and earls, becoming in theory their professional entertainers—the Servants of the Earl of Leicester, the Servants of the Earl of Lincoln, and the like.[13]

But these group allegiances did not bring respectability. They might offer elementary protection from arrest as vagabond or va-grant, but they did not enhance or even create social prestige. Players were never, jauntily, Lord So-and-So's *Men* as in current critical parlance; they were always the *Servants* of the Lord Chamberlain, the *Servants* of the Lord Admiral, the *Servants* of the Earl of Worces-ter. Further, peerage affiliations could not always protect them against group arrest when the city authorities did not want a com-

12. See Herbert Berry, *Shakespeare's Playhouses* (New York: AMS Press, 1987), pp. 1–44.

13. Clifford Leech and T. W. Craik, eds., *The Revels History of Drama*, 8 vols. (London: Methuen, 1975–), vol. 3, *1576–1613*, Barroll et al., pp. 3–40.

pany playing in a certain locale.[14] Nor were fixed salaries forthcoming from these nobles. The players, at the time Shakespeare came on this scene (1585–90?), had simply exchanged their marginal status as masterless men or workers-without-a-shop for the status of minstrels wearing the livery of some noble, but with no bed, board, pay, or state-wide protection.

Even a performing retainer, such as Shakespeare's own Touchstone, has a somewhat higher status. He seems actually to be living and eating his meals at the palace. But even if he is grand enough to run off romantically into the forest of Arden with the daughters of two dukes in *As You Like It*, he accompanies them because the last thing they fear from him is overfamiliarity or molestation; it is significant, too, that he is married off to a peasant girl. Also above Shakespeare's situation is Feste (whose employment becomes an issue). He, an entertainer, would seem to triumph over an enemy, yet even the Countess Olivia's absurdly presumptuous steward, Malvolio, is above Feste's level; for Feste, he is a great personage who must be brought down. Feste is as far below Malvolio as Malvolio is below the Countess Olivia.

Hamlet may summarize. Asking Rosencrantz and Guildenstern about a children's choir group that has become an acting company in "the city" and is satirizing adult companies, he asks:

> Who maintains 'em? How are they escoted [supported]? Will they pursue the quality no longer than they can sing? Will they not say afterward, if they should grow themselves to common players—as it is most like if their means are no better—, their writers do them wrong to make them exclaim against their own succession? (1.11, 345–51)

"If their means are no better." . . . In the end, playing was considered the essence of "base" for reasons beyond the masterless status that forced Shakespeare and his colleagues into artificial feudalism. Conceptually, in early modern England, any large crowd of people in itself suggested lowness of quality. They contrasted with the "few," at the apex of whom resided the aristocracy and the monarch—existing, as it were, as the genetic result of life processes in which a minute percentage had been sifted from the "many," as wheat from chaff, or as fire and air transcended the baser elements earth and water. Thus the players' introduction into early modern

14. See *Malone Society Collections*, 14 vols. (Oxford: Malone Society, 1907–1991), 1.2:180–181. Hereafter cited as *MSC*.

English leisure activity of a situation that welcomed anyone at all merely according to ability to pay admission, rather than according to individual station in life, defined Shakespeare and his fellows as common—"common players." Their theater was common too because mere money, not hierarchy, also defined preference of place within the playhouse. Players and playing place became the nucleus, the essential spring, of merely multitudinous activity. Players were the very spirit of the many. The common was their business.

Being a member of such a "profession" was socially quite removed even from the situation of another commoner who might seek to be a poet in the higher sense. Making common plays could give a Shakespeare neither the gentled leisure to create nor social prestige as a creator of writings considered literary in his time. Those with so-called literary ambitions—such as Samuel Daniel, John Florio, or John Donne—worked in a different way, writing to be read by the discerning, not to be seen at the public playhouse by the common crowd, many of whom might even be illiterate. A poet such as Phineas Fletcher sought to be understood as having moved away from his own social origins, not up into the aristocracy, of course, but up in another way, up into that transcendent (and politically harmless) class occupied for ages by Virgil, Horace, Seneca, Catullus, and more lately by figures such as Dante, Petrarch, Chaucer, and even Edmund Spenser. Samuel Daniel lived as a gentleman, his lack of funds remedied by financial support in patronage from the nobility or even from the merely rich.[15] Emulating Virgil or Ovid, such literati lived the gesture of gentility, making themselves fit for the cultivation of the countess of Bedford or Sir Robert Sidney, gaining food, shelter, and money from noble friends of the muses, becoming themselves enhanced in classical paradigm as latter-day Maecenases whose residences might be praised as Jonson, in classical ode, praised Sir Robert Sidney's Pennshurst. To those concerned with the accepted literary genres of sonnet, long poem, epic, and satire, the vulgar and its writings were simply irrelevant.

That dealer in common plays, William Shakespeare, if he ever envisioned such a classically poetic life for himself, did not seem to pursue it for long. Early in his career, with some versions of the

15. That Shakespeare was styled a "gentleman" in 1612—see E. K. Chambers, *William Shakespeare*, 2 vols. (Oxford: Clarendon Press, 1930), 2:91—and was probably richer than Samuel Daniel is evidence of a social vector worth separate exploration, especially since Daniel was then a groom of the queen's chamber and Shakespeare was not.

Henry VI plays and also *Titus Andronicus* already acted, Shakespeare apparently did make some kind of bid for the patronage of the earl of Southampton, as the dedication of his long poem *Venus and Adonis* (1593) attests. The move had some success: when the second long poem, *Lucrece* (1594), was published, the dedication, again to Southampton, seemed to thank him for previous favors. *Venus and Adonis* and *Lucrece* were republished often in Shakespeare's lifetime, but, though he was by 1598 known too for unpublished sonnets, Shakespeare either failed to assure himself of, or perhaps did not even want, the kind of patronage that might have enabled him to live the life of a gentleman-writer residing in an aristocratic household (if not of Southampton then of someone like him), or of a John Donne serving as secretarial assistant to a member of the political elite.[16] Shakespeare left the path suggested by *Venus and Adonis* and *Lucrece* to return to the common playhouse and its own financial possibilities.

It is not my purpose in this book to probe for Shakespeare's personal motivations in such a move. Even though awareness of the past creates its own conceptual paradoxes in that it inevitably conveys the appearance of teleology, one ought not to offer narratives that sketch historical figures making intelligent plans to implement intelligent decisions, experiencing consequences fully anticipated and hoped for. Such narrative, in Shakespeare's case, might suggest that, from the moment he was born, the circumstances of his mind and environment were bent to interact in the production of his oeuvre, and that his biography is best organized according to the sense of such inevitability. But a "life" is not to be structured as a well-made tragedy or comedy with emerging and developing plot lines. Theory must consider whether Shakespeare's narrated life is to retain its traditional symmetry or instead is to be described as a series of inconsistent episodes. Rather than an ideological advance, the "progression" of Shakespeare's existence may have been merely temporal: warped, challenged, diverted, or transmuted by the poet's culture into a series of discontinuities, perhaps not resolved but

16. Regarding the dates of the poems, Francis Meres' *Palladis Tamia* (London, 1598) mentions the "sugared sonnets among his private friends." As for *Venus and Adonis*, it had editions in 1593, 1594, 1595?, 1596, 1599 twice, 1602?, 1602 [1607?, 1608?, 1610?], 1617 and more. *Lucrece* had editions in 1594, 1598, 1600 twice, 1607, 1614, and more. I use dates from *A Short-Title Catalogue of Books Printed in England, Scotland, and Ireland: 1475–1640*, 2d ed., ed. Katherine F. Pantzer et al. (London: Bibliographical Society, 1976–1986), 2 vols. STC 22345ff. Hereafter cited as *STC*.

merely stopped by death. In this sense the poet's dramatic production, once he was well into the consequences of common playwrighting, might have resulted not from a smoothly articulated plan or a linear maturation of spirit but from a series of responses to the various circumstances of his time.

II

This essay in Shakespearean biography indeed opts for a sense of the discontinuous in his professional life and presents narratives showing that Shakespeare's chosen (or yielded to) way—to make the common his business—was fraught with unexpected difficulties that he barely surmounted, and at a considerable cost in creative energy. A most important consequence of Shakespeare's choice was the vulnerability of his creative efforts to serious social and environmental challenges. The common playhouses, as places of crowds, were policed—suppressed during times perceived as political emergencies and also closed every year by the observance of Lent. They were also shut down, in the early seventeenth century, by a persistent and long-lasting series of attacks by disease. After 1603, especially, Shakespeare and his fellows constantly battled threats of plague to continue their profession, and Shakespeare himself faced other rarely mentioned pressures that inhibited his writing. But because traditional Shakespearean biography still favors the story of a seventeenth-century idyll—a continuum of artistic creation, social success, and financial enrichment broken only by those inexplicable tragic moods that would enable the poet to write his greatest dramas—the dramatist's social vulnerability is a crucial issue here. Therefore this book begins by demarginalizing unpleasant possibilities and foregrounding calamities. Current criticism, has already shown the plays to be part and symbol of explosive ideological admixtures in early modern English society. The traditional packaging of the dramatic canon has been torn to reveal these works as societal symptom and commentary. But now we must also remove from around Shakespeare's "life" that insulation that has so often exempted him from mundane concerns.

Part of such removal must, for example, engage a powerfully attractive current theory. It is initially important to demystify the association of Shakespeare's company with King James, an association that has seemed fraught with privilege. Thus this study of

Shakespeare's working life begins with the court—and what the court was not for Shakespeare. In Chapter 2 I contend that the new patent that created Shakespeare and his fellows Servants of the King was largely irrelevant to their basic situation as common players and that their company remained the plaything of social circumstances, their welfare a matter in which the crown was not invested. In the first decade of the Stuart era, Shakespeare and his fellows did not become the wards of King James but continued in that social and artistic marginality they occupied at Queen Elizabeth's death.

To this effect, in Chapter 2 I present a reading of the salient texts that have traditionally and continually enhanced the social prestige of Shakespeare and his fellows for biographers. I argue instead that the Servants of the King occupied the same low level inhabited by other English actors; they continued to be treated as a lower order of servant, notwithstanding the traditionally held accounts of their receiving red cloth for the 1604 coronation celebration and of their attendance as grooms of the chamber upon the Spanish representative for the Spanish Peace of 1604, the constable of Castile. Indeed, their poor fortunes during the well-known plague of 1603 only reinforce all other indications that the company was offered little in the way of special treatment and that routine payments at court did not compensate for business losses in the playhouse.

Marginality brought other problems as well. In Chapter 3 I turn to the rather startling difficulties raised for actors by bubonic plague in London during the early Stuart period. This disease has not figured largely in recent studies of Shakespeare's life and times because so few well-known figures died of plague. Those of Shakespeare's contemporaries well enough educated to pen plays and tracts, compose poems, write letters, or govern the realm were not especially vulnerable to the disease which, unlike smallpox, could be avoided by members of the less poverty-stricken classes. Since William Shakespeare survived plague too, traditional biography has unthinkingly assumed his insulation from the problems that plague itself brought.

Chapter 3 offers an *annaliste* account of the activities of Shakespeare and his fellows in 1603 when the great plague came to London, showing the hardships that had to be endured by the company despite its alleged protection by the court. But this chapter also makes a second, more extended, point. The crown, being primarily interested in prevention, since no cures were available, did not wait for huge visitations of disease before the playhouses were shut down.

The perceived nature of plague, Renaissance approaches to gathering and applying statistics, the steps taken by the authorities to control plague—all these elements constitute the substance of Chapter 3. Personal danger aside, the primary difficulty posed for the players by plague was the steps taken by the authorities to control it. When recorded deaths from the disease—or from what the authorities thought to be plague—reached an agreed-upon number, the public playhouses in London were closed. And, it is important, they were closed not by the city magistrates but most often by the crown, acting through the privy council. Thus there is little indication of a scenario in which the Puritan city establishment urged plague as a reason to close the hated theaters while the crown, sensitive to cultural necessities, more benignly managed to keep the playhouses open. The crown perceived plague to be a clear and present danger to London as the seat of governance. Closing theaters, gathering places of the multitude, was one measure of preventing this danger.

Other authoritarian measures also curbed the life of the playhouses. Playing was regarded as too frivolous in Lent or at times of official mourning (as for the deaths of Queen Elizabeth and Prince Henry) and as too great a gatherer of crowds in times of political emergency. Thus Shakespeare's choice of profession led him to work within a social institution subject to suspension in times perceived as dangerous for any reason at all.

Such conditions, particularly those prevailing in plague times, figure in the discussions of Shakespeare's career throughout this book. After the famous plague of 1603, lesser outbreaks were endemic in London between 1604 and 1610. The deathrates were low, but often they were sufficient to induce the crown to close the playhouses. This chronic situation foregrounds the more important questions of when and under what circumstances Shakespeare was able to follow his profession during the final ten years of his career. In this regard, Appendix 2 lists the recorded number of plague deaths for each week of the years 1603 through 1611, and Figure 1, p. 173, offers a graphic synopsis of the conclusions reached throughout this narrative on the availability of London playhouses in this period.

Chapters 2 and 3, which remove Shakespeare from the protection of the royal court and subject his profession and playhouse to the increasingly disruptive conditions in his culture, are only the necessary preliminaries to the major narrative offered in this book, a reconsideration of the order and tempo in Shakespeare's production of his Stuart plays. To this effect, it is important to consider that Shakespeare had wedded himself to an artistic form whose conceptualization could be delimited by social factors. In Renaissance England before Shakespeare's death, public stage plays were seldom composed to be circulated in manuscripts or in printed books as was, say, Sir Philip Sidney's *Arcadia* or Edmund Spenser's *Faerie Queene*. Drama's existential mode was not print or manuscript but the motions, sounds, and colors associated with human actors in rehearsal or performance on the actual stages of the new London public theaters. Printed quartos of many such plays certainly appeared throughout Shakespeare's lifetime, but these books did not constitute even half of the plays performed in the period and they generally appeared some time after a drama had made its debut. For the playwright, then, such a printed quarto was not the definitive presentation, the gesture of the artist in his creative medium.

In Shakespeare's own case, many of the plays printed in his lifetime did not even bear his name on the title page (but *Venus and Adonis* and *Lucrece* did) and cannot, *as books*, have furnished their author with any personal sense of public presence. Additionally, and much more significant and dismaying from the point of view of an author aspiring to the literati, many Shakespearean dramas that did see print did so only posthumously. Such plays as *Twelfth Night, Julius Caesar, Macbeth, Measure for Measure* and *Antony and Cleopatra*, all printed first in the Folio of 1623, achieved their realization for Shakespeare not in print but only when he viewed them in rehearsal or in production. *Othello*, for example, was for Shakespeare always a manuscript or a series of performances; it was not a printed book until 1622, six years after his death and eighteen years after its first performance.

Shakespeare obviously seems to have acquiesced in this conceptual situation despite the fact that his times—though much less sophisticated about media than today—were yet attuned to the definitive prestige of the expensively styled manuscript and the printed edition—of the Bible, of Cicero, Virgil, Chaucer, and then Spenser and so on. By leaving the temporary path suggested by *Venus and Adonis* and *Lucrece* in 1593–94 to return to common plays, Shakespeare reaffirmed this crucial conceptual commitment. This conscious *literary* artist of the sonnets and the long poems now continued throughout his professional life to produce plays whose printing or wide documentary dissemination could never be assured—or even allowed by the professional company of which he was a member; for, of course, no copyright laws protected a script from being used by an acting group that did not own it.

This same acceptance, Shakespeare's subscription to the life of his art as inhering not in the publication but in the sensorial excitement of performance, subjected him to circumstance. His medium was the medium of the common, and when the state forbade common plays for purposes of public control—purposes that seldom obtained with printed books—there was no way for Shakespeare to view a new creation. Any play he might recently have completed had to wait until the playhouses were open again, although seasonal performances at the royal court, unaffected by such restraints, were an important (and complicated) exception to which I later advert.

The phenomenon of play restraint applied to all Renaissance public playwrights. But in Shakespeare's case there are indications that when, because of theater closings, he had no prospect of seeing a play in production, when denied that uniquely vivid kind of fulfillment offered by a dramatic production, his creative behavior changed. Denied the visual and auditory realization of his plays on stage, Shakespeare's creative drive for drama seems to have faltered. Such a situation seems intimated early in Shakespeare's career, in 1593, when the authorities closed the playhouses during an epidemic of plague that effectually erased the theater business for over twenty months.[17] In these circumstances, if plays were a writer's livelihood, he might reasonably continue producing them if only with an eye to the future, since presumably the plague visitation would not last forever. But during that first period of plague Shakespeare published his two long nondramatic works, *Venus and Adonis* and *Lucrece*. It is as if, with the theaters closed, Shakespeare simply did not wish to write plays. When they could not be rehearsed on stage or performed before the public—in these barren circumstances—his emotional and creative energy seems to have disengaged itself from plays to redirect itself into the writing and actual publishing of poetry.

This first instance in the early 1590s offers a hint only; it does not establish a pattern of behavior. The professional state of drama in 1593 may have been so disrupted by the plague that for a while Shakespeare belonged to no company at all and thus had no com-

17. See J. R. Dasent, ed., *Acts of the Privy Council of England* (1542–1604), 35 vols. (London, 1890–1907), 24:31–32 (hereafter cited as *Acts*), and *MSC*, I. 1:72–74. The first official restraint occurred January 28, 1593, and final permission to resume playing, October 8, 1594.

mercial reason whatsoever to write stage plays. But when the playhouses were reopened in late 1594, Shakespeare returned to the stage
with energy. And while the theaters remained open—until the end
of 1602, on the eve of James's accession—Shakespeare produced
perhaps twenty-seven plays, more than two-thirds of his entire dramatic achievement. It is therefore arresting that at the end of 1602
Shakespeare's output fell. The slackening is marked: between the
beginning of 1603 and 1611, Shakespeare produced only ten more
dramas. The scale of this abatement may be better imagined if one
applies this later rate to Shakespeare's first professional decade. In
that case, he would, before the end of 1602, have written not twenty-
seven but only twelve or thirteen plays, less than half his actual
output.

Perhaps this Stuart drop in production should not be surprising
in as much as Shakespeare's last professional decade was a period
of transcendent dramas. During those last ten years Shakespeare
was generating huge tragedies infused with such creative brilliance
and energy that mere numbers are beside the point. The output was
small but glorious. Yet to impose such arithmetic limits of psychic
energy on Shakespeare's career is, again, to substitute determinism
for alternate forms of historiography—as if Shakespeare wrote all
the plays he was capable of writing in this period because these were
indeed all the plays he wrote.[18] But could it not also be said that
during the prior decade Shakespeare's production also brought forth
many significant works—*Hamlet, Troilus and Cressida*, the Hen-
riad, the great comedies, and *Romeo and Juliet*—in addition to other
plays and long poems and the sonnets?

Because aesthetic arithmetic is at best fanciful, Shakespeare's drop
in production of dramas during the Stuart decade is not convincingly
addressed by the traditional practice of gauging intrinsic excellence
in plays as a function of the time taken to write them or by con-
trasting the vigor of youth with the relaxation of age.[19] Rather, the

18. See Richard W. Miller, *Fact and Method* (Princeton: Princeton University
Press, 1987), pp. 18–24. He speaks of such statements as examples of one of the
logical faults in historical narrative. He adverts to the frequent use of the covering
law in its deductive-nomological pattern: empirical general laws and statements of
initial conditions are presented which logically entail the statement that the event
in question has occurred. This maneuver can lead to such pseudoexplanations as
"Whoever is Napoleon [or: is born on Corsica of such-and-such parents on such-and-
such a date] becomes emperor of France."

19. For this kind of approach, see, for example, Stanley Wells et al., *William
Shakespeare: A Textual Companion* (Oxford: Clarendon Press, 1987), p. 92.

social difficulties surrounding Shakespeare's chosen medium have at least equal claim to relevance. To be specific, the response of the state to the resumption of bubonic plague in 1603 may have influenced Shakespeare's rate of production. Confronted by a Stuart decade riddled with playhouse closings, the poet who under similar circumstances divagated to write *Venus and Adonis* and *Lucrece* in 1593–94 may, for long periods between 1603 and 1611, have simply not written any plays at all.

I believe this to be the case. But if such a narrative of Shakespeare's creative life is to gain agreement, it must bring forward a complementary question: if Shakespeare did not wish to write plays throughout the periods when the playhouses were shut—when he could not see productions at the Globe—how could he have had the time to produce his last ten dramas at all? Between 1603 and 1611, the playhouses in London were closed off and on for a period of at least sixty-eight months. I respond to this question of available time by suggesting another of Shakespeare's behavioral traits. When the circumstances were favorable—when the playhouses were open and stages available—Shakespeare seems to have produced very rapidly indeed. In Chapters 4–6 I show that long periods of inactivity seem to have been followed by enormous productivity. The phenomenon is hinted at in the recollections of Ben Jonson: "I remember the players have often mentioned it as an honor to Shakespeare that in his writing, whatsoever he penned, he never blotted out line. My answer hath been, would he had blotted a thousand."[20] No matter Jonson's answer, it is significant that in some contemporary thinking about the way Shakespeare composed there is the notion of an unusual facility.

This study of Shakespeare's Stuart career, then, invites two considerations: first, that Shakespeare stopped writing plays when he knew that they would not immediately be put on stage—in performance, or in rehearsal—as he was completing them; second, that Shakespeare produced plays at great speed—at surprising speed. (He may, for example, have written three of his great tragedies in one year.) But this second observation, while not necessarily following from the first, is not inconsistently related to it, whatever the psy-

20. See Ben Jonson, *Works*, 12 vols., ed. C. H. Herford and Percy and Evelyn Simpson (Oxford: Clarendon Press, 1947), 8:583–584. In this context Jonson is blaming the "multitude" that commend writers on the same terms that they commend fencers or wrestlers, judging by the number of ostentatious flourishes rather than by the "slight touch" that wins the match.

chology of the pattern. For it is reasonable to imagine Shakespeare thinking that if, for him, composition came quickly, why write in advance against future needs? Or, if one could quickly produce plays whenever commercial need dictated, why write, it being . . . unpleasant(?) to do so when no stage was available?

There is no final way of telling whether Shakespeare's practice in these respects was attributable to individual psychology or to convention. Plays might not have been produced by any dramatist in those times unless the pieces could be rehearsed act-by-act with the players as the rest of the drama approached completion. Certainly the playwright Thomas Dekker penned numbers of pamphlets when playhouses were closed by plague and in these complained of inactivity. Thus, a study that would define Shakespeare's creative rhythm as responding to the larger motions of his environment must, while inscribing new narrative on the traditional records and texts pertinent to Shakespeare's life and times, try to avoid such merely essentialist notions of causation.

How then to make plausible this proposed narrative—this seeming dichotomy in Shakespeare of detachment and immersion, restraint and energy? When one examines the order and rate of Shakespeare's Stuart plays, the chief problem is that of method: how does one arrive at the probable dates of the plays? Theater closings, from plague or for other reasons, are not definitive; they can suggest to the historian only when plays could not be performed. What kinds of text reveal when a play was written? Short of authorial testimony, both the conception and then the time of the first writing of a play are unknowable. Even so, it is possible to pose an annalistic question that is answerable, at least in theory: when was the first public manifestation of an individual creative effort? when was the first known performance?

Such a question cannot be posed in hopes of achieving those certainties hoped for by positivist fancies. (Topical allusions and other presently privileged positivist modes of chronological measurement—stylistic tests, lists of metrical propensities—are all at best ambiguous concepts, with difficulties alluded to elsewhere in this book.) To gather annals is only to narrate in a certain rhetorical form from historical documents that allow, however, not one but a variety of interpretations. A history based on the records of events (letters, reports, proclamations) cannot be the only source of information about an English Renaissance playwright's creative behavior, but, in the end, such an approach is easier than other methods. It is easier, for example, than the superimposition of theories of (Renaissance? modern?) psychology on formalist criticism of Shakespeare's individual plays in order to define or establish developmental stages in the writings of a vanished human being whose psychodynamics are otherwise inaccessible and for whom the necessary pertinent social data are unavailable. If narratives about the sequence of a dramatist's works are drawn from the printed or written material of his culture which lies outside his work, they may not uncover the complexities of the author's motivations. But, by positing a series of external events, such narratives approach a different level of hermeneutics: they present historical loci which, existing as material for counterinterpretation, counternarratives, offer an escape from the redundancies of formalist argument.[21] One does not have to offer one's sense that *Romeo and Juliet* is a young play—and thus early—against someone else's sense that it is a mature play—and thus later in time.

Working within the confines of these methodological assumptions, I begin in Chapter 4 to examine Shakespeare's dramatic production from 1602 to 1606; using a variety of documents, including plague records, I argue that from 1602 to 1605 only two Shakespearean plays, *Measure for Measure* and *Othello*, were newly performed. In the following year, however, both *King Lear* and *Macbeth* may well have been produced. Chapter 5 adds *Antony and Cleopatra* to the 1606 scenario already occupied by *King Lear* and *Macbeth*; the Roman play may also have made its debut in that same Christmas season. Thus the productivity of this single year stands in significant contrast to Shakespeare's relative inactivity during the year and a half prior to *Othello*, as well as during the years between *Othello* and 1606, when plague kept the theaters closed.

Chapter 6 reviews Shakespeare's late career according to premises elaborated earlier. The pattern by which he composed plays in his so-called tragic period was not an orderly, evenly spaced chronological sequence but an erratic one with cluster points of concentrated productivity. His rate of composition and the company's schedule of performances appear to have been directly tied to opportunities dictated by the larger rhythm of playhouse accessibility in the confused London years before 1611. Traditional orderings of the Shakespeare canon for his so-called final period from 1606 to 1613, when

21. I offer such counternarrative for the case of *Richard II* and the Essex rebellion in Barroll, "New History."

presumably six or more plays were written and produced, often pro-mulgate a tapering off of Shakespeare's genius into his final come-dies. But again, the interesting correspondence throughout Shakespeare's Stuart career between opportunity and performance suggests a narrative that does not follow these traditional lines.

In the end, then, my general proposal foregrounds the ultimate subjugation of Shakespeare's dramatic creativity to environmental forces. But I also develop certain arguments about method. Shak-espearean biography, I maintain, must not only avoid assumptions about Shakespeare's importance to the ruling class of Renaissance England but also eschew unexamined principles of biographical sym-metry (such as Aristotelian processes of beginning-middle-end). Fur-ther, in efforts to refigure English Renaissance culture, the writing of literary history must discontinue the canonization of received narratives derived from merely traditional documentary loci. The potential relevance of nontraditional texts lying outside the canon of conventional and long-preserved historical vignettes, the evolu-tion of alternate narratives from traditional texts, the entertaining of concepts of discontinuity as well as continuity, of chaos as well as symmetry—all these are among the concerns that I attempt to bring to a rereading of Shakespeare's activity. Such concerns, dealt with here or elsewhere, can enable a new historiography of Shake-speare's time to recognize and deal with a variety of environmental and societal phenomena, a renewed sense of whose relevance has already been challenging twentieth-century models of historical so-cieties other than that inhabited by Shakespeare.[22]

22. See, for example, Christopher Lloyd, *Explanation in Social History* (Oxford: Basil Blackwell, 1986), chaps. 3, 7, 8.

2

Shakespeare without King James

Some recent views of Shakespeare and his company have deployed a narrative that is part of a larger ideology about the dramatist and his art, one that emphasizes the social importance of Shakespeare and his fellows in Renaissance London. Because the group became the Servants of the King just after James's accession, these views hold the performance of Shakespeare's works at court to be the expression of a particular political relationship in which the Stuart crown desired to use drama for its own political purposes to contain subversive forces attempting to employ the stage against the interest of the state.

Although "state" is the term generally used, the ideology of such an approach envisions early Stuart society not as a state but as an empire in Eisenstadt's sense, that is, as a political enterprise wherein the crown possesses all organized power and wherein the force to be contained by the crown is the single large mass of the populace.[1] Accordingly, this ideology problematizes the relationship of drama to the crown as the emergence of an important propagandistic medium the appropriation of which becomes crucial to the authorities; theatrical activity is a potential popular expression against the hegemony of the empire and, as such, it must be appropriated in order

---

1. See S. N. Eisenstadt, "The Causes of Disintegration and Fall of Empires: Sociological and Historical Analyses," *Diogenes* 34 (1961), 82–107.

to contain any subversive efforts by the populace that might be propagated through the drama itself.

The playing out of this ideology in many critical discussions of the dramas of William Shakespeare entails the assemblage of favored historical narratives. These works present documents that have seemed to place Shakespeare and his fellows in a special relationship to the crown. But such traditional recensions have overstated the power and significance of Shakespeare and also of plays in general at the royal Stuart court. The ideology underlying my own argument, on the other hand, assumes England during the life of Shakespeare to have been not an empire but a state in the sense defined by Fernand Braudel and François Chabod—a body politic with a prince, but composed of constituencies such as the peerage, Parliament, and the city guilds (which produced the lord mayor of London), constituencies that related to each other within a general formation characterized by the constant mobility of power centering.[2] Thus, although this position does not challenge the existence of a containment-subversion process generating political action in the state, it does not view the English crown as a hegemony in this early seventeenth-century political unit or the London acting companies as part of the formulation and implementation of an enveloping master plan for empire, including the detailed containment of subversion. Power—and thus the interest in containing subversion, however defined—was actually shared with the crown, by the peerage, by the city guilds, and by Parliament when it was in session. It was thus not relevant for the crown to exploit the theater in order to control the populace. From the crown's point of view, other constituencies were also forces of subversion requiring containment. The fact that members of the peerage (including the lord chamberlain) may have been behind the extremely inflammatory production of Middleton's *Game at Chess* (some years after Shakespeare's death) emphasizes the many locations of potential subversion in an early modern state.

In support of the ideology presented here, I offer in this chapter counternarratives from the same documents used in presently priv-

---

2. For these distinctions, see François Chabod, "Y-a-t-il un état de la Renaissance?" in *Actes du Colloque sur la Renaissance* (Paris: Lib. Philosophique J. Vrin, 1958), pp. 57–74; S. N. Eisenstadt, "The Causes of Disintegration"; Fernand Braudel, *The Mediterranean*, 2 vols., trans. Siân Reynolds (New York: Harper & Row, 1973), 2:681–701. See also John Guy, *Tudor England* (Oxford: Oxford University Press, 1988), chap. 13: "The Making of the Tudor State."

ileged biographies of Shakespeare. These documents have been used to enhance Shakespeare's relationship to the royal court and to foreground the interaction of his plays with the monarch. Critics, writing of James I, have implicated drama in the whole fabric of his theory, policy, and practice. In this more general claim about the political significance of drama in the time of Shakespeare, documents bearing on the king's own tastes, personality, and writing have constituted a pertinent locus. Organized as a narrative, this locus thus presents a situation in which Shakespeare's dramas, the plays of others, and court masques become important as part of a political dialogue between James I and some dramatists or as propagandistic material in the policy programs of the crown.

I

A priori assumptions about James's personality and tastes are best considered at the outset, for obviously the desires of a historical monarch can cut across impossibilities established by dozens of historians committed to their own versions of historical order or disorder. Crucial to such readings has been the idea of a personal preference in James, already intellectually inclined to the writing of poems and to the reading of history, for dramas and masques too. But what has been appropriated as a central text supporting this sense of James's theatrical orientation has been one locus in the *Basilikon Doron*, the long essay on kingship he wrote and dedicated to his five-year-old son, Prince Henry. This is the section in his book in which James likens a king to "one set on a stage whose smallest actions and gestures all the people gazingly do behold." But only a univocal response to the publicly disseminated and printed words of the dominant symbol of patriarchal authority in early modern England would regard such a text as complete testimony to the psychological bent of King James, their ostensible author. For even if this particular passage from the *Basilikon Doron* is to be interpreted as promulgating his partiality to performed drama (rather than his sense of patriarchal ruling techniques), another passage, never cited in this respect, seems much more specific on actors and acting:

> Abuse not yourself in making your sporters your counsellors; specially delight not to keep ordinarily in your company comedians, or balla-dines [mountebanks], for the tyrants delighted most in them and de-

lighted to make comedies and tragedies themselves. Whereupon the answer that a philosopher gave one of them there-anents is now come in a proverb—*reduc me in latomias.*[3]

To make his point, James cites no less a villain than Nero, a ruler traditionally associated with drama and performance, but also with capricious tyranny and matricide.

This counterexample is of course subject to the same methodological strictures already invoked regarding the making of narratives from documents. The complexities of intertextual relationships between biography and personal statement are, as Dominick LaCapra seems to imply, beyond any current achievement in psychohistory, and James's *Basilikon Doron* is not necessarily indicative of any direction in his views about the relationship of royalty to drama.[4]

Finally, still another traditional set of documents has served to promulgate Shakespeare's professional life as one closely connected with James and the court. Pre-dating the advent of the "new historicism," readings of these documents have foregrounded an upswing in the sheer number of plays presented during the holidays at court after James came to the English throne in 1603. This surge has suggested to many commentators King James's interest in drama and, by implication, in Shakespeare.[5]

Again, univocal interpretations of records are not the most sophisticated form of historiography. In this case, a performance before the king does not necessarily imply James's love of Shakespearean or other drama. Texts illustrating the larger social setting suggest that James, as king of England, inherited a long-standing tradition of court entertainment. The declared accounts of the treasurer of the chamber had been listing Christmas holiday payments to adult professional players since 1558, six years before William Shakespeare was born (*MSC*, 6:1–42). Accordingly, when several plays were performed at Hampton Court during James's first Christmas season (1603–4), this was no great departure in custom. In the previous Christmas season just before her death, Queen Elizabeth had seen eight plays by five different companies of actors between De-

3. James VI, *Basilikon Doron*, 2 vols., ed. James Craigie (Edinburgh: William Blackwood and Sons, 1944), 2 vols., 1:197–198. The Latin proverb says in effect, "I'd rather work in the stone quarries."

4. See, for example, Dominick LaCapra, *Rethinking Intellectual History: Texts, Contexts, Language* (Ithaca, N.Y.: Cornell University Press, 1983), pp. 39–41.

5. See G. W. Wickham, *Early English Stages: 1300–1600*, 3 vols. (New York, Columbia University Press, 1959-). 2.1:94.

cember 26 and Shrovetide. Thus the Venetian ambassador spoke truly when, in the following year, he noted: "All these last days have been devoted to fêtes, banquets, jousts, as is usual in England from St. Stephen's [Dec. 26] to Twelfth Night" (*SPV*, 10:129). If, during his first season, James attended nine performances by four adult, professional companies and two performances by a new group of child actors, he was not necessarily exhibiting a marked preference for drama over Queen Elizabeth.

The level of King James's enthusiasm for the plays he did attend, furthermore, seems to have been rather low, if the courtier Dudley Carleton—the future Lord Roscommon—is reliable. Another document, a letter Carleton wrote describing that first Jacobean holiday season, told John Chamberlain: "The first holy days we had every night a public play in the great hall, at which the King was ever present and liked or disliked as he saw cause, but it seems he takes no extraordinary pleasure in them."[6]

Carleton's observation seems reinforced by still other texts—those that pertain to King James's series of meetings with the prelates of England in this same first holiday season January 12, 16, and 18, 1604, to settle matters of religion: the Hampton Court conference. King James was absent from two plays given and paid for by crown moneys as he attended this important event. Additionally, his own idea of what constituted entertainment may be surmised, if not inferred, from his letter to a confidant, Lord Henry Howard (the future earl of Northampton), reporting on the conference: "We have kept such a revel with the Puritans here these two days as was never heard the like, where I have peppered them as soundly as ye have the Papists there."[7]

Because the term "revel" ordinarily described festivities and entertainments at court during the holiday season, it is significant that King James playfully used the word to convey his sense of entertainment in dealing with those advocates of the Puritan religious position who were allowed to attend the second day of the conference. Since the conference was held during the winter holidays, James seems to have regarded this activity, from his point of view, as his true "revels"; he obviously went out of his way to write a

---

6. See *Dudley Carleton to John Chamberlain (1603–1624)*, ed. Maurice Lee, Jr. (New Brunswick: Rutgers University Press, 1972), p. 53. Hereafter cited as *Carleton*.

7. *Letters of James VI and I*, ed. G. P. V. Akrigg (Berkeley: University of California Press, 1984), pp. 220–221.

letter expressing an exuberance not to be found in what is available about his responses to plays.

Nevertheless, there were payments for more than those eleven dramatic performances during James's first holiday season: nine additional plays are recorded. What of them? Is not their sheer number another kind of statement to be set against readings of other records? Yes, but the surviving financial information offers a significant distinction in these matters. Plays at the Stuart court were viewed not only by the king but also by other members of the royal family when James was absent. In fact, the nine additional plays of James's first holiday season, a number that has swelled James's reputation as a patron of the drama, were seen not by King James at all but by his queen consort and by Prince Henry. One important difference between Queen Elizabeth's and James's relationships to drama at court is that Elizabeth did not have a family. James did. The royal audience had increased in number.

Why, then, to conclude theoretical observations about the association of Shakespeare's career with the court, did James watch plays at all? He watched them because plays were traditional as court entertainment during the holidays from Advent to the day before Ash Wednesday. Why plays had become so imbedded a convention in this entertainment is quite another—and potentially fascinating—subject that demands discussion, but in the present context it is enough to note that plays were becoming traditional to court revelry. Their presence, however, was time-bound. During Shakespeare's career, very few plays were ever performed at court after Ash Wednesday. During the following eight or nine months until the arrival of the next annual holiday cycle of revels at Christmas the court paid for no plays at all.[8]

For this holiday season of royal entertainment, invitations were always sent to foreign emissaries and visiting foreign nobility, and plays seem to have been especially associated with such ambassadorial entertainment. In the first season of James's English kingship, such envoys were especially numerous, being present in London to offer congratulations on behalf of their sovereigns on James's accession to the throne.[9] The first two nights after James's first English

8. When James came to the throne, he began to celebrate All Saints' Day and All Souls' Day (November 1, November 2) as a brief time of revelry occasioned by the king's first return to the city after the summer, and, often, the opening of Parliament.

9. Plague had kept the majority of these special ambassadors from making their ceremonial visits because the new king had moved so often from place to place in

Christmas, the king honored such ambassadors—those from Spain and from Savoy on December 26, and those from Florence and Poland on the twenty-seventh. Their entertainment was a state dinner and then a play, as was often the custom.

Generally, James seems to have regarded the watching of plays in this context as duty, as part of the traditional noble revelry over which he was expected to preside. A final set of texts even suggests that drama otherwise held little or no interest for the king at all. These writings—letters from the collection at Hatfield House and papers held in Italian archives—appeared early in James's reign, during the second series of Christmas holidays (1604–5). They suggest that James began to evolve an interesting change in the traditional concept of kingly "solace."

The term "solace" was related to the idea that recreation was necessary to a monarch who otherwise might become dull and demoralized and, through his or her own ill health, in patriarchal theory, bring sickness to the body politic. The concept was inherent in many of the documents of the late sixteenth century which dealt with entertainment at court. A privy council notice to the aldermen and mayor of London of November 1581, for example, urged the financial relief of players to expedite their readiness for court entertainment "with convenient matters for her highness' solace this next Christmas, which cannot be without their usual exercise therein." Indeed, the rubric under which the actors were paid for court performances with crown moneys was precisely this idea of solace. Moreover, solace was a concept not confined, for the common players, to the palace precincts. The players, in theory, had to be well rehearsed for the Christmas solace; therefore they needed their own playhouses and audiences before whom to practice. In sum, as has long been understood, the idea of the monarch's solace was thus of some importance to the legitimacy of professional drama in the city and greatly helped to sustain professional drama before the revolution.[10] Consequently, it is significant to note what the Vene-

---

England during the previous summer and autumn. Ceremony required formal honors and entertainment to be extended to such visiting dignitaries. As Arabella Stuart, the king's first cousin, remarked in a letter to her uncle, the earl of Shrewsbury, just before these holidays: "the King will feast all the ambassadors this Christmas"; see E. T. Bradley, *The Life of the Lady Arabella Stuart*, 2 vols. (London, R. Bentley and Son: 1889), 2:195. Vol. 2 is an edition of Arabella's letters.

10. The concept of solace was well enough known even to be burlesqued in 1626 in a story told by John Taylor, who was also known as the "Water Poet," about a

tian ambassador Nicolo Molino wrote, in code, to the doge of Venice on January 31, 1605. James had apparently written a letter to the privy council reminding its members that he had been in London for nearly three weeks over Christmas (seeing, among other presentations, *Othello* and *Measure for Measure*). But, Molino reported,

> [King James] finds this sedentary life prejudicial to his health. . . . For in Scotland he was used to spend much time in the country and in hard exercise, and he finds that repose robs him of his appetite and breeds melancholy and a thousand other ills. He says he is bound to consider his health before all things, and so he must tell them that for the future he means to come to London but seldom, passing most of his time in the country in the chase; and as he thus will be far away from court he cannot attend to business, and so he commits all to them, relying fully on their [the council's] goodness and ability."

This situation apparently occasioned much sober comment at court. John Chamberlain wrote to Ralph Winwood on January 26 that "the hunting life" is "the only means to maintain [James's] health," which must be spared too much business. For it is this health which is "the health and welfare of us all." Even the very powerful earl of Worcester, master of the king's horse, spoke of this

---

man with a trained monkey. The man arrived at Looe in Cornwall and could find no audience until he forged a royal warrant announcing that the monkey was "the Queen's Ape"—the warrant going on "to will and require you, and every of you, with your wives and families, that upon the sight hereof, you make your personal appearance before the Queen's Ape, for it is an Ape of rank and quality, who is to be practiced through her Majesty's dominions, that by his long experience amongst her loving subjects, he may be better enabled to do Her Majesty service hereafter; and hereof fail you not, as you will answer the contrary"; see John Taylor, "Wit and Mirth," in *Works* (London, 1630), sigs. 2R3ᵛ–2R4.

11. Corroboration for *SPV* 10:218 comes from several sources—principally King James himself, who wrote the privy council as early as January 9, 1605, that during his absences for necessary recreation they should assemble to conduct business at the court of the queen. In a letter to Robert Cecil, the king later wrote that he would return to London only "if my continual presence in London be so necessary, as my absence for my health makes the councillors to be without authority or respect." For these matters see *Calendar of State Papers: Domestic Series, of the Reigns of Edward VI, Mary, Elizabeth, and James I (1547–1625)*, 12 vols., ed. Robert Lemon and M. A. E. Green (London, 1856–72), 8:186 (hereafter cited as *SPD*; *Calendar of the MSS of the Marquess of Salisbury Preserved at Hatfield House*, 23 vols., ed. M. S. Giuseppi (London: Historical Manuscripts Commission, 1883–1976), 16:399 (hereafter cited as *Hatfield*); Sir Ralph Winwood, *Memorials of Affairs of State*, 3 vols., ed. Edmund Sawyer (London, 1725), 2:46; and Edmund Lodge, *Illustrations of British History*, 3 vols., (London, 1838), 3:136.

hunting and referred to the king's health "that doth necessarily require these recreations."[12]

From the viewpoint of drama, solace had now moved. In January 1605, the second year of James's reign, the sovereign's necessary recreation left its Elizabethan domain of stage plays and courtly entertainments to focus on the traditionally royal pastime of hunting. Indeed, when James was absent from various dramatic performances that the queen and the prince attended during the first Christmas of his reign, he was at his hunting lodge at Royston.

Whether this publicly stated attitude was a reliable indication of James's private feelings is beside the point. It is enough that a public rhetoric served as a conceptual basis for his absence from palace life and from the attendant ceremony in which drama was a traditional part. The event in itself is thus sufficient to force a priori consideration of an alternate narrative about King James and stage plays, a narrative in which the requirements of monarchy exist in some plausible relationship to the question of occasional entertainment at court.

II

If one assumption about Shakespeare's relationship to the Stuart court has been that King James was a lover of plays and an active sponsor of the theatrical arts, a second seems to be that Shakespeare's genius was recognized by the aristocratic members of James's court in much the way it is assessed today. Having considered some of the a priori questions relating the English crown to court plays, we must now become annalistic to present a narrative that, in effect, minimizes king and court in both Shakespeare's artistic production and his professional life. Although after James's accession Shakespeare and his fellows bore the name of the king and acted at court, these advantages did little to alleviate the severity of the conditions in which they often found themselves or to improve the professional milieu for Shakespeare's own creative activity.

Specifically, it is time to explore 1603–4, the year of the accession of James, focusing on events often cited by cultural historians in

12. See *SPD*, 8:186; *Hatfield*, 16:399; Winwood, *Memorials*, 2:46; and Lodge, *Illustrations*, 3:136.

support of the view that Shakespeare and his company enjoyed a privileged position at the Stuart court—in particular, the patenting of the company as the King's Servants, the issuance of red cloth in the coronation procession, and the attendance of the company at the signing of the Spanish Peace. These events, it turns out, had no significant transforming influence on Shakespeare's career; the court milieu itself, as observed at the Spanish Peace and in the activities at Wilton in late 1603, was focused on issues of greater moment than the performances of professional players. If one is to examine the material conditions of Shakespeare's profession, and those of Shakespeare's own career, it is not the court but the public theater that must be emphasized—and the public theater was to be radically destabilized by plague.

The year 1603 did not begin well for Shakespeare and his fellows as far as their admittedly tenuous relationship to the court was concerned. Because the King's Servants were the first theatrical company to obtain royal patronage after the accession, and because the patent seems to have been issued rather speedily, it has been assumed that King James indeed intended to single out Shakespeare's company as his personal favorite and to make a public demonstration of his own preeminent interest in the theater. Certainly the circumstantial evidence for this view seems persuasive.

The patent naming Shakespeare and his fellows the King's Servants was issued with a speed so remarkable that it is surprising this in itself has not drawn comment. On May 17, 1603, approximately six weeks after James was proclaimed king, he signed the privy signet version of the document; by the end of the very next day the bill had worked its way through the bureaucracy of the court; and on May 19, less than a week after the king arrived in London to claim his throne, the actual letters of patent were issued to Shakespeare and his fellows.[13] Moreover, in a break with tradition, the

---

13. The course from creation to execution of letters patent such as the new King's Servants received was through seven stages: (1) A petition was initiated by or on behalf of the interested party setting out the conditions of the grant desired. (2) The request was granted by the crown and directions were issued for the preparation of the papers. (3) There was a *king's bill* in which the wording of the intended patent was settled. This king's bill was signed and then sent to the signet office as the authorization for preparing further papers. (4) These subsequent papers were the *privy signet bill*, addressed by one of the clerks of the privy signet to the lord privy seal (Sir Robert Cecil). The King's Servants bill dated May 17. (5) In the privy seal office, the wording of the bill in (4) was used as the basis for preparing the *writ of privy seal*, executed here and addressed to the lord chancellor (Sir Thomas Egerton). The

terms of the patent were unusually ample, allowing the newly created King's Servants to perform not only at the Globe but also at other "convenient places" throughout the kingdom.[14]

The issuance of this patent represented a significant improvement in the status of the company, formerly known as the Lord Chamberlain's Servants, vis à vis their competitors. From 1597, when George Carey, second Lord Hunsdon, was appointed lord chamberlain, to about 1601, when he stopped attending meetings of the privy council because of illness, Shakespeare and his fellows had theoretically enjoyed the protection of a noble in a powerful position. The chamberlainship was, of course, an important and powerful office, the coveted prize of many earls and barons, an anachronistic combination of royal household duties reaching back to the twelfth century and of much wider, seventeenth-century administrative responsibilities involving constant access to the monarch.[15] But Hunsdon had become ill by 1600, and when he was no longer able to carry out his responsibilities as lord chamberlain in the last year of Elizabeth's reign they were assigned on a temporary basis to Thomas, first Baron Howard of Walden. With the death of Elizabeth, the Lord Chamberlain's Servants had to wait to find out whether they would

---

King's Servants bill dated May 18. (6) In the lord chancellor's office were prepared the actual *letters patent* under the great seal. The King's Servants patent dated May 19. These letters patent were delivered to the persons concerned: Shakespeare and his fellows. (7) Meanwhile, the document prepared in (5) above, the writ of privy seal, was passed to the clerks in chancery, who entered the contents in the patent rolls. For reproductions of these documents, see *MSC*, 1.3:264–265, and J. O. Halliwell-Phillipps, *Illustrations of the Life of Shakespeare* (London: Longmans, Green, 1889) 2 vols., 1:82–83.

14. The previous privy council order concerned with the regulation of plays—promulgated March 31, 1602, a year previous—had barely done more than rule that each of the three permissible acting companies should "be appointed their certain houses, and one and no more each company," where the group should confine its acting. Strict in tone, the document used the word "toleration" twice. See E. K. Chambers, *The Elizabethan Stage*, 4 vols., (Oxford: Clarendon Press, 1923), 4:334–335.

15. The lord chamberlain was described by a contemporary as "the greatest governor in the king's house. He hath a greater command of the King's guard than the captain hath. He makes all the [court] chaplains, chooseth most of the King's servants, and all the persuivants." One of his many subordinates was the master of the revels, the official who supervised the mechanics of the entertainment at court and had jurisdiction over the actors, their playhouses, and even the content of their plays, both in the city and at court. For the lord chamberlain and the master of the revels, see Chambers, *Elizabethan Stage*, 1:36–42. For the lord chamberlain, see also David Starkey et al., *The English Court* (London: Longman, 1987), chap. 6 by Neil Cuddy. For the master of the revels, see also Barroll, *The Revels History*, 3.1.1–27.

remain so. They did not, for on April 6, 1603, James appointed the acting lord chamberlain, Baron Howard (nephew to Henry Lord Howard, the future Northampton and one of the powerful nobles instrumental in bringing James to the throne), permanent lord chamberlain at the Stuart court. At that point, Shakespeare and his fellows, who for three years had been without whatever effective representation their sponsor might have furnished them, lost the power of his title as well; they became simply the Servants of George Carey, second Lord Hunsdon, an ailing baron who was second cousin to the lately deceased queen.[16]

Their chief professional competitors—the Lord Admiral's Servants, headed by Edward Alleyn—were in a much better situation. This company's patron, Charles Howard, the earl of Nottingham—the only earl created by Queen Elizabeth in the last ten years of her reign—retained immense influence. King James continued him in the office of lord admiral (Nottingham had vacated the lord chamberlainship ten years earlier to ensure this position) and his prestige remained great. As J. K. Laughton observed, no important commission seems to have been considered complete in James's reign unless Nottingham was a member of it.[17] As for the third city playing company, the Earl of Worcester's Servants, their patron had been, and now continued as, master of the horse, the earl of Essex's old position.

The first inkling of what the Stuart era had in store for the theaters must have been disconcerting to all three companies, but under the circumstances particularly to the Servants of Lord Hunsdon. On May 7, James issued a lengthy proclamation from Theobalds that concerned monopolies but concluded with a ban on all public entertainments, including the theater, on the Sabbath.[18] Thus, as Easter term began in May, Shakespeare and his fellows presumably had much melancholy meat to digest.

The issuance of their patent less than two weeks later not only

16. In May 1600, Hunsdon had been at Bath for medical purposes; in September 1600 and June 1601, he was unable to work; ill again in July 1602, he had an attack on the thirty-first that compelled his wife to write Cecil; see *Hatfield*, 10:156, 162; 11:231; 12:219, 266. See also *Manuscripts of Lord de L'Isle and Dudley Preserved at Penshurst Place*, 6 vols., ed. C. L. Kingsford and William A. Shaw (London: Historical Manuscripts Commission, 1914–1966), 2:484. Hereafter cited as *L'Isle*.

17. See *Dictionary of National Biography*, 66 vols., ed. Leslie Stephens and Sidney Lee (Oxford: Oxford University Press, 1885–1901), 10:4. Hereafter cited as *DNB*.

18. See J. F. Larkin and P. L. Hughes, eds., *Stuart Royal Proclamations* (Oxford: Clarendon Press, 1973), 2 vols, pp. 11–14. Hereafter cited as *Proclamations: Stuart*.

resolved what had really persisted as a long-standing problem of patronage but marked an impressive leap in status for Shakespeare and his fellows. To make things even better, the company had moved far ahead of the nearest competition in this matter of image. Although many drama historians imply otherwise, the crown, at James's accession, did not immediately and automatically take all London acting companies under its protection.[19] The Lord Admiral's Servants were not inscribed as the Servants of Prince Henry until the following February 1604, when they began using the name; even so, their patent was not actually issued for another two years. In still another case, the acting company that would be allowed in that same February 1604 to style themselves as Servants of the Queen did not receive their official patent until April 15, 1609—five years later.[20] In startling contrast, the King's Servants had their patent in hand less than a week after the king was in London to first claim his throne.

That the company had a powerful intercessor at court therefore seems indisputable. What is not so obvious, however, is the identity of this helper and the political activity that made the patent possible. It cannot be assumed from the foregoing events that James himself instigated this action or even that he had much interest in it.[21] On the contrary, the issuance of a patent to a theater company—however momentously significant to the company itself—would have been a matter of extremely low national priority to King James at this time. James was, after all, concerned with the consolidation of his own power in these, the early months of his reign. This meant, among other things, the implementation of a well-formulated plan (developed primarily through secret correspondence with Cecil and Henry Howard) to gain the accession without strife, which culminated in a meeting at the house of the earl of Nottingham, the lord

19. See, for example, G. W. Wickham's interpretation of events in *Early English Stages*, 2.1:90–91; Jonathan Goldberg, *James I and the Politics of Literature* (Baltimore: Johns Hopkins University Press, 1983), pp. 231–239; and Stephen Orgel, "Making Greatness Familiar," in *Pageantry in the Shakespearean Theater*, ed. David M. Bergeron (Athens: University of Georgia Press, 1985), pp. 22–23.

20. The very popular boy actors, the Children of the Chapel Royal, to whose challenging competition *Hamlet* seems to have alluded, were not themselves licensed as the Children of the Queen's Revels until the following February 1604 either. For these matters, see *MSC*, 1.3:267–269, and Chambers, *Elizabethan Stage*, 2:48–49, 230–231, 187–188.

21. But see S. Schoenbaum, *William Shakespeare: A Documentary Life* (New York: Oxford University Press, 1975), pp. 195–196.

admiral, where a document was issued proclaiming James king, signed by all the powerful nobles.[22] James was also busy expanding the privy council as the core power group from fourteen to twenty-four to include key Scottish nobles.[23] There was also the matter of selecting Scottish and English nobles to provide counsel and protection in a strange land—taking actions such as relieving Sir Walter Ralegh of his position as captain of the guard and replacing him with a Scottish intimate.[24] There was the pardoning of political prisoners (such as Southampton) and the crafting of the symbolic statement represented by Queen Elizabeth's funeral, James's own progress to London, Queen Anna's similar progress to London that was to take place in June, and the planning for the coronation on July 25. All these matters were complicated, requiring immediate attention, and only in fantasy may it be imagined that the gilding of Hunsdon's old (and financially very solvent) company of actors with the name of the king ranked in priority with such affairs. In such an electric context, even the Hampton Court conference that laid out the un-

22. Although Sir Robert Carey, brother of the ailing second Lord Hunsdon, had raced north to be the first to tell James that Queen Elizabeth was dead and that James had been declared king of England, he was apparently blundering into an otherwise systematic removal of obstacles to James's peaceful accession; his authority was angrily repudiated by the privy council writing at 10 P.M. on March 24. The same letter designated Charles Percy and Thomas Somerset as the official messengers; see David Calderwood, *History of the Kirk of Scotland*, 8 vols., ed. Thomas Thomson (Edinburgh: Woodrow Society, 1842–49), 6:206–209. The delicacy of the succession process was noted in the letter of the French ambassador Marin Cavalli to the doge of Venice and to the senate in *SPV*, 10:7. Indicative also are the activities of Robert Cecil, who, for example, "stayed the journey of the Captain of the Guard [Sir Walter Ralegh]," who was in process of conducting many suitors north to the king on April 9; see *SPD*, 8:2; *Hatfield*, 15:57–58.

23. See *Hatfield*, 15:100–101; *SPV*, 10:10, 17. These appointments, for instance, included the earl of Northumberland, who had participated in secret correspondence with James during Queen Elizabeth's lifetime.

24. For opposition to Ralegh in the secret correspondence, see pp. 18–19. James I, *Correspondence with Sir Robert Cecil and others in England*, ed. John Bruce (Westminster: the Camden Society, 1861), pp. 18–19. Ralegh was summoned to the privy council on May 8 and relieved of his office then; see *Acts*, 32:498. But this dismissal was anticipated by April 28 or even earlier, for Cobham had a bitter argument with Cecil about the matter; see *Hatfield*, 15:61, and John Manningham, *Diary*, ed. R. P. Sorlien (Hanover, N.H.: University Press of New England, 1976), p. 224. Ralegh's replacement was Sir Thomas Erskine, a gentleman of the bedchamber since 1585. He became Viscount Fenton in March 1606 and a privy councillor January 31, 1611; see *Complete Peerage*, 13 vols., ed. H. A. Doubleday et al. (London: St. Catherine's Press, 1910–59), 5:294, and John Stow and Edmond Howes, *Annals* (London, 1615), sig. 4G5 (hereafter cited as *Annals*).

derstanding between James I and the religious establishment in England waited for almost a year.

What force, then, might have managed to bring forward the subject of Hunsdon's playing company at this time of urgent and complex beginnings?[25] Assuming that the status of Shakespeare's company could have been changed because of some esteem for William Shakespeare himself, the earl of Southampton's intercession here might be plausible.[26] Some scholars have been eager to connect him with Shakespeare as patron, lover, and friend.[27] Certainly the poet dedicated *Venus and Adonis* and *Lucrece* to Southampton in 1593 and 1594; and in 1599 when Essex was imprisoned in London after returning from Ireland, his associates, Southampton himself, and the earl of Rutland showed in interest in drama, "going to plays every day"—presumably while they awaited resolution of Essex's current problems (*L'Isle*, 2:401). But there is no text indicating a connection between Shakespeare and Southampton beyond Shakespeare's early poetry, and in May 1603 Henry Wriothesley, once earl of Southampton, must have had a great deal else on his mind.[28] A close friend and ally of Essex during the abortive attempt at a coup in 1601, Southampton was released by James on April 5, 1603, in one of several public actions taken by the new king to support the family and friends of Essex.[29] But, although Henry Wriothesley was free to

25. Because the English actor Lawrence Fletcher appears at the head of the list of Shakespeare and his fellows in the new patent, it is possible that Fletcher, who had acted in Scotland, may have been instrumental in helping Shakespeare and his fellows become Servants of the King. I do not think this probable, but I deal with the matter at greater length in a forthcoming article.

26. Shakespeare himself, if typical of his age, might have preferred a minor court position similar to that achieved by Samuel Daniel, or a monopoly such as Henslowe enjoyed in the business of bringing bears to court. But the change of name for the whole company served to enhance their group prestige.

27. For a review of these matters, see E. K. Chambers, *William Shakespeare*, 2 vols. (Oxford: Clarendon Press, 1930), 1:565–568.

28. The question of Southampton, Essex, Shakespeare, and the performance of *Richard II* is too lengthy to be dealt with here. I discuss it in Barroll, "A New History for Shakespeare and His Time," *Shakespeare Quarterly* (1988), 441–464, the thrust of the argument being that the crown did not view this performance by common players as particularly dangerous.

29. For James's letter delivering Southampton, see Charlotte C. Stopes, *The Life of Henry, Third Earl of Southampton* (Cambridge: Cambridge University Press, 1922), pp. 259–260, which quotes from British Library Add. MS. 33,051, f.53, in extenso. For James's other actions here, see *SPV*, 10:26. James was also careful to support those who had helped convict Essex, however. See his creation of Sir William Knollys as Baron Knollys of Rotherfield Greys (*DNB*, 11:286).

walk the streets by April 10, he had by no means been restored to his title, which was still attainted, or to his property. King James granted Southampton an audience on April 24, but it was not until May 16—only twenty-four hours before the processing of the privy signet bill creating Shakespeare and his fellows the King's Servants—that James confirmed an official grant of pardon and restoration to Southampton and his heirs. Even this act, however, restored only Southampton's property, not his earldom or the means by which to maintain it and recoup his financial losses. And, although on May 17 James continued to favor Southampton by appointing him as one of twenty gentlemen of the king's privy chamber, an important honor, Southampton still awaited the more fundamental restoration of his status and income.[30] It appears unlikely that Southampton, preoccupied with these concerns, would use his April 24 audience with the king to intercede for the player-servants of Baron Hunsdon, or to make the unconventional suggestion that they should become the King's Servants simply for the sake of some poet that Southampton had patronized ten years before.

To pursue this puzzle of the creation of the King's Servants, one might more plausibly turn away from the very busy Southampton to another noble appointed to the king's privy chamber, one who shared Southampton's early audience with James on April 24, the nephew of Sir Philip Sidney about whom James had written laudatory sonnets: William Herbert, third earl of Pembroke, son of Mary, countess of Pembroke, and editor of her brother's *Arcadia*. Pembroke's connection with Shakespeare surfaces in the dedicatory epistle by Hemmings and Condell in the Shakespeare First Folio, in which they allude to Pembroke's interest in the person and plays of the poet.[31] It is important, though, to remember that throughout James's reign—and prior to it—Pembroke, like other members of his illustrious family, was an active and general patron of the arts. Before he was twenty-three years old, Pembroke helped the young Inigo Jones to travel and study in Italy. Later this noble was also patron of, among others, Ben Jonson, John Donne, and George Chapman.[32]

30. Southampton was carver for the King at a dinner in late May. See Philip Gawdy, *Letters*, ed. I. H. Jeayes (London: Roxburghe Club, 1906), p. 132. For the date of Southampton's grant of pardon, see *SPD*, 8:8.

31. Dedicated to both the earl of Pembroke and his younger brother the earl of Montgomery, the epistle prefacing the Shakespeare First Folio refers to the two brothers as personages who "have prosecuted both them [Shakespeare's plays] and their author living with so much favor."

32. For these matters, see the "Life" prefixed to Inigo Jones, *Stonehenge Restored*

Pembroke seems to have been particularly interested in the theater and to have had a personal friendship with Richard Burbage, as we know from his heartfelt response to Burbage's death in a letter of 1619: "all the company are at the play, which I being tender-hearted could not endure to see so soon after the loss of my old acquaintance Burbage."[33] And in that same year, Pembroke used his authority as lord chamberlain to intervene with the stationers' company on behalf of the King's Servants in an extraordinary way. In a written communication, he directed all booksellers and printers to refrain from printing plays belonging to the King's Servants without prior consent of the company, granting, in effect, a kind of copyright authority to the company highly unusual for the times.[34]

Frequently an activist when it came to the arts, Pembroke was central to the new circle of patrons that formed around the court of Queen Anna shortly after the accession of James and continued well into his reign. This group, which included many of the former supporters of Essex, was the true center of intellectual activity at the court.[35] And Pembroke himself is the only one of the nobles in this circle, as we have just seen, whom documents directly associate with professional actors and especially members of the King's Servants.

That James himself was immediately taken with this wealthy

(London, 1725); "Conversations with Drummond," in Ben Jonson, *Works*, 12 vols., ed. C. H. Herford and Percy Simpson (Oxford: Clarendon Press, 1925), 1:141; and Sir Sidney Lee in *DNB*, 9:677ff.

33. See R. C. Bald, *John Donne: A Life* (Oxford: Oxford University Press, 1970), p. 351. The letter was written during June, but Burbage, Shakespeare's great acting associate, had been dead since March.

34. See W. W. Greg, *Shakespeare's First Folio* (Oxford: Clarendon Press, 1955), p. 24 n. D, and Chambers, *William Shakespeare*, 1:136 n. 1. It is true that later in 1623 the master of the revels read a regulatory statement to all the master printers of London concerning the licensing of plays; see the text furnished by Greg to Peter Alexander's *Shakespeare's Life 2nd Art* (London: James Nisbet, 1939), p. 41 and n. 1. But there is no evidence that this statement was intended to protect the *players*. It could, for example, have been a warning to printers to publish only plays licensed for performance by the office of the revels—plays thus already "allowed."

35. See L. Barroll, "The Court of the First Stuart Queen," in *The Mental World of the Jacobean Court*, ed. Linda Levy Peck (Cambridge: Cambridge University Press), in press. See also the description of the Christmas holidays of 1602–3 just prior to Queen Elizabeth's death, when the earl of Pembroke, with his uncle Sir Robert Sidney, spent Christmas with the countess of Bedford and the earl and countess of Rutland (who was Sir Philip Sidney's daughter and the Earl of Essex's stepdaughter); John Chamberlain, *Letters*, 2 vols., ed. N. E. McClure (Philadelphia: American Philosophical Society, 1939), 1:179. Hereafter cited as *Chamberlain*.

young earl (Pembroke was twenty-three in 1603) is apparent from
several accounts. It was Pembroke whom James selected to bear the
great banner at Queen Elizabeth's funeral.[36] Again, Pembroke, as
well as Southampton, was appointed to the king's privy chamber,
and on the same day he was made keeper of Clarendon Park. Most
important, on July 2, 1603, Pembroke, with Southampton, was one
of only two English earls initiated into the consummately prestigious Order of the Garter in a ceremony in which the four other
new inductees were King James himself, his queen's brother the
king of Denmark, the duke of Lennox (the king's cousin and the
peer nearest the throne during the minority of the prince), and the
earl of Mar (James's closest Scottish advisor).[37]

Finally, at the coronation of James in July, Pembroke was again
to be noted in relation to the new king, at least by Scaramelli, the
Venetian secretary in London, who described part of the coronation
ceremony in a letter to the doge and the senate:

> The Earls, [privy] Council, and Barons, one by one, kissed the King's
> hand, kneeling before him on a red brocaded cushion, and touched
> the crown, some even kissing it. The Earl of Pembroke, a handsome
> youth, who is always with the King and always joking with him,
> actually kissed his Majesty's face, whereupon the King laughed and
> gave him a little cuff. (*SPV*, 10:76–77)

This early familiarity was, in fact, to continue as a close relationship that lasted the entirety of King James's life.

If one had to choose, then, between Pembroke and Southampton
as intercessors for Shakespeare's company, odds might favor Pembroke because of his lifelong commitment to the arts, his interest
in theater, his friendship with Richard Burbage, and his unhampered
circumstances in spring 1603. Indeed, the connecting link after all
might not have been William Shakespeare but Richard Burbage. For,
nine months later, when this company and no other was awarded a

---

36. William Watson, one of the Bye plot conspirators, wrote his confessional letter
to Pembroke hoping thereby that this letter would reach the king directly because
of the "extraordinary affection and trust" the king reposed in Pembroke even in
Scotland; *Hatfield*, 15:242. For Pembroke's funeral assignment, see Doubleday et al.,
eds., *Peerage*, 10:412.

37. For Clarendon Park, see *SPD*, 8:9. For the Order of the Garter inductions of
this year, see *Carleton*, p. 35.

sum of money by the crown for plague relief, the award was signed over to "Richard Burbage, one of his majesty's comedians."[38]

Ultimately, it is not that important to our understanding of Shakespeare's Stuart career to choose between Southampton and Pembroke. What is important is the strong probability that King James himself would never have taken as a first order of business in his newly authorized reign the corporate patenting of a London company of common players nor have pursued the speeding of the patent through its three stages within five days. At the same time, someone must have intruded the acting company into a crown agenda crammed with matters of highest national priority requiring the swift attention of the king before his formal assumption of the crown in July. Both Southampton and Pembroke were early favorites of a certain kind and were close to the king at this time, and the patenting of an acting company was just the kind of unimportant favor James seems to have been prepared to grant such nobles as a way of showing respect for the memories of Sir Philip Sidney and of the earl of Essex. James lavished Pembroke and Southampton with favor and, in the case of the Order of the Garter, with an exceptional honor not even granted Robert Cecil as earl of Salisbury or the earl of Northampton until 1605.

These were, however, honors having little to do with the main thrust of English political affairs, in which a Scottish monarch was moving south at the invitation of the English ruling group of barons and earls to claim the throne of England. It was to this latter group, Cecil and the Howards, as well as to his few, close Scottish advisors such as the earl of Mar and the duke of Lennox, that James accorded real power. The Sidney–Essex group he showered with honors, but neither Southampton nor Pembroke (nor anyone else connected with the group) would be allowed real political power for many years. Instead, after being honored with the Order of the Garter, Southampton and Pembroke, although active in Parliament, became primarily the king's hunting companions. In such a context, should either earl in these days have requested a patent for the Servants of Lord Hunsdon to become the King's Servants, no significant jealousies would

---

38. See *MSC*, 6:39. The first part of the entry reads: "To Richard Burbage, one of his majesty's comedians, upon the Council's warrant dated at Hampton Court the 8th day of February 1603 [1604] for the maintenance and relief of himself and the rest of his company."

have been fomented by the granting of that minor suit, so easy to accord to such favorites.[39]

But would not the question of crown control over the drama of the city at the accession of James transcend the individual case of the company of Shakespeare and his fellows? Surely the privileged tradition, reasserted by Glynn Wickham, S. Schoenbaum, and Stephen Orgel, holds that James at his accession incorporated *all* of London's acting companies under the crown to assert royal control. The creation of the lord chamberlain's acting group as the Servants of the King should thus be seen as part of a new, general crown policy. It was in line with this crown approach, presumably, that the other two adult, professional companies of players in London also experienced changes in designation. As we have seen, these groups now bore the names of other members of the new royal family. The Earl of Nottingham's Servants became the Servants of the Prince, while the company which had hitherto been known as the Earl of Worcester's Servants became the Servants of the Queen. Furthermore, throughout the prerevolutionary period, all remaining groups of actors who were allowed to perform in the city (and sometimes those performing in the provinces) would henceforth bear the names of other members of the royal family.

This may in general (and for various reasons) be so, but the accession of King James, as I have just observed, was not immediately followed by the incorporation of all three public acting companies in London under royal names. For one thing, there was no need to gather the public acting companies under the control of the crown; they were already there. They were and had for decades been constantly answerable to the master of the revels, and he himself answered to the lord chamberlain, who was one of the more important and powerful officials of the crown, especially during the first several years of James's reign. Furthermore, when plays are compared to the governmental, political, and social preoccupations of those who surrounded the sovereign or his consort, it is difficult to envision any plausible scenario in which actors would be directly administered

---

39. In any event, one should compare the granting of a patent to Shakespeare and his fellows to the May 14 grant of the office of the keeper of the manor house and park of Temple-Newsham in the County of York bestowed by the crown for life on Thomas Pott, as well as to the May 17 grant to Sir Amias Preston of the office of the keeper of stores and ordnance in the Tower of London. In both these equally trivial cases, the recipients had the advantage of Shakespeare and his fellows in that they gained significant financial opportunities.

or supervised by any high officials of the crown at all—let alone by the sovereign himself.

But then what is to be made of the proliferation of the royal names associated with the adult acting companies so early in King James's reign? One must view and follow the situation from the theoretical vantage point of the actors themselves. The year 1603 had begun, we saw, with Shakespeare and his fellows in somewhat deteriorated condition with respect to possible patronage. The advantage that this acting group might have anticipated from its nebulous association with the lord whose name it bore seemed to be coming to an end. Reverting to his baronage as second Lord Hunsdon of middling wealth, son of the first cousin to a queen who was now dead, Hunsdon was not a promising patron, especially when compared with those men whose names the competing acting companies bore. These were, of course, the Servants of earl of Nottingham who lost nothing by the change in reign, and the Servants of the very prestigious earl of Worcester, who himself remained master of the horse. If something were to be made of the prestige of one's lord in this curiously archaic situation in which financially independent acting companies pretended (for good reason) that they were the household servants of some highly placed nobleman, Worcester's and Nottingham's Servants, compared to those of Baron Hunsdon, seem, at the beginning of the new reign, to have been in superior positions.

When Shakespeare and his fellows then rebounded as the instantaneous "Servants" of no less a personage than the king himself, actually holding in their hands the physical patent, the parchment warranting their new status, and this only sixteen days after the new lord chamberlain, the future earl of Suffolk, himself received the white rod, and only fifteen days after the new Jacobean privy council was all sworn, it is easy to envision the reaction of competitors. Shakespeare and his group had obviously gained some kind of upper hand while the two other companies had become nothing royal at all. In this same May, the latter remained as they had been— servants of the lord admiral and of the earl of Worcester. Had the crown intended to control all London actors by changing all their company names, the process had been somewhat careless.

The uniqueness in "royal" status for Shakespeare and his fellows is suggested by activity in Coventry the following summer, when several of the companies performed at some point during the year-long time span in which the well-known 1603 plague closed the London theaters. For Coventry there are entries which, though them-

selves undated as to day and month, follow after a notation made
November 17, 1603.[40]

To the King's Players	40s
To the Earl of Worcester's Players	20s

.
.
.

To the Earl of Nottingham's Players	20s

In this account book, Shakespeare and his fellows may well be
known as the King's Players, but Worcester's Servants and Nottingham's Servants are not called the "Queen's" and the "Prince's"
players at all.

Lest this entry seem idiosyncratic, another entry earlier in the
summer, in Leicester where Worcester's Servants had visited often
and were well known, reinforces the picture of his group as not yet
(as they would be) Servants of the Queen, just as it persists in calling
Alleyn's company the Lord Admiral's Servants. The last indication
of date in the document before these entries is April 3, 1603.

Itm	given to the Earl of Worcester's players	x s
Itm	given to the Earl of Worcester's players one other time	xx s
Itm	given to the Lord Admiral's players the xviii of August	x s

When the Worcester group next played in Leicester, in 1605, they
were referred to as "the Queenes Majesty's Playars."[41]

By these indications, then, Shakespeare and his fellows were the
only company bearing a royal name for several months after the
accession of James in 1603, hardly an indication of a royal policy
concerning all London players.

The narrative offered here depicts a situation different from traditional historical descriptions. I suggest that the other two companies, far from rejoicing in their freedom from crown control in
the spring of 1603, must have seen themselves at some sort of com-

40. See p. 364 of the chamberlain's and warden's account book II for 1603 in
Records of Early English Drama: Coventry, ed. R. W. Ingram (Toronto: University
of Toronto Press, 1981), p. 362.

41. See William Kelly, ed., *Notices Illustrative of the Drama . . . of the Borough of
Leicester* (London: John Russell Smith, 1865), pp. 236, 245.

petitive disadvantage. Although the King's Servants seem to have gained relatively little from the implied association with royalty, it is difficult to imagine any group in the competitive entertainment business not expecting some helpful publicity from such an association. From such a truism one might then surmise the steps that the other companies might have taken in response, seeking the social status that too many recent critics overelaborate as the crown's effort at the containment of potential subversion.

The competing companies shared an obvious difficulty. The earl of Nottingham and the earl of Worcester, two of the most politically powerful earls in the kingdom, might not lightly be approached by their player-servants actually seeking to leave the incredible honor of their "service." Nottingham, for example, had been one of the three persons, with the lord chancellor of England and the Archbishop of Centerbury, to escort James to his octagonal dais for the ceremony of his coronation (*SPV*, 10:76). Nor would the crown itself wish to go out of its way to offend such earls by appropriating their own nominal servants, common players, disturbing these earls' sense of their own honor, that highly volatile Renaissance commodity. Therefore such a change would have to come from some other direction. A possible course of events in such a situation is, I think, adumbrated by documents that were produced by the first Christmas of the new reign.

When plays were performed at court during this holiday season of 1603–4, the warrants for paying the actors were, as usual, processed rather later than the occasion. On February 19, 1604, the crown reimbursed both Worcester's and Nottingham's Servants in different warrants, but both warrants referred to these companies by new names, the payee in the Worcester group named for the first time as one of "the Queen's Majesty's players" and two payees in the Nottingham group described by the payment warrant as "two of the Prince's players" (*MSC*, 6:39). Thus, by February 1604, if not by May 1603, all the London playing companies had names of royal family members.

Critics generalizing this situation into a coordinated movement of crown policy have, I think, been overly dependent on an account of this situation from Shakspeare's time which tends to make all these changes of the dramatic companies to royal patronage seem simultaneous and thus planned. In *Time Triumphant*, a small, celebratory description typical of those publications that attended public events of the period, Gilbert Dugdale commemorated the king's (deferred) coronation procession of March 15, 1604. Entered in the

Stationers' Register on March 27, the book, in a typical effusion, observed that

> [His Grace, the King,] together with his Queen and children, pro-
> gressed in the country, and dealt honors as freely to our Nation as
> their hearts would wish, as creating knights of gentlemen, Lords of
> knights, and Earls of lords, and no doubt hereafter Dukes of earls, and
> raised up an honor to England, that to this day have been long in
> oblivion, which as now it is honorably living, so it will never die—I
> mean our noble Knights of the Bath, young and gallant, worthy and
> valiant. Nay, see the beauty of our all-kind sovereign. Not only to the
> indifferent of worth and the worthy of honor did he freely deal about
> these causes, but to the mean gave grace. As taking to him the late
> Lord Chamberlain's Servants, now the King's Actors, the Queen taking
> to her the Earl of Worcester's Servants that are now her actors, the
> prince their son Henry, Prince of Wales, full of hope, took to him the
> Earl of Nottingham his servants, who are now his actors, so that of
> Lords' servants they are now the Servants of the King, Queen, and
> Prince.[42]

Within a context in which the writer is balancing contrasts for effect, and writing in 1604—not 1603, Dugdale makes the acts with the players seem simultaneous even though we know they were not.

The means by which the Prince's and the Queen's Servants came to their new names in 1604 is indicated with somewhat greater clarity by another remark, long after the fact. The observer here is a much more significant one than Dugdale—the actor and dramatist Thomas Heywood who himself had been one of the Earl of Worcester's Servants. With the change in patrons in 1604, he became one of the Servants of the Queen and remained so for many years. But Queen Anna died in 1619, and her company seems to have fallen to pieces by the summer of 1623, so that Heywood, fifth in the list of the Queen's Servants allowed to wear black in her funeral proces- sion, presumably turned more directly to writing.[43] In 1624, he pub- lished a book on celebrated women, *Gunaikeion*, which he dedicated to his company's old patron, the earl of Worcester, who was now even more powerful at court than he had been in 1603, twenty-one

42. John Nichols, *The Progresses...of James the First*, 4 vols. (London: J. B. Ni- chols, 1828), 1:413.

43. For the fate of the Queen's Servants and for Heywood and the queen's funeral, see G. E. Bentley, *Jacobean and Caroline Stage*, 7 vols., (Oxford: Clarendon Press: 1941–68), 1:170–174; 2:473.

years before. Heywood's prefatory bid for patronage in the dedication remarks:

> I was, my Lord, your creature, and amongst other of your servants, you bestowed me upon the excellent Princess Queen Anne to whose memory I have celebrated in these papers the zeal of a subject and a servant. But by her lamented death your gift, my Lord, is returned again into your hands, being still yours, either to keep unto yourself or to confer where your most noble disposition shall best please.[44]

All due allowance being made for the necessary preciosity, "bestowing" by the earl, one might imagine, was more appropriate in such cases than confiscation by the crown. The transaction had to be voluntary, especially since, from the viewpoint of crown control, the issue was meaningless.

However the mechanics of the transfer were effected, the reason for it seems quite clear, for the change happened after Christmas had begun. At the outset of the plague-delayed first Christmas season, the first six performances of the holiday interval at court were very uncharacteristically engrossed by one company. Shakespeare and his fellows played every consecutive available date through New Year's. Why? In the previous year, under Queen Elizabeth, there had been a fairly even division of honors in these respects.[45] It is unlikely that this proliferation of performances by Shakespeare and his fellows was at the demand of King James. Rather, I suggest that the master of the revels, who was responsible for such entertainment at court, assumed (as may have Shakespeare and his fellows in that age of monopolies) that the group now patented as Servants of the King was the only one indeed eligible to play at court. Yet, as Elizabethan court records show, the English crown was accustomed to be fairly evenhanded in its extension of grace to common players by inviting them to entertain the sovereign at Christmas and Shrovetide. The Renaissance virtue of magnificence comprehended outreach to commoners at such times, and several companies were usually represented. Indeed, the city players might reasonably have come to expect this. When Shakespeare and his fellows now proceeded to present in this new Christmas season at court the first

---

44. Thomas Heywood, *Gunaikeion* (London, 1624), sig. A3. He praises Queen Anna on sig. M2.

45. In the previous season, Queen Elizabeth had seen eight plays by five different companies. Nottingham's Servants had performed thrice, Shakespeare and his fellows twice, Worcester's, Hertford's, and Paul's boys once apiece; see *MSC*, 6:35–37.

five or six plays in a row, however, Worcester's and Nottingham's
Servants may have been genuinely alarmed. Their theaters had been
closed from plague since May or June, and companies were usually
awarded ten pounds per play when performing at court—not a small
sum, especially when the weekly norm was now nothing.

In this situation, the comments of Dudley Carleton seem quite
pertinent. Carleton had written on January 11 that there had been
a play at court almost every night during Christmas. "The first holy
days we had every night a public play in the great hall, at which the
king was ever present and liked or disliked as he saw cause, but it
seems he takes no extraordinary pleasure in them. The Queen and
Prince were more the players' friends, for on other nights they had
them privately and have since taken them to their protection."
(*Carleton*, p. 53).

Indeed, the prince and the queen saw several plays without King
James present, and many of these were by Worcester's and Nottingham's Servants. But, despite the eventual change in nomencla-
ture (complete, one assumes, by the time these companies were
designated as Prince's and Queen's servants in February 1604 payments by the crown), James himself did not see Nottingham's Servants (the new Prince's) for the first time until January 21 and he
did not see Worcester's (the new Queen's) Servants until December
30, 1604, a whole season later (*MSC*, 6:38–42, 115b–137b).

Though now free to use these new royal names, the other two
companies, as previously remarked, did not quickly receive their
official patents. The Prince's Servants would not be issued theirs for
another two years, while the Servants of the Queen, although there
exists a draft patent for them that cannot be exactly dated (and not
necessarily prepared by the crown), did not receive an official document until April 15, 1609 (*MSC*, 1.3:265–271).

The new monarch, then, contrary to critical tradition on the subject, was apparently not so concerned with drama as immediately
to have placed all the city acting companies under the protection
and control of the crown by changing the names of all companies
at once. Indeed, it cannot be too heavily stressed that the structure
of the lord chamberlain's office and the office of the revels that
reported to him had long been in place. As for Shakespeare and his
fellows, they were indeed fortunate in their name change, whatever
this might do for them, but the event does not argue the king's close
interest in or respect for the power of drama. If it argues anything,
the early patenting of the King's Servants bespeaks an interest in

the company by an unknown figure at court who effected the patent through special influence and through the ability to insinuate the matter early into the crown agenda. Whatever this interest, however, the basic social status of the company, and their consequent vulnerability to social hardship, would remain unchanged, unprovided for by any planned policy of the crown.

III

The indications of King James's personal interest in Shakespeare and his company are sparse, and the king's role in their obtaining of the royal patent questionable. Even so, several episodes in 1604 have also served as the basis for claims that at the beginning of the Stuart era the crown enhanced the social status of Shakespeare and his fellows, singling them out for royal favor and bolstering their status. These claims stem from two events of King James's second year: the coronation procession which at last took place in March 1604, and the visit of the Spanish constable of Castile to England in the following August. In both these events, the King's Servants are supposed to have enjoyed a special role.

But the first instance, the long-deferred coronation procession, did not involve Shakespeare and his fellows alone among the city actors. Each member of Shakespeare's company was given, as is well known, four yards of red cloth "against his Majesty's said royal proceeding through the City of London." Additionally, ten of the two-months-old Servants of the Queen were each given the same amount of cloth, as were the nine members of the company now known as the Servants of the Prince. That any of them actually marched in the procession, however, has been doubted by three scholars, one of whom noted that the red cloth these men received was the lowest grade of such cloth awarded to crown servants in such circumstances—scarlet, for example, going to a higher grade of household retainer.[46]

More stock has been put in the activities of Shakespeare and his fellows later in the same year during the state visit of the constable of Castile. As grooms of the chamber, they waited upon the constable in what E. K. Chambers and G. W. Wickham implied was an ex-

---

46. See F. J. Furnivall, who reproduces the authorization of payment in *Transactions of the New Shakespeare Society* (1877–79), pp. 15´–17´; Ernest Law, *Shakespeare as a Groom of the Chamber* (London: G. Bell and Sons, 1910), pp. 8–9; and Chambers, *Elizabethan Stage*, 2:211.

ceptional role; S. Schoenbaum reinforces this view of the acting group as "in attendance on a sensitive diplomatic occasion."[47] These critics have unwittingly established a tradition that exaggerates the role of Shakespeare's company in crown affairs.

In 1604, now that Philip II of Spain was dead, King James was anxious to ratify the relatively quiet international status quo with an official peace treaty as his first open act of foreign policy. Preparation of the articles of peace was accomplished in committee, but the work culminated in a highly publicized, official, and largely ceremonial signing of the peace agreement, to take place first in England and later in Spain.

Most of the nations of Europe maintained regular embassies in London for such day-to-day business as filing protests about pirated ships, urging trade agreements, spying, bribing English court officials to give the right advice to the decision makers, or simply keeping their own masters up to date. But on unusual occasions such as James's accession to the throne or this signing of a peace treaty, a foreign power would send as a representative some special individual who stood high in nobility and political prestige. This individual would be designated an ambassador-extraordinary with a one-time mission only—such as the embassy of the marquis de Rosny for Henry IV of France to congratulate King James on his accession, or, as now, the visit of a Spanish noble to sign a peace treaty on behalf of his sovereign. The ambassador-extraordinary himself had to be welcomed by his hosts with appropriate recognition of the honor being extended—with appropriate protocol. This protocol demanded not only a show of respect for the greatness of the monarch who had sent the ambassador but considerable personal attention to the ambassador himself.

The Spanish ambassador-extraordinary for the occasion of the signing of the Spanish Peace was Don Juan Ferdinando de Velasco, duke of Frias and constable of Castile, one of the most eminent members of the nobility in his country and lord great chamberlain of Spain. Every effort was made to acknowledge the highly distinguished status of the visitor; thus Shakespeare and his fellows acted as grooms of the chamber on this occasion in a rather large context. For example, the constable and the 234 gentlemen in his party (a group analyzed by Edward Lord Wotton of Maherly in his report to

47. See, for example, Chambers, *William Shakespeare,* 1:76–77, and Schoenbaum, *WSDL,* p. 196.

Robert Cecil as comprising "eight of very good quality, some few other gentlemen," and "the rest all household officers and servants") formally debarked at Dover and were ceremonially greeted by Wotton of Maherly at the head of six hundred horsemen. Sir Lewis Lewrenor wrote Cecil that Wotton's company was so well turned out and equipped that the constable thought they "had all been gentlemen of the court."[48]

King James, on a hunting trip, was not in the vicinity at the time of the ambassador's arrival, and Queen Anna, in residence at Whitehall, apparently represented the crown. As welcoming gifts, King James arranged for a diamond ring worth £1,000 to be presented to the constable, and Queen Anna sent the constable's wife a necklace of pearls valued at £1,400 (*SPD*, 8:141, 148). The queen also sent to Don Juan himself, presumably to match his diamond ring, a tablet of diamonds containing a miniature painting of herself and King James, the whole costing an additional £1,000. The royal couple was equally generous in arranging accommodations. The lord chamberlain of England, the earl of Suffolk, made sure—since here his duties lay—that Somerset House, one of the most splendid residences in London, now Queen Anna's property, and the constable's residence while in England, was well decorated and well stocked. The most gorgeous hangings belonging to the crown adorned the walls, and £300 per diem was allocated for the food and maintenance of the visitors.[49]

The constable proceeded overland from Dover to Greenwich, where he took barge for Somerset House on the Thames, and the vessels had almost finished making their way up the river when another and more splendid craft hove into view, approached the Spanish, and saluted. On this ceremonial barge were Lord Cecil, the earl of Nottingham, the earl of Suffolk—the king's first secretary, the lord admiral, and the lord chamberlain—along with a mysterious lady wearing a mask. Later her identity would be revealed to the constable of Castile, who would feel himself much honored, for this was the queen.[50]

Saluted again by the massed and assembled guards of the king of England, the 234 members of the Spanish party debarked at the water-stairs of Somerset House, passed through two anterooms, and

48. See *Hatfield*, 16:208, 211. See also *Carleton*, p. 61, for a similar analysis of the constable's train.

49. See *SPV*, 10:175, and Winwood, *Memorials*, 2:26.

50. See Law, *Shakespeare as a Groom*, p. 18.

came at last to the lavishly decorated presence chamber, where were
lined up the large number of pages and grooms-in-waiting of the
king's own chamber who had arrived the previous day. Among this
crowd were twelve men, William Shakespeare and his eleven fellows, who were being paid a total of £21.12 to wait on the party of
the constable of Castile for eighteen days, from August 9 to August
27. The document that authorized payment to the group for their
services describes them as "His Majesty's grooms of the Chamber
and Players."

Presumably, then, this is the scene according to which tradition
dictates that Shakespeare and his fellows were especially honored
and thus in some special relationship to the king of England himself.
But the company's position within the larger activity at Somerset
House is not the only relevant point; the general occasion of the
signing of the Spanish Peace provides additional insights into the
relationship between the King's Servants and the crown. For elsewhere there was a second welcoming group employing a second
assemblage of players not from Shakespeare's company. Instrumental in the negotiations for the peace with Spain was Albert, archduke
of Austria and ruler of the Spanish Netherlands, those provinces of
the Low Countries still being occupied by Spain. The cooperation
of the archduke in the negotiations was crucial because of the central
importance of the Low Countries to the peace agreement. Early in
May, Austria's ambassador-extraordinary for the peace conference,
the count of Aremberg, had arrived to organize Austria's agenda for
the occasion. He had taken a modest house in London and conferred
at several times from May through July with the Spanish and French
ministers. When the time came for the official signing of the treaty,
however, the count of Aremberg moved from his more modest lodgings and, like the constable of Castile, established formal residence
in palatial surroundings for the duration of the elaborate ceremonies
(*SPV*, 10:138, 171). This residence was Durham House, like Somerset
House owned by the crown, approachable from the river by water-
stairs, and large enough to have a hall supported by lofty marble
pillars.[51] Indeed. the count of Aremberg and his large group of re-

---

51. See E. B. Chancellor, *Annals of the Strand* (London: Chepman and Hall, 1912),
pp. 278–280. Three hundred years old, Durham House had passed into and out of the
control of the See of Durham, being bestowed by the crown upon various favorites,
the latest of whom had been Sir Walter Ralegh, who lost the palatial residence after
his conviction in the Bye plot of 1603.

tainers resided at Durham House for the same period that the constable of Castile and the Spanish party resided at Somerset House.

The count, to continue the parallel, was also presented with gifts for the occasion by the English crown. Queen Anna gave him a jewel worth £260 with an "A" and an "R" worked into it (presumably for "Anna Regina"), to match her gift to the constable of Castile.[52] Durham House was lavishly furnished and peopled with attendants to act as grooms of the chamber and pages for Aremberg's retinue. Among these grooms were Thomas Green and "ten of his fellows grooms of the chamber and the Queen's Players," who were paid a total of £19.16—in effect, the same sum as Shakespeare's group— for waiting on the count of Aremberg and "the rest of the Commission at Durham House."[53]

Because the level of special treatment accorded Shakespeare and his fellows on this occasion is at issue, the presence of the Queen's Servants at Durham House raises several points. The first concerns the status of the King's Servants as grooms of the chamber. When the King's Servants and the Queen's Servants had been awarded red cloth for the coronation procession in March, they had not actually been described as grooms of the chamber at all; instead, they were referred to as simply players. In fact, both companies became grooms of the chamber for the first time five months after the coronation procession, in the August warrant paying them for this summer attendance at Somerset House and Durham House.[54] This document is, in fact, the basis for the scholarly tradition that strangely conflates the assignment of coronation red cloth to Shakespeare and his fellows with their appointment as grooms of the chamber and often omits reference to the Servants of the Queen altogether.

The second point is that the number of each acting group seems to have been inflated for the occasion. According to the "Apparelling" section of the chamber account, the chamberlain's office paid Shakespeare and his fellows for twelve persons, the payment simply

52. See Frederick Devon, *Issues of the Exchequer* (London, 1836), p. 16.

53. *MSC*, 6:38. The payment to Green and the group of players now called the Queen's Players was identical to that bestowed upon Shakespeare and the members of his company. The twelve people of Shakespeare's group were paid a total of £21.12; thus each person received £1.16. The eleven Queen's Players at Durham House were paid a total of £19.16; thus each man in this group also received £1.16.

54. For these matters, see Law, *Shakespeare as a Groom*, pp. 8, 21–22. In the payment for Somerset House, Shakespeare and his fellows were described as "his Majesty's grooms of the Chamber and Players."

indicating "Augustine Phillipps and John Hemmings and ten of their fellows." But the 1603 patent for Shakespeare's company authorized only nine names as Servants of the King, and nine were again listed when Shakespeare and his fellows received the red cloth for the coronation procession. Comparable inflation occurred with the Servants of the Queen in this instance of the Spanish Peace. Ten persons from the company were issued red cloth for the coronation procession, and the same ten names appeared in 1609 at the time the patent legitimizing the company was granted.[55] Yet, when the Queen's Servants were paid for attendance at Durham House, the payment was not to ten persons but "to Thomas Greene for the allowance of himself and ten of their fellows, Grooms of the Chamber" (*MSC*, 6:38).

The reason for this inflation may lie in the requirement of attendants for this large affair. The nature of this requirement is suggested by Edmond Howes, who wrote in his continuation of Stow's *Annals* that the Spanish and Austrian commissioners and ambassadors were "dieted [fed] at the King's cost, served and attended by the special servants and officers of the King, Queen, and Prince, viz. the gentlemen ushers, sewers, cooks, yeomen of the guard, and grooms of the chamber" (sig. 4B2ᵛ). But during this August the crown was manning at least three palaces: Somerset House, Durham House, and Whitehall, where King James's full court, combined with the court of his consort Queen Anna, was in residence for the duration of the visit. The situation may well have occasioned a shortage of gentlemen ushers, cooks, extra yeomen of the guard, sewers, and grooms of the chamber. Therefore it may have been necessity, not honor, that brought Shakespeare and his fellows to Somerset House. It is true enough that they were the King's Servants. But whether or not their title was an artistic accolade, these actors, as King's Servants (and as Queen's Servants), were obviously a resource for solving the great problem in logistics posed by the entertainment of literally hundreds of foreign guests and their servants.

The third point raised by the presence of the Servants of the Queen at Durham House has to do with the acting company that was *not* present on the occasion of the peace meetings. Most scholars assume that the primary competition for Shakespeare and his fellows during the Elizabethan period was from the Servants of the Lord Admiral, the earl of Nottingham, who had in their number the famous Edward

---

55. See Chambers, *Elizabethan Stage*, 2:231.

Alleyn and who were financed by Philip Henslowe. In 1603 and 1604 these actors were playing at the Fortune playhouse, the newest and perhaps the most gorgeous playhouse in the city after the Globe. As we have observed, during the previous Christmas the group had become the Servants of Prince Henry, an affiliation that accorded with their former status as servants of the prestigious Nottingham; the heir apparent, though young, was theoretically more important than his mother the queen consort.

In the coronation procession of March 1604, this company too had received their four and a half yards of red cloth as footmen to the prince. But now, in August, even though their status as actors was still high and they seem to have been a more successful group than the Queen's Servants—they had presented five plays at court the Christmas before while the Queen's Servants had presented only two—they were not attendants at the Spanish Peace.[56] From this it would seem that the appointing of actors as grooms of the chamber at the palatial river residences was not necessarily a function of artistic excellence as perceived by contemporaries. In fact, the Queen's Servants themselves had been a provincial company that became Servants of the Earl of Worcester a year or so before Queen Elizabeth died, when the two major acting companies of the city were already quite well established. Worcester's Servants were most likely the poorest in quality of the three groups.

The absence from these proceedings of the Servants of the Prince suggests, then, the coincidence of the status of "Servants" in general with the political activities of the patrons to whom these acting "Servants" were nominally attached and the lack of any necessary relationship between the promulgation of actors and questions of public policy. In this particular case, the ten-year-old Prince Henry would play a small, though highly symbolic, role in the peace ceremonies, but he was not actively concerned in the social activities. He was a child with no greater court of his own than a small household composed of noble boys. But because the future prince of Wales's acting servants were absent from the large ceremony, this does not mean that the prince himself was in disgrace—that the

56. If frequency of court performances at Christmas be any criterion, Shakespeare and his fellows, in the Christmas 1603–4 holidays, gave nine plays, the Prince's Servants gave five plays, and the Queen's Servants gave two. In the Christmas season celebration that would follow the August of the Spanish Peace, Shakespeare and his fellows presented eleven plays at court, the Prince's Servants eight, and the Queen's Servants one; see *MSC*, 6:38–42.

treatment of actors bearing his name was any function of his honor. The players were not the personalities in this affair. The Queen's Servants were probably present for the following reason. Queen Anna was very much a part of the proceedings of the peace meetings, especially because James had chosen to absent himself from London until the very last moment, delegating the royal representation to her. Further, protocol in this situation dictated the staffing of Somerset House, the residence of the highest ranking ambassador-extraordinary, with persons nominally from James's household, while Durham House would be staffed with retainers nominally from the court of the queen. In the end, however the logistics were administered, both ambassadors-extraordinary—and by inference the king of Spain and the archduke of Austria—received elaborate courtesies from the king and the queen through the donation of both their palaces and their own household servants.

The often celebrated sojourn of Shakespeare's fellows at Somerset House (and of the Queen's Servants at Durham House) may finally be viewed within the context of the other servants surrounding them. The royal "chamber" was a large concept. The bed chamber and the privy chamber, for example, were highly formalized groupings of people with a great deal of influence at court. Shakespeare and his fellows, however, were merely grooms and merely of the chamber in general—not gentlemen of the privy chamber or ushers or even grooms of the privy chamber. A contemporary manuscript listing annual court household expenses suggests the structure of the privy chamber.[57] In descending order, there were gentlemen of the privy chamber, gentlemen ushers of the privy chamber, gentlemen ushers not of the privy chamber, grooms of the privy chamber, grooms not of the privy chamber, and so forth. The players in the queen's and king's acting companies, however, were ambiguously "grooms of the chamber"—and probably for this one event.

Their pay is significant. Each man received two shillings per day. Very few court jobs were paid on a per diem basis; more than nine-tenths of them were paid according to annual rates. In fact, the only other group participating in the Spanish Peace to receive the same wage as these actors were the guards: each of the 250 ordinary yeomen of the guard received two shillings per

57. *Mss of Lord Montagu of Beaulieu*, ed. S. C. Lomas (London, HMSO:1900), 62–63.

diem too. It is true that the actors and the yeomen of the guard fared well in comparison to the customary recompense provided to masons, joiners, and tailors, who were also paid on a per diem basis. But in the context of expenses accrued during the entire ceremony of the Spanish Peace, the thirty or so men including Shakespeare, his fellows, and their colleagues at Durham House were an almost negligible financial item, even compared to the many guards who were paid at the same wages.

The marginality of Shakespeare and his fellows to things royal during the ceremony of the Spanish Peace is also indicated by the activity of King James at this time. The king had been hunting in the country since July. Long before, he had decided not to arrive in London until the Tuesday following the Spanish constable's Friday arrival and not to deal personally with the constable at any great length until the Sunday of the lavish ceremonial signing. He planned to return immediately to Royston, the location of his hunting lodge, on the Monday following the signing in London. James carried out this plan, coming to London in stages on horseback and by coach and arriving at Whitehall five days before the signing. In the time intervening between his arrival and the Sunday ceremony, James allowed the constable a total of two hours and fifteen minutes (*SPV*, 10:175,178). Of course the king devoted Sunday to the constable. But as the constable, escorted by the earl of Devonshire, proceeded in state to Whitehall at 11:00 A.M., Shakespeare and his fellows presumably remained at Somerset House. And they were presumably there when the constable returned from the Whitehall ceremonies late in the afternoon to dine in private.

Nevertheless, at the end of this affair the players briefly came closer, so to speak, to King James. Sunday night the constable experienced a kidney attack and was confined to bed all day Monday, when he was scheduled to go to Whitehall and bid the king of England farewell. James, anxious to leave town on this day, came calling on the constable instead. He appeared at Somerset House at 4:00 P.M. and mounted the steps to the constable's personal chambers to bid him a royal and forgiving farewell. The king then departed for Durham House, where he visited the chambers of the bedridden, gout-stricken count of Aremberg, who had missed the Sunday ceremony, to bid him a formal farewell as well. And thus, as the Venetian secretary observed, the king attained his own objects while honoring these noblemen all the more through his gracious visits.

Late Monday evening, but pretty well on schedule, King James departed the town (*SPV*, 10:180).

Viewing James's relationship to the ceremony of the signing of the Spanish Peace, it is difficult to determine where William Shakespeare could have fitted into the king's plans—a rapid visit to the city, a rapid return, and an avoidance, when possible, of the principal figures participating in the drama of the signing. Indeed, if there was anything James was thinking of in London at this time, it was not a dramatist but something with whiskers and four paws, which had lived for a while but unfortunately was now embalmed: the new lion cub born in the Tower of London.[58]

As for the question of cultivating literary persons to ornament the crown, a perennial and wishful fantasy of literary historians, a remark made by King James during the audience with the constable of Castile is, finally, pertinent to this whole affair. According to a Spanish pamphlet describing the peace-signing process (printed in Spanish at Antwerp, surviving in a single copy once in the royal collection before it came to the British Library), the constable of Castile had a brief interchange with the king during the audience of introduction which lasted three-quarters of an hour. Complimenting King James, the constable observed what a wonderful thing James's love of the noble pastime of hunting was, especially when this love was coupled with a love of letters—a combination rarely met with among those who are crowned kings. King James, continues this account, promptly replied that it was strange that kings and common men of letters had to be lumped together like this. For among a group of monarchs only one king might indeed be found who loved hunting *and* learning; yet this one king was certainly one more than could ever be found in any group of common men of letters. Evidently, James assumed that letters did not ennoble him, but he letters. If we assume that James would not have included actors and playwrights among such common men of letters, his opinion in *Basilikon Doron* seems to argue otherwise (see above, p. 25).

During the signing of the Spanish Peace, Shakespeare and his fellows may indeed have been in attendance to swell the train, but neither the actions nor the words of King James provide the slightest

58. See *Hatfield*, 16:207–208. Although James in Royston had commanded Sir Thomes Lake to write Robert Cecil to tell the lieutenant of the tower to see that the lion cub was fed, kept warm, and protected from sightseers, the cub did not survive its first day; the lieutenant then preserved it for James's inspection.

suggestion that the occasion was a significant milestone in their social advancement. If indeed the episode must be regarded against all indications as significant in this way, then it must serve equally as a complimentary adornment of the earl of Worcester's old company, the Servants of the Queen; they served in identical circumstances, receiving identical pay and probably identical exposure to the person of the king. By the same token, one would be constrained to argue that the Prince's Servants, the old Servants of the Lord Admiral, by virtue of their absence from these proceedings were deliberately humiliated. Given the context, however, none of these options seems realistic.

IV

A final and more immediately pertinent response to the important question of English royal priorities as they applied to Shakespeare and his Stuart career is to be found in the activities of the new Stuart court in the west during 1603, several months before the coronation procession and the Spanish Peace. I am referring specifically to the early part of the 1603 Christmas season and the circumstances surrounding the first performance known to have been given by Shakespeare and his fellows at court during the reign of King James.

In a number of ways, to be sure, 1603 was not typical. Since his plague-ridden accession and after his July coronation, James had moved the temporary seat of crown activities away from London— first to Oxford and then west to the Salisbury-Winchester-Southampton area, finally settling in at Wilton, the young earl of Pembroke's palatial estate in that region some distance from London. The latter move was to make room for the trial of the Bye and Main Plot defendants in Winchester, a key event continually postponed by the plague. Remaining at Wilton not only allowed James to focus on administrative matters in a stable, because less peripatetic, context but also to attend to diplomatic responsibilities that had been postponed during his many removals. It must therefore have seemed, in early December 1603, when official court documents were being dated as if Wilton was serving as the royal palace, that Christmas was, for all intents and purposes, to be held there in the west.

Drama historians rarely recall that Wilton was the site of the Stuart debut of the King's Servants, while those who do tend to overestimate the implications of the event. This first performance took place within a general context in which King James was attending to two immediate problems, one large, one small. The smaller was the necessity of finally receiving at Wilton some of the many ambassadors-extraordinary who had come to pay him special homage on the occasion of his accession and who were literally following him around the country waiting for audiences. The larger context was the prosecution of the treason trials by the crown, a practical as well as symbolic necessity finally to be attended to at this same time in the Wilton-Salisbury area. Both these concerns, embassages and the trials, more largely define, in the end, the limits of the relevance of Shakespeare and his fellows to the court of King James, significantly establishing these limits as operative at the very beginning of the reign.

Ambassadors-extraordinary had begun making their way to England ever since James's accession, for international courtesy required congratulatory gestures toward the new monarch. Most of the relevant states sent such ambassadors, and, as in the case of the constable of Castile, the resultant protocol dictated that such ambassadors receive double recognition: as personal representatives of their monarch, and as figures of exalted rank in their own right. The visit of Piero Duodo, ambassador-extraordinary from the Republic of Venice, was not the only such embassage, but taking place at Wilton in late November 1603 it has special relevance to the context of the first known performance by Shakespeare and his fellows in the Stuart reign.

The Venetians were highly valued by the English crown for their wealth, their trade, and their command of the Mediterranean. The privy council regarded Venetian influence as important in suppressing Turkish and other piracy on English vessels, and Venetian potential for conflict, as a Catholic state, with Spain and with the pope as useful. Venice kept up a large volume of trade with heretic England, and James himself seems to have had a personal liking for the idea of Venice. He had written a youthful poem on the Battle of Lepanto in which the Venetians had been pitted against the Turks, and he would continue to evince a strong political interest in the affairs of Venice throughout his reign (manifested perhaps in his attraction to Shakespeare's *Merchant of Venice*, as we see in Chapter 4). For all these reasons, Piero Duodo's visit to Wilton was treated with the greatest attention to ritual expressions of esteem by the

English crown.[59] A brief description of the welcoming and farewell
ceremonies should serve to illustrate the royal panoply of the occasion—court spectacles of great dramatic impact that certainly
competed with players' interludes for the attention of the court.

During the late autumn of 1603, on Sunday, November 20, the
day appointed for the Venetian embassage's audience of introduction, Lord Henry Howard, a member of the privy council, Sir Lewis
Lewkenor, James's master of ceremonies, and twenty-five carriages
arrived in Salisbury, where Duodo, Nicolo Molino, the ambassador-
in-ordinary, and the rest of the entourage were staying several days
after they had arrived by ship near Southampton. The Venetian emissaries proceeded under their escort from Salisbury to Wilton, arriving at three in the afternoon. After the ambassadors had rested
briefly in a chamber, the entire entourage moved across the courtyard of Wilton to the great hall for the audience with the king. In
the windows above the courtyard of Wilton stood the king, the
queen, and Prince Henry, while many ladies and gentlemen watched
from similar vantage points. The ambassadors wrote later: "We believe that our suites must have made a fine show, both for numbers,
for variety of livery, for the robes of silk and gold, the crowd of
gentlemen, not merely from Venice but from other cities, all [being]
sumptuously dressed" (*SPV*, 10:116).

Although the protocol for the king's subsequent reception of the
emissaries in the crowded presence chamber in the great hall was
prescribed, James made several exceptions to it in order to bestow
special honor on these Venetian visitors. As the entourage halted
before his elevated throne in deep obeisance, he himself removed
his hat in respectful deference to the Republic of Venice. He then
rose from his throne and actually descended the steps of his state,
and with hat still in hand moved outside the shelter of the royal
canopy. There he solemnly accepted the ambassadors' letters of credentials and the greetings of Piero Duodo. Although the king often
spoke through an interpreter, as he had when the Spanish ambassador-extraordinary had paid his congratulatory visit a few weeks
earlier, on this occasion James responded to Duodo's speech in
French, thus indicating that he and Duodo could converse personally
in this international common language. Moreover, he offered an
apology for what had turned out to be inadequate lodgings for the

59. For these matters, see *SPV*, 10:113–116.

Venetians in Salisbury, with a promise of royal retribution against those Salisbury citizens who had refused the Venetian group more opulent quarters. Duodo and Molino protested their satisfaction with the hospitality, unwilling that any English subjects should be punished for their sakes, thus setting the tone for the exchanges to follow during the one-week series of formal visits.

James persisted in showing the Venetian embassage high favor, sometimes laced with his own variety of humor. For example, on Monday, November 28, Duodo and Molino issued from Salisbury a rather conventional interembassy invitation to the ambassadors of France and of Tuscany as well as to some gentlemen of the English court to dine as guests of the Republic of Venice. Shortly thereafter, they were informed that the nine-year-old Prince Henry, who had taken a small but significant role in the audience of introduction, wished to join this dinner. After excited and hasty preparations, all was in readiness and Prince Henry arrived at the Venetian lodgings in Salisbury with an assembly of "chief officers of the state."[60] Sir Thomas Chaloner, the young prince's "governor," then proceeded to explain to the excited Venetians the reasons for this royal presence. King James, he said, was still distressed at the quality of the lodgings offered the Venetians in Salisbury, and he wished to make amends. Therefore the king was sending to the Venetians the prince, his own son and heir, as a hostage—never doubting that the Venetians would return their prize.

The Venetians observed to the doge and to the senate of Venice in their report that the prince had never before taken a meal outside the palace; he had even refused an invitation from the Spanish ambassador. Therefore, at a time when conspirators against the lives of the royal family were on trial, the honor done by the prince's visit was obviously great and noted by all. Moreover, they added, the king himself had been twice on the point of calling his own carriage to attend this dinner but had desisted, fearing to inflict too much weight on what had begun as second-level diplomatic entertainment. In any event, Duodo and Molino concluded, "God be thanked it all passed off in perfect order" (*SPV*, 10:120).

Such regal courtesy and pomp achieved its apogee during the ceremony of farewell on Tuesday, November 29. Prior to an elaborate

60. See p. 248 of the extremely useful but not yet widely consulted journal (1595–1605) of Levinus Munck, a member of Sir Robert Cecil's secretarial staff. This journal has been edited by Howard Vallance Jones, "The Journal of Levinus Munck," *English Historical Review* 68 (1953), 234–258.

midday dinner that was usually the final act of royal hospitality to a departing ambassador-extraordinary, Duodo and Molino had a private audience with the king. Then, conducted to the great hall by the lord chamberlain, James and the two Venetian ambassadors arrived at a sixteen-foot-long table attended by the elaborately dressed nobles who would act as servitors so as to attest to the king's largesse and the favored status of the Venetians. After elaborate ceremonies of hand washing and seating, the dinner began. It featured a rich abundance and impressive variety of food. The rest of the court, dining in a second room, hastened through their meal so as to be able to watch the main dinner in progress. There King James was not simply attentive to his guests; he conversed at great length and animatedly about the government and laws of the Venetian republic. On several occasions he rose from his seat and, removing his hat, offered toasts in honor of the doge of Venice and his distinguished emissaries. In all, the dinner lasted two hours and concluded with a second series of ceremonial hand washings attended to by a different group of nobles.

Although they had made their formal adieux to King James immediately after the dinner, the Venetian embassage remained in Salisbury because the ambassador-extraordinary had not yet made his final visit to Queen Anna, who had been ill and unable to attend the dinner. He waited, in fact, from Wednesday, November 30, until Friday, December 2, the date on which Shakespeare and his fellows performed a play at Wilton. On that same day, the queen sent to inform Duodo that because she was still too indisposed to grant him audience she would consider Duodo's formal farewell visit as having occurred so that the Venetians could get on with the arduous winter journey back from Southampton to Dover and then to Venice. As a consequence, Duodo and his entourage did not form part of the audience for the first court performance of Shakespeare's company that night. Nor, presumably, did Queen Anna, who could hardly appear after having announced her indisposition, the existence of which is affirmed by other documents.[61]

Spectacular though it was, the visit of the ambassadors was not the only drama generally coincident with the December 2 debut of the King's Servants at the court of James I. A far more important form of political theater overlapped Duodo's visit—the resolution of the Bye and Main Plots. The trial was of key importance to James,

61. See E. T. Bradley, *Arabella Stuart*, 2:190.

who also seems to have used the occasion to exploit the political opportunities implicit in the situation.

Briefly, the Bye and Main Plots had apparently been a scheme to assassinate or gain control of the person of King James on Midsummer Day, June 24, just one month before his coronation. Because of dissension among the conspirators, however, the attempt was aborted—but not soon enough to deter the authorities from uncovering the plot. Arrests began in early July and, as the conspiracy unfolded, officials discovered that the threat involved highly ranked persons well situated to negotiate with James's enemies. Thus the distinction between the "Bye" or "Priests'" Plot, featuring such malcontents as the Catholic priests William Watson and William Clark, as well as Sir Griffin Markham and Sir Anthony Copley, and the "Main Plot," which reached into the peerage.

The conspirators of highest rank were two barons: the Catholic Henry Brooke, Lord Cobham, who as warden of the cinque ports held a post crucial to the defense of England; and Thomas, fifteenth Lord Grey of Wilton, a Puritan activist and bitter enemy of Essex and Southampton. A week before the coronation, the plots having been discovered, Lord Cobham's brother George Brooke implicated Cobham in a correspondence with the count of Aremberg, ambassador-extraordinary from the archduke of Austria, who was the Spanish king Philip's son-in-law and ruler of the Spanish Netherlands; this at a time when the faith of anyone who succeeded Queen Elizabeth was still a potentially inflammatory issue. Lord Cobham, his brother, Lord Grey, and also Sir Walter Ralegh were all sent to the Tower of London, Ralegh because Cobham's confession implicated him too (*Carleton*, pp. 38–39).

By the time of the November trials, scheduled at Winchester because of the plague in London, public interest in the conspiracy was high, and the authorities feared that the city would become a circus—and a possible source of contagion—if appropriate steps were not taken. Accordingly, the proclamation adjourning the Michaelmas law term (when cases could be tried) to November 9 (*cras martini*) and to Winchester also ordered that no person could gain entry through the gates or other openings into Winchester without fully explaining his business, as well as his state of health, to those guards appointed by the lord chancellor of England, Lord Ellesmere.

The trials of the lesser defendants—that is, everyone except Sir Griffin Markham, Sir Walter Ralegh, Lord Grey, and Lord Cobham, who would be judged separately by their peers—began on Sunday,

November 13. This was coincident with the arrival of the Venetian ambassadors in the Southampton area. James had sent them word that, although he would be delighted to receive them sooner, he recommended Sunday, November 20 for the audience of introduction, when most of the privy council attending the trials would have returned from Winchester.

The commissioners were, in fact, back by Saturday, November 19, having found all the Bye Plot defendants guilty. On November 25 and 26, in the midst of the Venetian embassage, the trial of the peers for the Main Plot took place in Winchester with all the most powerful nobles in the country present. Lord Grey of Wilton, Lord Cobham, and Sir Walter Ralegh were all condemned to die.

The executions of the lesser conspirators, starting with Watson and Clark, began in Winchester on November 29, the day the Venetians had their audience of farewell with James, and continued until December 5, the Monday following the Friday performance at Wilton by Shakespeare and his fellows. Those not of the nobility were condemned to that gory and spectacular end that was the standard punishment for traitors—hanging, drawing, and quartering—but apparently some leeway was allowed in the carrying out of such sentences. Sometimes the victim was not cut down until he was, in effect, clinically dead or nearly dead, and unconscious. Then his members were hacked off, including his genitals, and his body chopped into quarters. But Watson and Clark, both cut down while alive and conscious, were "very bloodily handled." And Clark, wrote Dudley Carleton to John Chamberlain, "to whom more favor was intended, had the worse luck, for he both strove to help himself and spake after he was cut down." The quarters of both priests were set on the gates of Winchester and the heads impaled on the first tower of Winchester Castle (*Carleton*, p. 47).

However compelling such spectacles might be, an even greater drama was anticipated at the beheading of the condemned nobles on December 7, five days after the performance by Shakespeare and his fellows. With the issuance of the warrants for the execution of Sir Griffin Markham, Lord Grey, and Lord Cobham (Ralegh was to be executed later), the state was set for a scene of high tragedy, effectively eclipsing any interludes staged by mere players.

The story of these "executions" is well known. James, in a theatrically brilliant manipulation of ritual, arranged for the conspirators to be brought to the scaffold individually, where each bade farewell to friends, said the appropriate prayers, and readied himself for execution. Markham, who went first and was visibly shaken, was told at the moment of execution to return to the castle for further meditation. Lord Grey, who appeared to Dudley Carleton like "a dapper young bridegroom," confessed his crime with a religious fervency, only to be informed that the order of executions had been reversed and he would have to wait another hour. After a similar charade was staged with Cobham, the three conspirators were reunited on the scaffold.

> So as Grey and Markham, being brought back to the scaffold, as they then were but nothing acquainted with what had passed no more than the lookers-on with what should follow, looked strange one upon the other, like men beheaded and met again in the other world. (*Carleton*, p. 51)

In these highly dramatic circumstances, the sheriff announced that the king "hath sent hither a countermand and given you your lives." The results were sensational:

> There was then no need to beg a plaudite of the audience, for it was given with such hues and cries that it went from the castle into the town and there began afresh, as if there has been some such like accident. And thus experience was made of the difference of examples of justice and mercy, that in this last no man could cry loud enough God save the King, and at the holding up of Brooke's head [Cobham's younger brother executed on a previous day], when the executioner began the same cry, he was not seconded by the voice of any one man but the Sheriff. (*Carleton*, p. 51)

The chief significance of the pseudo-executions at Winchester in the present context is again to emphasize the general social situation within which Shakspeare and his fellows found themselves at Wilton and could often find themselves whenever they performed plays at court. The early part of December 1603 featured political and public spectacles of primary and absorbing interest to courtiers: the pomp, ritual, and politics of ambassadorial activities; the consummate theater of the Main and Bye Plot extravaganza. The first performance of Shakespeare and his company could not possibly have been a central event at the time—however primary it may be in the imaginative reconstructions of critics who, over the centuries, have chronicled Shakespeare's career. And, although the Stuart court in 1603 may have been subject to unusual disruption because of plague, the activities I have reviewed here do suggest, not only what the preoccupations of a court environment were, but also how they defined the social and political scene into which Shakespeare and his fellows were summoned as entertainers.

Indeed, it was most probably because of the embassages that Shakespeare and his fellows were even present at Wilton if Dudley Carleton, again, is accurate. On November 27, when all thought that Wilton or even Windsor, another location away from London, would hold the royal court through the plague-filled Christmas holidays of 1603–4, Carleton observed to John Chamberlain that "the court is like to Christmas at Windsor, and many plays and shows are bespoken to give entertainment to our ambassadors" (*Carleton*, p. 42).

In early December, the French, Spanish, Polish, and Florentine congratulatory embassages were in the vicinity of Wilton (*SPV*, 10:114–117). Since plays seem to have been standard fare as ambassadorial entertainment, Shakespeare and his fellows were most likely summoned to Wilton late in 1603 to be available for these events, and to be used as needed. There was nothing singular or special about their presence there except that no other company had similarly been summoned. But Shakespeare's company was probably chosen for the same reason that it later gave the first five performances at Hampton Court when the Christmas season moved back there; that is, the master of the revels must have assumed that the King's Servants were the only acting group authorized to play at the time.[62]

V

Shakespeare's traditional biography has been informed by two unproved assumptions: that King James was a lover of plays and a royal sponsor of artistic activity, and that Shakespeare's genius was recognized by his aristocratic patrons in much the same way we recognize it today. Neither of these premises is warranted by the texts that survive from the great dramatist's lifetime, and so efforts at describing Shakespeare's professional life in the decade from 1603

62. In Edinburgh, several years before James came to England, there was only one playing company and it too was called the King's Servants. See my forthcoming article on this subject.

to 1613 must entertain narratives other than those that currently argue Shakespeare's relationship to the Stuart court and James's own investment in the theater. Indeed, it is important to conclude this consideration of the social status of Shakespeare and his fellows in the early Stuart period by recalling the general circumstances under which Shakespeare and his fellows, or any acting company, appeared before a royal audience in the first place. For, finally, the circumstances did not necessarily mirror a royal love of drama.

Playing companies appeared before the sovereign at specified periods and for particular purposes. From the time of James's accession until the death of Shakespeare, a span of thirteen years, the companies were paid by the crown only twice outside their regular Christmas appearances: for the visit of the king of Denmark in the summer of 1606, and for the delayed wedding festivities of Elizabeth of Bohemia. Otherwise, the professional acting companies played only between the end of October and several days before Lent, and then only on particular dates. For example, when James came up to the city every year for All Saints' Day and All Souls' Day, November 1–2, there seems to have been ritual festivity.[63] Then, in December, in Advent, there were traditional performances of plays at court on various major holy days extending to and culminating in the Shrovetide sequence before Ash Wednesday.

The Christmas season especially, that two-week period clustered around Christmas day, was an annual demonstration of royal pomp and power. London was packed with courtiers, nobles, ambassadors, and other dignitaries, at the ready to take part in a series of resplendent and politically important court spectacles. Occasionally at the palace would be the marriage of a noble couple—one of the principals a court favorite—with masques in which noblewomen or noblemen celebrated the bride or groom. Ambassadors would make formal calls to express their season's greetings to the monarch and required formal entertainment. And, in James's reign, Queen Anna would institute masques as important social events of this season. Plays by professional actors were a part of the spectacle, but their

63. The very convenient Appendix A of Chambers, *Elizabethan Stage*, vol. 4, "A Court Calendar," does not make this fact obvious. But *Othello*, for example, was performed on November 1, 1604, and *Tempest* on November, 1 1611. A play was canceled for November 1, 1612, and *Bartholomew Fair* was presented November 1, 1614. Queen Elizabeth did not celebrate All Saints' Day or All Souls' with plays, perhaps because her Accession Day fell in the middle of November and was, of course, annually celebrated.

importance in the scheme of things has been greatly exaggerated. The playing companies were not in attendance at court for this entire period. They would be called to one palace or another for a performance or a series of performances as necessary.

Moreover, as already suggested, there is nothing to indicate that plays by professional actors were the new king's preferred form of court entertainment, that plays were central to the festivities and— with the ear of the king bent attentively to its script—perhaps politically charged. Despite the number of plays performed in the first Christmas season of James's reign, for example, there is no suggestion in the comments of James's contemporaries that he had a special interest in drama. Finally, and contrary to traditional assumption, King James did not always attend plays that were presented at court. Because commentators on the subject have not hitherto differentiated between plays shown before a full court and plays shown before Anna or Prince Henry, it seems that the artistic tastes of his wife and son, both of whom saw a great many plays (but even then, never out of season), may have been ascribed to James. The emergence of Queen Anna's court as the center of artistic activity and patronage in the Jacobean period is too large and complex a phenomenon to be dealt with adequately here; that there was, however, a decentering of the monarch's role in the promotion of the arts is relevant to my consideration of Shakespeare's own professional career in his Stuart decade.[64]

The court and the king were not implicated in the dramatist's professional activities. Plays there were at court, in season, But Shakespeare and his fellows, at the most, in the best circumstances, might give ten to fifteen plays at court between November and Lent and be paid for them at a rate that had not risen with inflation since the early days of Queen Elizabeth: £10 per play. A maximum gross under such conditions of £150 would not support the company and its expenses throughout any calendar year. Nor, apparently, was the prestige edible or useful in keeping the actors warm. Common players were not beyond the reach of disaster. In Chapter 3 we are concerned with the greatest of these troubles, bubonic plague. The years following 1603, when plague was less intense, were, paradoxically, even more difficult for Shakespeare and his fellows. It is these years, in fact, which would have a marked effect on Shakespeare's productivity.

64. I discuss Queen Anna and her circles in "First Stuart Queen."

3

Pestilence and the Players

Although it acknowledges the epidemic plagues of 1593–94 and 1603–4, Shakespearean criticism has not closely considered the interaction of this disease with the business activities and plans of the King's Servants or with Shakespeare's own dramaturgical career. Yet the effect of the 1593 plague alone both on the economics of the London playing companies and on Shakespeare's own creative activities is highly suggestive. The economic impact in 1593–94 is apparent from decreasing numbers: several companies that were operating in London before the plague of 1593 seem to have disappeared by 1595.[1] Indeed, it is after the cessation of this plague, with the privy council permission to play again in October 1594, that history first identifies both the Lord Chamberlain's Servants and Shakespeare's membership in that group. As for the effect of plague on Shakespeare's creative activities at that time, the poet's production of *Venus and Adonis* and *Lucrece* during the closing of the playhouses has already been discussed. Had the plague not occurred, it is quite possible he would never have written these works.

The plague of 1603 is the one most often noted by scholars, and in the second section of this chapter I focus on its implications for Shakespeare and his fellows. My immediate concern, however,

---

1. See E. K. Chambers, *The Elizabethan Stage*, 4 vols. (Oxford: Clarendon Press, 1923), 2:122–140.

is the effect of plague on London drama between the major visitations of 1593 and 1603. Taking their cue from F. P. Wilson's seminal study of the subject, *The Plague in Shakespeare's London,*[2] most critics who refer to plague—and they are few—have examined the great epidemics, at the cost of looking away from the less sensational endemic upsurges in the times between major epidemics and of ignoring the action of the authorities in trying to control these upsurges. Thus those periods when plague combined with Lenten stoppages or privy council special measures to extend the playhouse closings for prolonged periods have remained especially blurred.

One can easily see why the effects of plague between the "peaks" have been generally ignored. It is difficult to believe that Shakespeare's early Stuart period suffered regular play stoppages of some duration; difficult to believe that a society lacking microbiology and antibiotics would not simply allow these visitations to run their courses unhindered rather than press home such measures as the shutting of playhouses. Wilson's good book even inadvertently encourages skepticism on such a point by emphasizing major visitations while at the same time including rather droll contemporary references to various plague officials carrying out such duties as killing dogs and disposing of organic sewage—into the rivers. Was not the closing of theaters, or the attempted closing in milder periods of plague, simply another such instance of token but rote and futile official behavior—an effort recognized as futile by all and so given only lip service? Were not plague-related closings, in the final analysis, merely another shallow and unregarded excuse by city officials to impose ideological control over the subversive threat that plays seemed to them to represent?

But it was not the city, it was the crown, the original supporter and licenser of drama as the monarch's special solace in traditional times of revelry, that was most often the agent of such theater closings. The lord mayor and the aldermen did not often close playhouses, even though their connections with the city guilds might indeed have placed these officials alongside other antitheatrical elements. The theaters were most often closed in plague time by the privy council of England, if records are any indication, for the council not only carried on much of the day-to-day governance of the realm

2. F. P. Wilson, *The Plague in Shakespeare's London* (London: Oxford University Press, 1963).

but was composed of the most politically powerful nobles in the kingdom.[3] To understand why plague was dealt with at this level, we should consider not only what was implied by a visit of bubonic plague in London but also how the disease was understood by the authorities. Current Shakespearean criticism is too quick to dismiss the prescientific and practical steps adopted for plague suppression in the Elizabeth era merely as the futility of superstition and ignorance. Because this approach conceals an assumption that, really, the playhouses were closed only when plague was so dramatically prevalent that any desperate preventive measure was gladly embraced, it is important to view with some care the interaction of the London and crown authorities with the problems posed by this fearful disease.

The first section of this chapter positions plague in its English historical context and then closely considers the symptoms and forms of the disease and its mode of spread. In several instances, plague-prevention measures in Renaissance England (though less sophisticated than those on the continent) accorded with just those preventive steps recommended by twentieth-century medical theory before the discovery of antibiotics and still recommended today for third-world countries when antibiotics are unavailable. The methods being similar, then, one must consider the possibility that the crown authorities observed results that encouraged them to repeat the measures they adopted when plague threatened. And, although there can be no detailed history of plagues averted, the absence of plague in many instances could be as telling as its presence.

3. The reason that the privy council does not loom larger in plague orders for the first decade of James's reign is that the 1619 Whitehall fire destroyed records of the council proceedings between January 1, 1602 and April 30, 1613; see *Acts*, 33:v-ix. As John Chamberlain then noted, what were lost were "all, or most of the writings and papers belonging to the offices of the Signet, Privy Seal, and Council Chamber." A brief abstract of the privy council register covering the period 1603–1610, perhaps belonging to Sir Julius Caesar, forms *British Museum Additional MS* 11402; it is this brief abstract that has supplied the three privy council orders (1604–5) cited in this study (see *MSC*, 1.4/5:370–372). There are no further orders pertaining to drama in this abstract until 1615. Thus it may often seem as if the lord mayor and his council of aldermen wrote to the privy council suggesting restraint of plays because of plague, and then received no answer from the crown—as if the city authorities were being evaded. This picture is a misleading one, especially since the crown itself had no duplicate agency for gathering plague statistics. The city controlled the figures, and I presume that therefore city recommendations in these matters were ignored only at great risk.

I

Bubonic plague had been in London long before Shakespeare's time. In November 1348, a pandemic of plague first gripped the city. This visitation endured until the late spring, and by Easter hundreds were still being buried every day.[4] Endemic thereafter, this strange and fearful sickness struck with force again in 1405, and 30,000 died in the next two years. According to J. F. D. Shrewsbury, London experienced the plague ten more times in the next hundred years.[5]

Between 1526 and 1560, the pestilence constantly caused the authorities of city and realm to put off the beginning of the law terms in the autumn and drove the royal court to seek refuge in the country, and so the generations of Shakespeare's parents and grandparents were familiar with this fear. But, in the fifth year of the reign of Queen Elizabeth, what some think was the worst of all visitations to Renaissance England arrived in late March 1563, thirteen months before Shakespeare's birth. During that July, only one hundred died in London in one week, but during a seven-day period in September over 1,800 perished there. Plague also spread at alarming rates over the rest of England, and during the year of Shakespeare's birth it entered Stratford-upon-Avon itself. Although this town annually sustained an average deathrate of some 55 of its 800 inhabitants, in

4. For this level of mortality, see Leslie Bradley, "Some Medical Aspects of Plague," in *The Plague Reconsidered*, ed. Paul Slack (Local Population Studies with the S.S.R.C. Cambridge Group for the History of Population and Social Structure: Matlock, Derbyshire, 1977), pp. 17–19. For the statistics of 1349, see Charles F. Mullett, *The Bubonic Plague and England* (Lexington: University of Kentucky Press, 1956), p. 21.

5. See J. F. D. Shrewsbury, *A History of Bubonic Plague in the British Isles* (Cambridge: Cambridge University Press, 1970), chap. 5, which argues that some of these incidents of plague in England were really other diseases misperceived by writers and civil authorities as bubonic plague. Shrewsbury's reasoning, often cogent but challenged by others—see Christopher Morris, "Plague in Britain," in *The Plague Reconsidered*, ed. Slack, pp. 37–47 —is not relevant here, since the subject is what London authorities in Shakespeare's day took to have been the case. Visitations of plague in England are recorded for August 1433, May 1449, November 1451, September 1454, 1466, 1467, 1471, 1500 (when 20,000 died in London), and October 1513 (between 300 and 400 deaths per day). For a different view of the incidence of plague in fifteenth-century England and for further commentary on Shrewsbury's disintegrationist view of these statistics, see Robert S. Gottfried, *Epidemic Disease in Fifteenth-Century England* (New Brunswick, N.J.: Rutgers University Press, 1978), pp. 238–240. Gottfried adds to the number of nationwide plague epidemics in England by referring to visitations also in 1452, 1457–59, 1467, and 1473.

that year of pestilence 254 persons were buried—more than a quarter of Shakespeare's fellow citizens.[6]

Throughout William Shakespeare's boyhood and youth, London itself continued to experience strong outbreaks, particularly in 1569 and 1582, but in Shakespeare's own lifetime none was wholly comparable to the violence of the pestilence that struck as Shakespeare's dramatic writing career was beginning in 1593. In one year at least 15,000 persons of a London population of 123,000 died—more than 12 percent.[7] Then, though rife in the north of England throughout the remainder of the 1590s, the pestilence was mercifully absent from the city for almost ten years but eased into London again in 1603 (as observed in Chapter 2) just after the accession of King James.[8]

Thus, by the beginning of James's reign, plague had been coming and going for more than three hundred years—a span of time exceeding that stretching between the founding of the first colonies in New England and the present day. So the necessity of bending one's behavior to this lethal invasion time after time had shaped an administrative tradition in London within which the great-great-grandfathers, great-grandfathers, grandfathers, and fathers of the city aldermen and their contemporaries had frequently wrestled with the mysterious, evasive, and savage disease. By the time of Shakespeare, the London council's response to the incursions of this ugly, rapid, and ready way of dying was a settled routine. It was a routine not without a certain justification, even in that period before the development of modern medicine, and therefore not without a certain predictable success. But, of course, these happy results could not have come from such nostrums as odor purifiers, perfumes, and laxatives, talk of which filled the pages of the various printed remedies for the plague—nostrums not without some backing, too, from the authorities who themselves could be as weirdly theoretical as the veriest Paracelsan.

Then, as now, the aldermen and the mayors, the practical directors

---

6. Shrewsbury, *History of Plague*, pp. 197, 202. Between August 30 and October 20, 1564, the corporation of Stratford-upon-Avon met four times to collect money for plague relief for the poor; see Mullett, *Bubonic Plague and England*, p. 101.

7. Mullett, *Bubonic Plague and England*, p. 86.

8. On the 1603 plague, see C. Creighton, *A History of Epidemics in Britain*, 2 vols. (London, 1891; rpt. New York: Barnes and Noble, 1965, with introductory material), 1:474–493.

of the everyday affairs of a Renaissance city of approximately 120,000 men, women, and children, lived in a rather different world from that inhabited by much literary history. This was a world of wagons, shops, hospitals, streets, docks, ships, slums, fields, and warehouses; of merchants, immigrants, messengers, horses, vagrants, apprentices, burghers, and drunks. Immersed in the rattling details of this urban tumult, these part-time administrators, and the lord mayor himself, might have been opposed to players, to acting, and to plays, but when they took measures to legislate the control of public behavior for the suppression of plague they were under the more pressing imperative of dealing with the question of public safety and the maintenance of commerce. Further, because the crown had an important interest in the governance and safety of the city, evincing continual concern about plague in London, the privy council often urged the city officials to more severe measures.

The forms and symptoms of plague are multiple and complex and were recognized as such in Shakespeare's time. Renaissance physicians and observers attempted (in a rudimentary way) to isolate the variants of the disease and to make distinctions between those symptoms general to all types and those peculiar to some. Their commentary in some senses withstands comparison with what is known today. Indeed, as a way of assessing Renaissance medical theory and practice concerning plague, we can observe an intermediate text that intercepts our long-distance gaze on an earlier age.

Great visitations of bubonic and pneumonic plague swept China, Mongolia, and Korea in the early part of the twentieth century. The victims of these huge epidemics, most of whom were then living at a medical level comparable to that of Europe in the sixteenth century, were treated by physicians trained in modern medicine. These doctors understood the microbiology of the rat flea cycle and the manner in which the plague bacterium attacks the human body, but they did not have the broad-spectrum antibiotics that today easily treat the disease if administered early enough, nor was there yet preventive inoculation. So, despite the sophistication of these physicians, their approach had to be largely preventive and environmental. As a result of their extensive experience with these great oriental visitations of bubonic plague, some of this group of physicians—Wu Lien-Teh, J. W. H. Chun, and C. Y. Wu, and R. Pollitzer—compiled a manual for fighting plague which was published in 1936, but then superseded by R. Pollitzer's *Plague* published by the World

Health Organization in 1954.[9] Although the level of medical sophistication in the (unrevised) preventive sections of the Wu manual
might now seem old-fashioned in view of antibiotics and insect-
control methods available since World War II, this work, however,
remains particularly appropriate to the situation experienced in
Shakespeare's time.

Elizabethan England shared with late nineteenth-century China,
Mongolia, and Korea a low level of general sanitation, inferior quality
of construction in slums (mud and thatched roofs), and modes of
transportation (horse and wagon). In such conditions, the responses
of trained physicians familiar with the microbiology of the disease
accord startlingly with the methods in use in Shakespeare's London,
suggesting that, although the Elizabethan and Jacobean authorities
could not break the back of a major plague visitation, they could
make perceptible progress in impeding its spread. Such progress, in
turn, would validate measures taken against the theaters in time of
plague and ensure their enforcement.

The very nature of plague is sufficient to vindicate the attitude
of the London authorities and the privy council. The bacillus of
bubonic plague, once it has penetrated the body of a human being,
is vigorous and aggressive.[10] It reproduces itself rapidly and spreads
throughout the entire biological system. The incubation period—
that time in which the number of plague bacilli is increasing within
the body while the victim as yet shows no obvious symptoms—can
last for as long as a week and a half, but most often the span from
initial infection to sickness itself is three days. Then the onset is
sudden. Body temperature rises to at least 102°F, pulse increases,
the victim breathes faster than usual and needs to lie down. A sixteenth-century description of initial plague symptoms notes: "Many
one is so strait-winded that he cannot speak and when he breatheth,
it is with great labor and difficulty."[11] A severe headache also strikes
in the early stages. There are pains in the back and legs, and often
in places where the lymph glands are located: the groin, the armpits,

9. Wu Lien-Teh et al., *Plague: A Manual for Medical and Public Health Workers*
(Shanghai: National Quarantine Service, 1936), and R. Pollitzer, *Plague* (Geneva:
World Health Organization, 1954).

10. I am drawing here on the observations of Wu et al., *Plague* and Pollitzer, *Plague*.
Also pertinent is Jean-Noël Biraben, *Les hommes et la peste*, 2 vols., (The Hague:
Mouton, 1975), 1:9–12. This section of Biraben is also translated by Leslie Bradley
and Roger Schofield in *The Plague Reconsidered*, ed. Slack, pp. 27–29.

11. Jehan Goeurot, *The Regiment of Life*, tr. Thomas Phayre (London, 1546), sig.
O7 (ten eds. between 1544 and 1596).

or the neck. A victim who tries to walk at this juncture is not well coordinated, often staggering as if drunk. Victims also begin to feel very thirsty. In the words of one of Shakespeare's contemporaries: "Great dolor of head with heaviness, solicitude, and sadness of mind. . . . The second sign is if ye feel a great pricking and shooting in your body, and specially in any of the three cleansing-places: that is to say, the neck, the arm-holes, and the flanks. . . . The eleventh sign is heaviness, and dullness of all the whole body, and swooning and weakness of the limbs."[12] It is at this point that pregnant women almost always abort, a point also noted in Renaissance documents.[13]

Next accumulations of bacilli in the bloodstream begin to obstruct the tiny dilated capillaries, causing hemorrhage and bruises on the skin. The bacilli also begin to infiltrate the nerve fibers in the lymph nodes and to distend them, causing pain in the lymph glands. One's skin becomes hot and dry. Miniature blisters begin to appear on the hands, feet, and chest, becoming small, poxlike skin irruptions or coalescing into carbuncles sometimes as large as an inch in diameter. Sometimes, too, ulcers form on the skin near the lymph glands, and these ulcers may eat deeply enough into the skin to cause hemorrhage as the vein or artery is exposed. Yet none of these skin symptoms is the famous "bubo" of bubonic plague, and Thomas Lodge, who was a physician as well as a writer (one of his novellas was a source for Shakespeare's *As You Like It*), was aware of this fact. Lodge isolated the former symptoms before moving to the specifically "bubonic" element of plague: "Whenas fevers are accompanied with small pox, or measles, with spots or red marks like to the biting of fleas, it is a sign of pestilent fever."[14]

As the patient becomes weaker, her attention begins to wander.

12. For the commentaries on the "second" and "eleventh" signs of plague, see ibid., sigs. o6ᵛ–o7ᵛ, and cf. Gilbert Skeyne, *Ane Breve Description of the Pest* (Edinburgh, 1568), sig. A7.

13. John Graunt, writing in 1665, inadvertently alluded to this symptom in his discussion of the plague statistics: "The question is, whether teeming women died, or fled, or miscarried? The later at this time, seems most probable, because even in the said space, between March, and July [1603], there died not above twenty per week of the plague, which small number could neither cause the death, or flight of so many Women, as to alter the proportion 1/4 part lower. . . . Now the cause of this must be flying, and death, as well as miscarriages, and abortions; for there died within that time about 25,000, whereof many were certainly women with child, besides the fright of so many dying within so small a time might drive away so many others, as to cause this effect"; *Natural and Political Observations Made upon the Bills of Mortality*, ed. Walter F. Willcox (Baltimore: Johns Hopkins University Press, 1939), p. 49.

14. Thomas Lodge, *A Treatise of the Plague* (London, 1603), sig. C3.

With diminished brain function, she cannot control speech. Other symptoms also manifest themselves. Victims either become apathetic or go into wild deliriums marked by an impulse to wander or even run away. The pulse is now extremely high (120–180 per minute vs. a normal count of 72–80) and frequently sufferers may experience air hunger that causes them to wish to leave an enclosed room in order to sit or lie down outside. In sixteenth-century parlance: "Raving and walking occupies the last."[5]

Death comes from heart failure and can occur at any time from two days to four weeks after the onset of sickness, even after a seeming remission and recovery. In a manual available in Shakespeare's time, Jehan Goeurot wrote: "Sometimes also he shall think himself whole because that Nature in the first brunt drave the venom from the heart, and yet anon after, his life passeth from him for that Nature was not strong enough at the next assault."[16] In late nineteenth-century China, a third of those persons who perished during an epidemic of plague died after only two days of sickness; the remaining two-thirds were dead in three weeks—the first and, curiously, the third weeks thus being the most dangerous for the sufferer.

Such are the general symptoms produced in humans by the plague bacillus *Yersinia Pestis*.[17] But plague also takes several different forms, one of which, again without the buboes, modern medicine terms septicemic. Here, from the beginning, the infection is so overwhelming that the defenses of the body have no opportunity to react at all. The onset is sudden and the victim falls into an immobile state. There is often hemorrhaging both outside and inside the body of the victim, with bloody vomiting and diarrhea marking the course of sickness in which the patient dies after three or four days. Even now diagnosis of this virulent version of plague without a microscope is said not to be easy, which is unfortunate since it tends to appear at the very beginning of a general plague visitation. Seventeenth-century writers too were aware of this phenomenon:

15. Skeyne, *Breve Description*, sig. A7.
16. Goeurot, *Regiment of Life*, sigs. o7ᵛ-o8.
17. See Pollitzer, *Plague*, Ch. 8. The Plague bacillus has been called *Pasteurella pestis*, but in recent terminology it has been renamed after Yersin, its discoverer. Certain biochemical and enzymatic properties of the bacillus are markedly different from those characterizing the genus *Pasteurella*; see Biraben, *Hommes et la peste*, pp. 8–9.

Every man infected with the pestilence hath no such ulcers, botches, or sores, wherefore ye must take heed of the other signs hereafter that ye be not deceived for lack of the said apostemes [abscesses]. But what is the cause that such apostemes sometimes doth appear and sometimes doth not? No doubt but because that when the venom is so vehement and so furious, and hath gotten hold in the body of man, Nature, by reason of the swiftness of the infection, is so troubled, letted, and entangled that she cannot tell which way to succor, and so can drive out none apostemes. And that is more perilous than if there were many sores.[18]

By far the most common species of plague, however, is bubonic, and hence, after a point, easily recognizable. In addition to the various generalized plague symptoms, on the second or third day painful swellings in the lymph glands—buboes—also appear. The primary bubo occurs in the lymph gland that drains the infected area of the body nearest the place where the fleabite injected the plague bacillus. Thus, if the victim is bitten in the right leg, a bubo of the right thigh or the right side of the groin appears. If the victim is bitten on the head, the swelling occurs in the neck; if on the right arm, in the right armpit. Thomas Lodge and his contemporaries had a similar understanding of the bubo.

Whenas the plague sore appeareth in any of the emunctories, it is a sign that Nature by her power would discharge the member principal of that venom which assaileth it. . . . For under the armpits there are certain kernels that serve the heart, and these are the emunctories of that member, as behind the ears also there are the like which serve to discharge the brain, and in the groins, for the liver. And whenas the venom invades any of the principal members, Nature, to warrantize the nobler part, dischargeth and sendeth the venom to his proper emunctory. . . . We ought to take great heed lest, by cold repercussive or astringent medecines we drive the sore inwards. But rather, because the said sore is of a venemous nature, it ought to be driven and forced outward by medicines that draw and are in quality hot and fit to draw.[19]

18. Goeurot, *Regiment of Life,* sig. o6. Chun, writing in 1936, agrees with this observation (Wu, p. 316).

19. Lodge, *Treatise of Plague,* sig. I^v-I2. See also Wu et al., *Plague,* pp. 315–316. Lodge's source for this information was John of Bordeaux, a professor of medicine in Liège during the middle of the fourteenth century. For a copy of his shorter treatise on the plague and for some indication of manuscripts—John of Bordeaux was popular in England—see David Murray, ed., *The Black Book of Paisley* (Paisley, Scotland: Alexander Gardner, 1885), pp. 79–90.

Shakespeare's contemporaries, incidentally, were in the habit of distinguishing among the various skin manifestations accompanying plague, as doctors do today. Indeed, the cursing Thersites of Shakespeare's *Troilus and Cressida* was rather an authority on these matters. The swelling over the lymph gland today called a bubo was then called a plague sore or a botch, while the individual poxlike irruptions often covering the body affected by general plague were known as blains. The carbuncles, which may also accompany plague, becoming sometimes an inch in diameter, were then also referred to as carbuncles. These were quite painful and, in fact, the excruciating pain of plague was understood by physicians of the time as coming not from the rupturing of the bubo (as per Shrewsbury, *History of Plague*, p. 5) but from the unbearable burning of these carbuncles. Last, to conclude this rather sordid inventory, were the small, measlelike discolorations then known as tokens. Tokens were not in themselves fatal signs, as Scarrus thought when in *Antony and Cleopatra* he spoke of the "token'd pestilence where death is sure."[20] Nor were these tokens particularly bluish or black. "The Black Death," as Shrewsbury remarks, is a phrase invented by a nineteenth-century amateur historian. I have found no medical writer of the sixteenth or seventeenth century who gives darkness or blackness of the skin as a symptom of the "pestilence"—the name by which plague was ordinarily known in Shakespeare's England.

A third variation of plague, finally, is pneumonic plague. In this variety, the victim experiences the same general plague symptoms before buboes appear—rise in temperature, headache, back pains, stagger. But in a day or so there is extreme prostration, the headache is worse, and the face becomes red and bloated, giving the sufferer the peculiar facial appearance characteristic of pneumonic plague. There is chest pain and a fast pulse, but no coughing or blood as yet. Later, however, there develops a frequent and deep coughing,

20. For "plague sores" see Lodge, *Treatise of Plague*, sig. I^v; Goeurot, *Regiment of Life*, sigs. O5^v–O6^v, and *Especial Observations in the Last Time of Pestilence* (London, 1625), sig. D^v. "Botch" is used by Simon Kellway, *A Defensative against the Plague* (London, 1593), sig. K3; Goeurot, *Regiment of Life*, I.W. sig. R3; *A Brief Treatise of the Plague* (London, 1603), sig. B2; and John Woodall, *The Surgeon's Mate* (London, 1639), sig.3D3^v, who also uses the term "bubo." For "carbuncles" as excruciatingly painful, see Goeurot, *Regiment of Life*, sigs. R-R2, and Lodge, *Treatise of Plague*, sig I4. For "blaines" see Woodall, *Surgeon's Mate*, sig. 3D4^v, and Kellway, *Defensative*, sig. K3. "Tokens" are discussed by Lodge and especially Woodall. A somewhat later discussion of "botches," "blains," "tokens," and "carbuncles" may be found in Stephen Bradwell, *Physic for the Sickness* (London, 1636), sigs. G2 ff.

with so much blood that the miserable patient's bedding and the floor around are quite covered. A plague abscess in the lungs has ruptured. The rupture reduces the pain but causes shortness of breath, the victim gasping for it several hours before death, which comes mercifully soon. In Harbin, Manchuria, for example, the 1,128 deaths from pneumonic plague in 1910–11 occurred within an average of 1.8 days from onset.[21]

Pneumonic plague was almost always fatal. In the Manchurian outbreaks of 1910–11 and 1920–21, no diagnosed cases were known to have recovered. Furthermore, pneumonic plague spreads quickly, especially in winter when people spend more time indoors, because the disease travels from person to person via minute droplets from coughing and sneezing, as does the common cold. Because pneumonic plague is extremely difficult to diagnose without the aid of a microscope, researchers have found identifying its historical occurrences highly problematic. It is quite difficult, for example, to determine from contemporary accounts whether Londoners of Shakespeare's time (or earlier) suffered in any great number from this extremely contagious and almost invariably fatal form of plague; although contemporary writers indeed referred to the spitting of blood, this symptom occurs in various diseases.[22]

Diagnosing plague, in any event, especially before the appearance of obvious bubonic cases, would not have been easy in Shakespeare's time.[23] The lines of demarcation between the various forms would not have been particularly clear, especially when one variety of plague could develop in the course of another. Septicemic plague or secondary pneumonia could occur in bubonic cases, and buboes could also develop in the course of a case mainly pneumonic. One

21. See Wu et al., *Plague*, pp. 318–319.

22. C. Morris, in his review of Shrewsbury ("Plague in Britain," pp. 39–40) argues for the presence in England of pneumonic plague; but, although evidence for the continent is abundant, there is little direct testimony for England. "Death in three days" or "plague during the winter" are not evidence of pneumonic plague, Morris notwithstanding. Bubonic plague carried away its victims in three days—sometimes sooner—and also could occur in the winter. Skeyne listed as a symptom of plague the spitting of blood, (sig. A7^v) and Kellway, *Defensative*, sig. K3, spoke of carbuncles as lodging in the lungs (a bubo in the lungs is indeed pneumonic plague; see above), and he also referred to the spitting of blood as one of the deadly signs in a patient. But see *Annals*, sigs. 4C2^v–4C3, for strong indications that pneumonic plague was not known in Elizabethan or early Jacobean London; this is an account of what are obviously pneumonic plague symptoms during the Black Death of the Middle Ages but seem alien to the experience of the author in the early seventeenth century.

23. See Graham Twigg, *The Black Death* (London: B.T. Batsford, 1984), chap. 11.

could argue, then, that Londoners might easily have confused plague with other communicable diseases and that therefore the city authorities would not have zealously sounded prophylactic alarms whenever some epidemic seemed in progress. According to this view, one could hardly disrupt the activities of a large city—the money-making center of England and its chief port—in which smallpox, chicken pox, measles, influenza, cholera, diphtheria, typhoid fever, polio, and rabies were all present. Perhaps to cry plague on the basis of some exotic-seeming and contagious sickness was impractical in the administration of a port city in 1603. Where would one draw the line about taking extraordinary emergency measures (including the closing of playhouses) in the absence of sophisticated medical knowledge?

Plague would have been an exception if only because of the high and quick mortality it brought to a society a good proportion of whose members seem able to have survived a host of other diseases that might have severely affected unprotected modern populations. This being so, the aldermen of London and their medical advisers, even though they might indeed have confused plague with other communicable diseases, seem to have acquired a respectable measure of prescientific familiarity with this menacing and mortal exception. Inevitably based on empirical observation of linkages, seeming or actual, among the various phenomena of plague—on some notion of cause and effect—their perceptions, however, were hardly ignorant. They seem, in fact, to have been extremely astute.

This sophistication is again illustrated by the writing of Thomas Lodge. He translated and added to a French treatise, dedicating the sum to the lord mayor and the aldermen of London. No simpleminded search for astrological signs, justification of God's will, or dramatic declamation over buboes, this treatise is careful and fairly accurate about plague symptoms, even warning the reader to be alert to the subtleties:

> Otherwise the said sickness is very often times so fraudulent and deceivable that, for the most part, it deceiveth both the patient and the physician, as Avicenna after Galen doth testify. For divers of those that are infected, supposing themselves to be free from the plague, make no account thereof in the beginning. Nay, during the first and second days they only suffer a gentle fever without any other appearances so that nature desisteth not to perform her functions, being as yet unassailed by the venom. For which cause the patient will have a good pulse and healthful urine, almost as perfect as when they were

in health, when as suddenly they are seen to die without any manifest occasion, which breeds doubt and trouble in the physician, as Galen and Avicenna do testify.... This notwithstanding, whenas with the fever, the tokens, tumor, or carbuncle do appear, there is no cause of suspicion or doubt of the disease.[24]

Lodge was also aware, as we see from a separate context, of something like an incubation period. He observes: "A venom of that nature is accustomed to lie hidden in the body a long time without any effect or at leastwise notable impression—after the nature of the biting of a mad dog which suddenly, before it be discovered, takes a lamentable effect."[25] When the local authorities, or the privy council itself, were informed by their medical advisers—presumably of Lodge's level of knowledge or better—that plague indeed was in London or its suburbs, they took specific steps to limit the outbreak. To modern eyes these measures might seem superstitious, blindly traditional, desperately random, or at least so separated from epidemiological reality as we know it as to cause the authorities—the non-Puritan privy council, if not the play-hating city fathers—to be lax in their enforcement of these regulations. But modern understanding of the way plague spreads is surprisingly vindicating of those London methods—given the Renaissance ignorance of microbiology. Indeed, modern knowledge suggests how close the city officials were to reality in this matter and thus how determined they might have been to enforce the regulations they adopted.

To follow the procedures of plague prevention, we need a brief microbiological review. The microorganism that causes plague, *Yersinia pestis*, grows best at a temperature of 77°F, but it can survive for months—and sometimes even for years—if kept in the dark at a constant temperature: especially underground, within the miniature, warmish climate of a rodent's burrow.[26] In moist garden soil, the organism can survive for up to seven months. Cultures of *Y. pestis*, if refrigerated, can retain their virulence even up to ten years.

24. Lodge, *Treatise of Plague*, sigs. G2-G2ᵛ. See also Goeurot, *Regiment of Life*, sigs. o8-Pᵛ; I.W., *Brief Treatise*, sig. B2; and Woodall, *Surgeon's Mate*, sig. 3D2. In his preface (sig. A4), Woodall notes that he himself practiced in London during the first plague of James's reign (1603).
25. Lodge, *Treatise of Plague*, sig. Lᵛ.
26. See Biraben, *Hommes et la peste*, pp. 16–17. On the other hand, a mean temperature of over 85° so reduces the number of plague bacilli in a flea's stomach that fewer successful plague transmissions are possible.

This survival strength is significant, because plague is first a disease not of humans but of rats, or of other specific rodents.

Rats die quickly of plague, a disease enzootic among them. But before their deaths they manage to infect their own fleas (*Xenopsylla cheopis*). The flea must urgently find a new rat, because the plague bacilli in the blood ingested from the rat host multiply in the flea to such an extent that they form a plug big enough to block the entrance to the flea's abdomen. At this point, *X. cheopis* begins to starve; every time it tries to draw blood from a new rat, the blood only rebounds against that plaguey plug separating the flea's stomach from any newly entering nourishment. The flea is ravenous and continues a restless, perpetually unsatisfied search for new hosts. Whenever the flea pricks a new rat, the undigested new blood rebounding back from the flea becomes infected with plague and flows back into the minute wound on the rat. This rat contracts plague, and so all the rats in any given area are soon wiped out by these itinerant, hostless, "blocked" fleas. The dead rats, in turn, give up their own newly infected, blocked fleas to the atmosphere.

It is when every locally available rat has died that *X. cheopis* goes after humans. And because this infected flea is "blocked"—because the plug of bacteria separates its stomach from nourishment—the flea continues to be ravenous and quite aggressive. Despite its lack of nourishment, if the weather is suitably damp this flea will not be short-lived. Blocked fleas can stay alive and infective for a long time. Indeed, because fleas hibernate, one infected in October can awake to transmit plague in the following March.[27]

Heat and cold are obvious parameters in this situation, but it is humidity that controls the flea's life. At a humidity of 70 percent, with the temperature at 68°F, the flea dies. At this same temperature, but with the humidity at 80 percent, a starving flea can survive for seven or eight days. If the temperature rises and the humidity stays relatively high, the flea is still happier: at 74°F, with the humidity at 76 percent, a blocked flea can function and be infective for twenty-eight days.

The ideal humidity for the flea is between 90 and 95 percent. In this range, with temperatures from 59° to 78°F, a flea can live without nourishment for fifty days. In such humidity, even at 80°F an in-

27. See Wu et al., *Plague*, pp. 270–272. For a discussion of dormant plague at lower temperatures, see L. F. Hirst, *The Conquest of Plague* (Oxford: Clarendon Press, 1953), pp. 262–280.

fected flea can transmit plague as long as fifteen days after separation from its host—although, if the air were drier, the flea could not live much longer than thirty-six hours at this temperature.[28] If, finally, the temperature is within the range of 58° to 69°F—a not uncommon English span—but the humidity is below 80 percent, fleas live only a few days. Hence humidity is crucial. It can not only be too cold for fleas; it can also be too hot and dry.

The flea lays its eggs in the dust or in crevices in floors; these eggs survive and hatch only if the temperature and humidity are suitable. In moderate conditions, the eggs can survive for two to three months until a rainfall makes them all hatch at once.[29] Because rats invade storehouses, their fleas can lay eggs on the grain or in debris found there, and the larvae can also feed. Thus a container of grain kept in such places can itself become a flea nursery. Once hatched, young adult fleas can live up to fourteen days without food. With access to dry wood or grain, which they seem to enjoy, these young fleas can survive as long as six or seven weeks without animal hosts. Hostless fleas prefer all sorts of cracks and crannies, in fact, and rat fleas are thus found not only in grain but also in baggage and in human clothing. They are quite attracted to objects that are white, preferring fabrics, bedclothes, or clothing.[30]

Plague depends as much on the movement of the rat as on the habits of the fleas who are its parasites. The particular rat in question is *Rattus rattus*, a black rat, the principal rodent involved in seventeenth-century plague. This rat cannot survive far from human habitation in a country such as England that (in contrast to some Middle Eastern and Oriental areas) becomes quite cold in winter. Because it feeds principally on grain, the seventeenth-century black

28. Wu et al., *Plague*, p. 293, and Hirst, *Conquest of Plague*, pp. 322–331. Pollitzer, *Plague*, p. 327, states that optimum conditions for the rat flea *X. cheopis* are a temperature of 59°–68°F, with a relative humidity of 85–95 percent (but see pp. 318–319 for these fleas as not subject to changes in humidity). Gottfried, *Epidemic Disease*, pp. 272–280, omits this crucial etiological factor in the transmission of plague, and Leslie Clarkson, *Death, Disease, and Famine in Pre-Industrial England* (New York: St. Martin's Press, 1975), pp. 60–61, makes the same error. Both Gottfried and Clarkson associate plague only with temperature and thus with summer and autumn. In Clarkson, whose study correlates climatic conditions with known records of diseases, the omission may be of some consequence.

29. See Biraben, *Hommes et la peste*, pp. 12–16.

30. The rat flea is repelled by the smell of certain food oils (olive oil, nuts, peanuts) as well as by the odor of certain animals (horses, cows, sheep, goats). Biraben, ibid., p. 15, has observed that these characteristics were widely recognized in the Renaissance; such odors were regarded as protection from infection.

rat was thus to be found in shipments of grain, or in grain ware-houses, or in the granaries and larders of households. This rat likes to dig, burrowing into close spaces. It would therefore make holes in the mud walls of huts or build nests in the straw thatchings of such rudimentary dwellings—and it is an excellent climber. A house in an Elizabethan slum, with a wooden framework filled in with clay and plaster, with a refuse heap before the door and filthy rushes on the floor, was probably the nearest thing to paradise an English rat could imagine. On the other hand, dwellings made of stone or brick would not be nearly so congenial, since stone obviously tends to resist burrowing—hence the relative immunity of the better-off members of early seventeenth-century society to the pestilence which, in normal times, was often considered a disease of the poor.[31]

Being an agile climber, *R. rattus* gained access not only to the eaves of mud and lathe houses but also to ships. A sailing ship, dark, quiet, and with private wooden corners amenable to much gnawing and digging, was a good situation for a black rat, especially if it held attractive cargo. England, a maritime nation, was thus obviously susceptible to the importation of plague-stricken rats from the continent.[32] Indeed, when plague did come again to England in 1603, it came as part of a pandemic raging on the continent.

But the way in which pestilence came, and would continue to come, was not simply a function of seafaring rats and their ships. The arrival of plague in England depended on the interplay of the habits of the black rat with the life cycle of the rat flea and with the weather—especially with the humidity. Complex enough to lead modern authorities to debate niceties, these relationships can scarcely have been mastered by even the most intelligent of the physicians, aldermen, or privy councillors of Renaissance London and England.

Generalization, nevertheless, can paint a fairly accurate picture. Matters can theoretically begin with an epizootic of plague in the rat population on the continent. A rat dies of plague, and its fleas seek new hosts until all available rats are dead. At this point, the fleas change their behavior. Fleas are repelled by the odors of certain animals—horses, cows, sheep, goats—and they tend to be host-

31. For a description of an Elizabethan slum and for slum conditions in general, see Wilson, *Plague in Shakespeare's London*, pp. 2, 24–26.

32. For a description of the global cycles of plague as it issues from its birthplace in the foothills of the Himalayas, see Shrewsbury, *History of Plague*, pp. 17–20, and *Annals*, sig. 4C3.

specific. Different species of flea have marked preferences for specific kinds of animal and usually stay with their preferences, seeking a different kind of host only when starving: a rat flea likes rats, a dog flea likes dogs, a cat flea likes cats. A human being is by no means the host of preference for the rat flea, *X. cheopis*. In fact, this species of rat flea, experimentally starved for three or four days, when offered access to humans *and* rats did not attack the humans. Thus, it has been inferred (and, in Egypt, observed) that rat fleas can be conveyed from place to place by humans without their being bitten at all, at least for a time.[33]

In the seventeenth-century scenario being sketched here, the infected fleas whose rat hosts are now all dead, in the absence of new hosts, make for some favorite material: cloth, wool, or cotton. These—or, just as easily, bales of grain—may all have been loaded on a ship in France about to leave for England. Or the flea may inhere in the clothing of a crew member or passenger. When the ship arrives in England, it is the activity of the French flea, not of some infected person, that is important. If an infected Frenchman comes ashore, he will not be bitten by a healthy English rat flea (which would not leave its healthy English rat host). The Frenchman thus cannot transmit his (French) plague via an English rat flea to an Englishman.

The immigrant French flea is the problem: those fleas that have been living on infected French rats which, as the ship is docking, are presumably dead or dying. The remaining infected French rats and infected ratless French fleas come ashore, the last French rats shortly dying of plague to cast off their own infected and voracious fleas who join the others to search for healthy (English) rats. Or, if none of the French rats have survived the crossing, the infected French fleas will be inhering in the grain, in the wool, on bolts of cloth, or in the clothing of humans on the ship. The French fleas come ashore riding cargo or passengers.

The ratless and thus ravenous infected French fleas may now attack those Englishmen handling cargo from the ship to the shore, and thus, as Shrewsbury has suggested, a small flurry of plague deaths among English humans will soon occur, generally on the Bankside in London where cargo was unloaded.[34] After this initial contact, other humans will be left alone as the French rat fleas find their preferred hosts, the (English) rats. These will then become

33. See Wu et al., *Plague* p. 265.
34. Shrewsbury, *History of Plague*, pp. 264–265.

infected, and because they burrow together they will transmit fleas and experience epizootic. Or, in a slightly different scenario, a London rat on the dock may dig into a French grain shipment from the French vessel and there pick up contaminated and blocked French fleas who have found no rats and have hidden.

Humans, in theory, will not be bothered until all the local English rats have succumbed to plague, causing their own (now infected) English fleas to search for some other kind of host. In this gradual process, human plague in England begins. The process could be even more gradual. If cold weather started, infected fleas would hibernate and be inactive through the winter. With the warmer weather, they would come out, still infected with plague. Plague thus seems to "come back" in the spring. Or, it becomes endemic in the land, constantly reviving without extraterritorial importation.

After the entrance of infected fleas into the port of London, or after the revival of infected, hibernating fleas in spring, it might appear to the careful but microbiologically naive observer that random persons were coming down with the sickness in widely scattered locations throughout the city. Whole households would not contract plague; rather, one person only might succumb, the victim having suffered a fleabite when handling trade goods purchased away from home. On the other hand, whole households could come down with plague if the flea were transported home and either attacked the household rats or, lacking them, the other persons in the family. Infected fleas have been found, for example, in the dust on the beaten earth floors of the houses and huts of what are now regarded as backward villages but in Shakespeare's England were simply slums.

Given these facts, and lacking preventive inoculation, antibiotics, and modern pesticides, what principles and guidelines should ideally form the basis for the prevention of plague? The series of carefully controlled experiments in plague prevention carried out during the oriental plagues, first reported in 1908 by the Plague Research Commission and reprinted in the Wu manual of 1936 and its 1954 Pollitzer update are especially significant, since no epidemics of plague have been observed in the West by practitioners of modern medicine. The experimental results can be summarized as follows:[35]

1.   A direct spread of the infection from bubonic patients was most unlikely, because (a) their excreta as well as those of the rats were found

35. See Pollitzer, *Plague*, p. 484.

to be noninfectious when tested in the laboratory under conditions anal-
ogous to those in nature, and (b) the pus from healing buboescontained
few, if any, virulent *Y. pestis.*

2. There was no convincing evidence to show that the human flea played
any important role in the conveyance of the infection from person to
person.

3. Those attending bubonic plague patients remained singularly free from
plague infection, the plague hospitals in fact being the safest places during
outbreaks.

4. The contacts of patients who developed bubonic plague after arrival
in a hitherto unaffected locality invariably remained well.

5. The great majority of patients whose history was accurately known
had had no contact with previous cases before falling ill.

6. If bubonic plague appeared in a settlement, in the great majority of
instances not more than one case occurred per house.

7. If multiple cases occurred in any house, they often appeared simultaneously, as if infected from a common source.

8. If successive cases appeared in a house, invariably there was evidence
of a higher rat mortality than that found in houses yielding single plague
cases.

Techniques of plague prevention or inhibition formulated in terms
of these observations appear in the Wu manual as a series of
statements:[36]

In the case of an infected village or rural district, the headmen and
certain selected citizens should be co-opted; their duty would be to
organize, under supervision, squads for house-to-house visits.

The general public should be induced to observe cleanly habits, to
keep their houses in a sanitary condition, and to avoid overcrowding.
They should be taught to avoid crowded places such as theaters, tem-
ples, churches, schools, inns, brothels and refuge homes.

Sanitarians entrusted with plague prevention are aware of the dangers attending transportation of infected rats and fleas from one place
to another through the medium of ships, cargoes of grain, rice, and
cotton, forage, or crated goods, clothing, baggage, railway trucks, peddlers' goods, etc.

[In addition to other measures] the following should be carried
out:—Isolation of patients, convalescents and carriers; proper disin-
fection and disinfestation; disposal of dead bodies and rat carcases
(both these are best cremated); prophylactic inoculation; and com-
pulsory inspection of corpses. Isolation of all bubonic plague patients

36. Wu et al., *Plague*, pp. 461, 363–364, 427, 429.

is strongly advocated because, although an uncomplicated case is not infectious, secondary pneumonia may intervene at any time which may, under certain circumstances, give rise through droplet infection to an outbreak of primary pneumonic plague.

The regulations adopted by the authorities of Shakespeare's London are quite interesting in their close correspondence with the recommendations of the 1908 commission. These Renaissance London regulations included the closing of playhouses—as did the report of the Plague Commission—but the action in regard to theaters was merely a part of a larger preventive effort by the city.

In 1583, when Shakespeare was nineteen, regulations were first compiled by the city authorities with the help of the privy council for preventing the spread of plague in London. Then, in 1592, during the first great plague visitation of Shakespeare's writing career, the regulations were supplemented by orders issued by the privy council for the rest of England, orders also recommended by the council on July 16, 1593, to the lord mayor and aldermen of London.[37]

The most intrusive feature of these directives, as far as Londoners were concerned, was the order for houses within which plague had appeared. The doors, windows, and other openings of each house were to be kept shut at all times, all residents to remain inside for twenty-eight days after the last person there died of plague—or twenty days after the final plague case recovered, whichever came last. Meanwhile, the house was to be marked in the middle of the front door with a sign; from such a house no clothing or bedding was to be removed for almost a month after the dwelling had first seen infection. Should this restriction be broken, as penalty, the clothes remover's own house "shall be shut up as infected, and so shall continue shut up twenty days at the least."[38]

Such stringent regulations were based on experience, not on superstition. One need only consider these orders in light of observations from the 1936 plague manual:

---

37. For the two sets of orders, see *Present Remedies against the Plague*, ed. W. P. Barrett (London: Shakespeare Association, 1933), p. xiv. One set of orders was issued by the city (Barrett, pp. viii-xiii, has edited them from ms: *Journal of the Proceedings of the Court of Common Council*, 23, f.129 ff. September 7th, 1592). Another set was issued by the privy council for outlying districts and recommended for the city—*Orders Thought Meet* (London, 1592): *STC* 9199, 9200—and is also reproduced in Barrett.

38. For details of the orders, see Barrett, *Present Remedies*, p. ix; paragraph 13 of *Orders Thought Meet*.

Bundles of clothing and bedding taken from plague houses were kept in a flea-proof godown [warehouse] for several days and were then replaced with fresh lots. Twenty-six guinea-pigs were [then] let loose in this godown for an average period of four days each. Examinations revealed that three fleas were caught on these animals, of which one [guinea-pig] had a cervical bubo and died of plague.[39]

It is clear that infected fleas or infected flea eggs from bedding and clothing can remain in a house even after the bedding or clothing itself has been removed. Fleas can then move to fresh bedding or clothing inserted in a house and transmit plague to someone who subsequently enters the dwelling. In Rennaissance London the authorities, even if they did not know the precise causes, time and again showed their awareness of the plague dangers from the bedding or clothing of plague victims. In fact, householders were specifically charged that "no clothes, stuff, bedding or garments" be carried out or sold, but either destroyed or purified.[40]

The authorities did deem it safe to allow one of the quarantined household to go out to shop for provisions. Judging from the modern understanding that few if any of the other members of a victim's household are likely to contract plague, the dispensation probably was safe. In any event, this designated person had to carry a three-foot red wand and was required to avoid crowds. Thus, even if infected rat fleas were on his person, he was not too likely to infect anyone else unless he came close enough for the flea to jump the

---

39. Wu et al., *Plague*, p. 286.

40. London: Royal College of Physicians, *Directions for the Plague* (London, 1636), sig. H2. It has not been noticed, incidentally, that this section reprints hitherto unrecorded privy council plague orders for July 30, 1603; see sig. F^v. For similar viewpoints, see Lodge, *Treatise of Plague*, sigs. F3-F3^v; Francis Herring, *Certain Rules* (London, 1625), sig. A4^v; *Orders... by Her Majesty* (London, 1592), sig. B4; and Thomas Dekker, *The Meeting of Gallants at an Ordinary* (London, 1604), in *The Plague Pamphlets*, ed. F. P. Wilson (Oxford: Oxford University Press, 1925), p. 116. The contemporary concern about textiles should be taken into consideration in such a study as John Hatcher's *Plague, Population, and the English Economy: 1348–1530* (London: Economic History Society, 1977), p. 18, which takes issue with J. M. W. Bean on the subject of cloth exports as an index of steady or diminishing trade, in turn an index of the impact of plaque in the fifteenth century. Neither Hatcher nor Bean, "Plague, Population, and Economic Decline in England in the Later Middle Ages," *Economic History Review*, n.s., 15 (1962–63), 423–437, takes into account the restriction by continental ports of cloth imports for fear of plague infection. See, for example, Carlo M. Cipolla, *Fighting the Plague in Seventeenth-Century Italy* (Madison: University of Wisconsin Press, 1981), Ch. 2.

gap.[41] Finally, if someone were illegally conveyed, when ill, to some other parish, that person was to be forcibly returned and the house of the illegal receiver shut up for twenty days. This was either punishment or, again, locale-consciousness.

The prospect of a twenty-eight-day confinement not only threatened a shopkeeper's business (no customer could come in) but prevented a laborer from leaving home to work elsewhere. Hence the obvious need to keep plague in one's house a secret, and hence the sums of money often appropriated for relief of the poor during plague time.[42]

The competence of the London authorities of Shakespeare's time also appears in regulations that have been smiled at by modern scholars because they are directed against animals that themselves might have been natural enemies of the rat: "No person from the sixth day after such proclamation shall keep any dog or bitch, but such as they will keep within their own doors without suffering them to go loose in the streets, nor led in slip or line." Any dog caught outside was to be killed by the appropriate official and buried at least four feet deep. The London plague orders for 1646 (indicated as a republishing of 1603 ordinances) also stipulated that "no hogs, dogs, or cats, or tame pigeons, or conies be suffred to be kept."[43] Naive it might seem, but here are the opinions of several modern authorities:

> It must be noted that cats (and possibly to a lesser extent, dogs) are liable to be infected with plague so that their presence in a house during an epidemic may be fraught with danger. Cats should not be used for hunting rats during epizootics. Infected fleas may also be carried in their fur and the disease thus spread from place to place.

41. *Xenopsylla cheopis* can jump vertically 4 inches when starved and 3 inches when gorged. *Pulex irritans* (the flea parasitic on humans) jumps 7.5 inches vertically and 13 inches horizontally; see Pollitzer, *Plague*, p. 385.

42. Wilson, *Plague in Shakespeare's London*, p. 57, notes the gradual tightening of rules regarding the segregation of infected persons. In the first half of the sixteenth century, for instance, members of an infected household who needed to continue earning their livings were allowed to leave their houses for this purpose if they carried white rods. The 1646 orders of the London council, on the other hand, insisted that anyone in an *uninfected* household who visited the home of a victim of plague would consequently have to have his or her own house shut up.

43. See Barrett, *Present Remedies*, p. xi, and sig. B[v] of the 1646 orders and sig. B4 of the 1636 orders. See also Kellway, *Defensative* sig. E[v]. For other records of this legislation against dogs, see Creighton, *History of Epidemics*, 1:316, who also sees this action against domestic animals as naive.

On rare occasions, dogs may contract plague under natural conditions. Certainly, however, instances of this kind are of little importance when contrasted with the far more dangerous role dogs are apt to play by picking up plague-infected rodent-fleas and conveying them to their masters.

The incidence of plague among cats was not high enough to play a conspicuous role in the spread of the infection to man. However, the cats, like dogs, are apt to be dangerous by bringing infected rodent-fleas into the house.... Carnivora and birds of prey may play a role in the spread of plague, even though they are resistant to infection, because they are apt to pick up, and later to disperse, infected rodent-fleas.... Many species of bird were apt to seek temporary refuge in the burrows of wild rodents.[44]

With the quarantine of houses, with the emphasis on destroying clothing, sheets, or blankets associated with the houses of plague victims, with the emphasis on a strenuous washing and raking of the area outside all infected houses, and with the ban on crowds, there was actually little in the London plague orders that, from the present-day viewpoint, might not have served at least to ameliorate the plague situation. Of course, any real control of plague was doomed, given the seventeenth-century inability to deal effectively with all vectors of the bacteria. But observation must have confirmed that the enforcing of antiplague measures, probably with the help of contemporary physicians who could apply their knowledge of continental literature on the subject, did get some results—enough for the orders to be applied again and again. Who can say how many isolated outbreaks might not thus have been smothered?

That the city authorities, furthermore, sometimes accepted and sometimes seemed tacitly to reject the theorizing about plague to be found in the Renaissance plague manuals may seem illogical, but it is not inconsistent. In those instances in which the authorities followed the "book solutions," empiricism seems to have underlain any acceptance of theory. For example, one of the chief theoretical causes of plague was thought to be the air: "the stench and filthy savors that corrupt that air which we live in, for we cannot live

44. See Wu et al., *Plague*, pp. 450–451, and Pollitzer, *Plague*, pp. 306–308. David van Zwanenberg, "The Last Epidemic of Plague in England?" *Medical History* 14 (1970), 63–74, describing plague in Suffolk in 1906 and 1910, notes that rabbits, hares, ferrets, dogs, and cats were all involved in the spread of this disease. For a similar observation about the seventeenth-century attitude toward animals, this time in Italy, see Cipolla, *Fighting the Plague*, p. 74 n. 47.

without drawing of the breath, and we have none other breath but of the air round about us. Which if it be stinking, venomous, and corrupt, and we by necessity draw the same unto us, immediately corrupteth and infecteth the heart and the lively spirits of the same."[45] By an obvious association it seemed to follow that the breathing of a diseased person would spread (bubonic) plague too, because this breathing was a miniature conveying of the same kind of plague atmosphere. As Goeurot put it, "the venomous air itself is not half so vehement to infect as is the conversation [social intercourse] or breath of them that are infected already."[46] But "infected air" could be perceived or detected only in terms of odor (such modern amenities as carbon monoxide fumes and nerve gas being absent from Elizabethan awareness). Thus, if theory regarded plague as resulting from bad air, the idea underlying many preventives would have to do with air sweeteners. A repellent smell meant noxious air; ergo, an air sweetener dispersed the noxiousness, and such sweeteners were most logically directed to be carried in the vicinity of the nose and mouth.

Seemingly absurd, a "miasma" theory of plague was not, however, completely useless to the pragmatic observer in Shakespeare's London. When Elizabethans and Jacobeans spoke of corrupt air, they thought of "thick, cloudy, moist, and ill-smelling vapors," or of "air full of fogs and vapors, making a show of rain without any showers," or of "very much rain," a "watery sign" in the Zodiac.[47] Today one speaks of the conditions that cause an air-pollution index to rise in major cities as the heat, and especially the humidity, rise in the summer months. And one is aware that the effects of what is now called an inversion are to turn the air smelly with modern odors—exhaust fumes downtown, the river and garbage elsewhere—until the whole is mercifully dispersed by a dry wind from a high-pressure cold front bringing blue skies and relief.

In Shakespeare's time, the presence of miasma or noxious vapors was announced by organic odors—garbage, animal entrails, and animal corpses—held in place by a humid inversion causing the uncomfortable feeling of atmospheric closeness. This closeness and

45. Goeurot, *Regiment of Life*, sigs. M2ᵛ-M3; see also Lodge, *Treatise of Plague*, sig. C2ᵛ; and STC 1679, sig. C2.
46. Goeurot, *Regiment of Life*, sig. M3; see also Lodge, *Treatise of Plague*, sig. C6.
47. Lodge, *Treatise of Plague*, sig. C2ᵛ, and Goeurot, *Regiment of Life*, sig. M2ᵛ. See also Wilson, *Plague in Shakespeare's London*, p. 5, who quotes Ficino and others as the source for the concept of poisoned atmosphere.

corruption were, in effect, the ideal atmospheric conditions for the propagation of the rat flea which, one recalls, does best in temperatures of 64°–74° F with high humidity. It is important to remember that heat in England is associated with such temperatures rather than with the 90s of continental climates and of those areas of the northern hemisphere lying south of Gibraltar and the fortieth parallel.

In such humid English conditions, in the low 70s, the rotting organic matter would draw rats while the summer congregations would aid in the survival of infected rat fleas. Thus Thomas Lodge's treatise comes close when he writes of the "increase of such creatures as are engendered of putrefaction, as worms of the earth, flies, gnats, eels, serpents, toads, and such like" and says that "long and continued rains, accompanied with southerly winds, dispose the air to sickness and putrefaction."[48]

In the long run, the miasma theory, in the absence of microbiology, was as reasonable as any to explain the seeming caprice with which a flea-borne infection from rats would seem to operate. One plague scenario we might assume for the Elizabethans is that in which a person bitten by a rat flea when away from an (uncontaminated) house returns home without carrying infected fleas and is the only one in the household to die. Another is that in which a block of Elizabethan tenements becomes so infested with sick rats and their fleas that large numbers of human deaths result, all in the same neighborhood. A theory of bad air could explain both these situations. In the first, the sole victim wandered into corrupt air at the markets, or in a garbaged slum, before returning to a fragrant and clean home. In the second situation, the smelly tenement is riddled with corrupt air, presumably infecting almost everyone who lives there.

Whether miasma was the basis of their thinking or not, the London authorities were so convinced that plague was spread by infection— not an obvious fact, really, before microscopes—that they ignored some important religious tenets that one might expect to have given them pause. In fact, it is crucial for theater historians to realize that the city fathers, without actually saying so, turned their backs on the highly providential orientation to be found in preludes to most treatises on plague. These remarks asserted the usual theme: God, in his infinite and unknowable providence, was, through plague,

48. Lodge, *Treatise of Plague*, sigs. C2^v-C3.

scourging humankind for sin, warning the survivors to mend their ways and go about the main business of attending to their salvation. But infection contradicted any rational theory of God's punishing ways, because the punishment seemed unselective. If plague was really infectious, how did one explain that, after bubonic death had descended as punishment upon some hapless sinner, it then leaped infectiously, with seeming moral randomness, to possibly innocent persons coming into close physical proximity with said sinner. A theory of infection made it easy to view God's punishment, blindly seeking out both sinner and sinless, as random celestial swatting— Gloucester's "as flies to wanton boys are we to the gods." If those who argued for providence might reason that providence was ample enough to embrace the choosing of who would be infected, skeptics could respond that determined avoidance of plague-infected persons often turned out to be a gratifyingly easy way of fleeing God's avenging wrath.

But since infection was not provable in Shakespeare's time, religion could plausibly deny the notion of contagion. Plague was God's punishment for sin, and infection, a quaint, unproved theory, was an atheist pipedream. Thus, perhaps the very best steps to take against plague would be to ignore the various quarantine rules and to gather in the churches to pray for God's mercy and forgiveness. This was, at any rate, the position of Henock Clapham presented during the plague of 1603 in three separate small quartos.[49] Clapham also preached in person against the idea of infection, presumably using as one argument a point appearing in his writings: plague was God's punishment for sin, and one of the facts bearing this out was that "now of late many are killed up (as report goeth) without having upon them either sore or former marks."[50] Apparently septicemic plague was not altogether uncommon in 1603.

It is important to note that so convinced were the city authorities about the existence of an infectious element in the propagation of plague that, as Clapham himself told his readers, they imprisoned him from November 13, 1603, to the end of August 1604, a nine-

---

49. Henock Clapham, *An Epistle Discoursing upon the Present Pestilence* (London, 1603: *STC* 5339), reprinted with additions in *STC* 5340, and *Demands and Answers Touching the Pestilence* (London, 1604: *STC* 5343). Wilson, *Plague in Shakespeare's London,* pp. 3–4, alludes to a representative number of Renaissance English works making the providential point from Biblical example, but he does not attend the important difficulty this idea would have posed for a theory of contagion.

50. Clapham, *Epistle,* sig. B3ᵛ.

month period within which plague was rife. It seems clear that, since lengthy imprisonment was ordinarily restricted to debtors and to plotters against the crown—physical punishment being the usual mode of dealing with felons—this incarceration was meant to keep Clapham off the streets and to stop his dangerous preaching. The London authorities thus seem to have agreed with Francis Herring (against whom Clapham argued in his writings), who associated "open and large streets," "roomy" houses, and lack of crowding with the absence of plague. "Shall we imagine," he had asked, "that fair and ample streets, that sweet and goodly houses, are privileged from the stroke of the Angel [of death], or from the arrows of the Almighty, more than poor and smoky cottages?"[51]

In these contexts it is therefore not difficult to imagine the authorities as adamant against the crowding caused by such new and unusual structures as public playhouses. Indeed, plays, as public gatherings, were first prohibited for health reasons during the great plague of 1563, a year before Shakespeare was born, the London proclamation on the matter being promulgated on February 12, 1564. There were also play prohibitions by the lord mayor and the aldermen of London on May 3, 1583, when Shakespeare was nineteen, and a similar proclamation against public plays in plague time by the privy council itself on February 3, 1594, when Shakespeare was beginning his London career.[52]

But the London court of common council had already processed plague orders to cope with the 1593 epidemic in March and April of that year, and they had resolved "that restraint be made of interludes, of plays, assemblies of fencers, or other profane spectacles, and of going with drums, proclamations, or calling of people to the same within this city or liberties thereof. And humble suit be made to the most honorable [privy] Council that the like restraint be in places of other counties adjoining the said city."[53]

The regulations were refined slightly at the end of the second great plague of Shakespeare's London career. On April 9, 1604, a warrant was issued to allow all the city players to act again, now that the plague was gone. But in the warrant appeared for the first time the

51. Herring, *A Modest Defence* (London, 1604), sig. B; see also Kellway, *Defensative*, sig. Bᵛ.
52. See Wilson, *Plague in Shakespeare's London*, pp. 52–54. This caution about public assembly, including plays, was echoed by Herring in *Certain Rules*, sig. A4ᵛ. These rules were actually reprinted from a 1603 edition (see sig. A2ᵛ).
53. Barrett, *Present Remedies*, p.xii.

stipulation that the playhouses might remain open "except there shall happen weekly to die of the plague above the number of thirty within the city of London and the liberties thereof. At which time we think it fit they shall cease and forbear any further publicly to play until the sickness be again decreased to the said number."[54]

This "numbers game" had been first suggested in 1584 or 1585, when the group of actors known as the Servants of Queen Elizabeth had themselves tried to promote the notion that the playhouses should be closed in plague epidemics only when deaths from the disease rose to fifty per week. The city, in its response to those representatives of the crown who took up the notion and presented it to the London Corporation, put forward a rationale that one might think a modern epidemiologist, aware of rats, rat fleas, and plague vectors in general, would find congenial, even if not wholly accurate. Perhaps the London authorities, as some historians of drama claim, were typically Puritan and antihistrionic, but, for all that, their position about plague death numbers in their 1584 answer to the crown, although containing some misinformation, cannot finally be faulted:

> Touching the permission of plays upon the fewness of those that die in any week. It may please you [the privy council] to remember one special thing. In the report of the plague, we report only those that die, and we make no report of those that recover and carry infection about them either in their sores running or in their garments—which sort are the most dangerous. Now, my lord, when the number of those that die groweth fewest, the number of those that go abroad [around town] with sores is greatest, the violence of the disease to kill being abated. And therefore, while any plague is [in existence], though the number reported of them that die be small, the number infectious is so great that plays are not to be permitted.
>
> Also in our report, none are noted as dying of the plague except they have tokens. But many die of the plague that have no tokens. And sometimes fraud of the searchers may deceive. Therefore it is not reason to reduce their toleration to any number reported to die of the plague.... If your lordships shall think reasonable to permit them [the players] *in respect of the fewness of such as die*: this were a better way. (*MSC*, 1.2:170–174; emphasis added)

The better way would be to think in terms of the London death norms, if numbers are to be used for opening or closing playhouses.

54. W. W. Greg, ed., *Henslowe Papers* (London: A. H. Bullen, 1907), pp. 61–62.

The London death norm, the city fathers go on to point out in this letter, is forty or fifty per week when there is no plague. All additional deaths, however these deaths might finally be otherwise described or diagnosed, should, therefore, be attributed to plague. (The city fathers were factoring in smallpox, measles, and other endemic causes of death except plague when they produced the number forty or fifty). Thus, they concluded, playing should be permitted only when the weekly London death toll from *all* causes was under fifty.

This issue was not resolved in the 1580s and, in the end, death counts were regarded as only part of the evidence on which a judgment regarding theater closings was based—a point of some importance if one is trying to determine when the London playhouses were closed during Shakespeare's career. The privy council under James, did, as mentioned, establish thirty plague deaths per week as the criterion for theater closing, but the number was never considered an absolute. As F. P. Wilson opined, the privy council, supported by the city rulers, "were so anxious to ward off the infection that they usually closed the theaters long before the plague deaths rose to 30 or 40, and sometimes refused to take the risk of permitting them to reopen until some weeks after the mortality had fallen below that number."[55]

I think that the authorities closed the theaters whenever plague deaths, no matter how many, seemed to them dangerously high.[56] To take but one of many examples, the patent warranting the creation of Shakespeare's company as Servants of the King on May 19, 1603, states that they may "show and exercise publicly... when the infection of the plague shall decrease." This statement could only have been based on the plague death figure published the prior Thursday, May 12. But the number of plague deaths reported was nowhere near thirty: there were only eighteen deaths from plague reported for the week. Whatever the basis for individual judgments by the privy council or city authorities, it is virtually certain that they closed the theaters when they thought plague threatened. Over the

---

55. Wilson, *Plague in Shakespeare's London*, p. 55.
56. G. E. Bentley, in *Jacobean and Caroline Stage* 7 vols., (Oxford: Clarendon Press, 1941–68), 2:652–653, makes the same point for the period 1625–37, noting, for example, that "after the plague of 1625 the players of the Phoenix were commanded to stop playing by an order of 6 December, though only fifteen were reported dead of the plague in the last bill," and that "in 1636 the theaters were closed on 12 May and not opened for nine months, though the bills for 19 and 26 May recorded twenty-two and thirty-eight deaths respectively."

years, furthermore, the aldermen and the privy council had developed a thoroughgoing and systematic response to the hazards of the plague, and we have seen that the regulations for its prevention were in all likelihood at least partially efficacious. But any narrative in which plague closings play an important part cannot usefully be structured on the premise that playhouses were closed whenever the authorities became concerned; such concern is not satisfactorily demonstrable. Accordingly, for the sake of the argument, I conservatively adhere to the figure alluded to in the permission granted to the city acting companies in 1604 to play again since plague was considered past. In this permission, the proviso was added that if there occurred thirty plague deaths in a week, the playhouses would be closed again. Thirty plague deaths per week is thus my standard for judging when the playhouses were closed, although I mention additional texts that describe instances in which the theaters were closed when deaths from plague were fewer than thirty.[57]

In the balance of this chapter I suggest how Shakespeare and his fellows had to conduct business during the events that followed the death of Queen Elizabeth. Although at other times during Shakespeare's career crown affairs and Lent combined with plague to force extended closings of theaters for greater periods, the first twelve months of James's reign saw a complete stoppage of the ordinary

57. F. P. Wilson in *Plague in Shakespeare's London*, p. 54, thought that by 1610 the number of plague deaths that closed the theaters was forty, basing this on a remark in Lording Barry's *Ram Alley* (entered in the stationer's register November 9, 1610): "I dwindle," says one character, "as a new player does at a plague bill certified forty." Because the comedy's 1611 title page describes it as played by the Children of the King's Revels, a fleeting London company that cannot be traced after August 21, 1608 (Chambers, *Elizabethan Stage*, 2:64–68), Wilson (and Bentley) thus see a change in the closing figure from thirty to forty at about that time—1608. The difficulty is in determining whether the number alluded to was updated in the *Ram Alley* manuscript the publisher entered in 1610, for Bentley, in *The Profession of Player in Shakespeare's Time* (Princeton: Princeton University Press, 1984), p. 182, notes this passage in Middleton's *Your Five Gallants* (published in 1608): "'tis e'en as uncertain as playing, now up, now down, for if the bill rise to above thirty, here's no place for players." For the purpose of the present study, the issue is moot. Situations in which plague deaths were between thirty and forty speedily yielded deathrates of fifty and above that would close the two theaters whichever of the two figures seems plausible. It is also significant that a company reestablished in the first decade of the 1600s—the Children of the King's Revels—was partially organized around the prospect of plague closings. The agreement between the group and the player Martin Slater stipulates that "if any restraint of their playing shall happen by reason of the plague or otherwise . . . the said Martin shall travel with the children, and acquaint the magistrates with their business"; Chambers, *Elizabethan Stage*, 2:65.

business of the London playhouses. This was a year of politics and plague, a situation in which Shakespeare was probably not writing plays (see Chapter 4).

Early in 1603, just before the accession of James, Shakespeare and the other members of the company had been acting plays at the Globe on the Bankside until March 9, Ash Wednesday, when they presumably stopped for Lent.[58] On March 19, ten days after Ash Wednesday, it looked as if this Lenten suspension might be extended beyond Easter. An order was passed by the privy council of England to the lord mayor of London and to the justices of the peace for Middlesex and Surrey—the recreation areas outside the city limits to the north and south, respectively—an order for "the restraint of stage-plays till other direction be given" (*Acts*, 32:492).

This was not an order reenforcing Lent but a sign of concern about what would prove to be the mortal illness of Queen Elizabeth. In fact, even the Admiral's Servants, on tour away from London because of Lent, were prevented from acting in Canterbury because of the town council's sense of the queen's impending death (*MSC*, 7:18). On March 7, Elizabeth had been troubled with a cold, was briefly better, and then on March 12 was described as recovering after a dangerous sickness. There was much quiet worry, not only about the queen but about the prospects of civil disorder if she indeed should die, and this latter concern was deeper, in fact, than has generally been noted by dramatic historians. In a letter written by the earl of Northumberland to King James VI of Scotland two days before the March 19 play restraint, the earl observed that Queen Elizabeth had been ill for almost a month and that now the privy council was preparing for the worst. Therefore, according to Northumberland's letter, steps were being taken to preserve stability: "Order is given for pressing of all such rogues as might be apt to stir, and are sent unto the low countries. The city of London is commanded to keep strong watch lest discontented persons might make any head there." Papists and recusants were being watched too, with those of greatest note detained lest they also try to use this occasion to foment uprisings in an effort to put a Catholic monarch back on the throne: "Every county hath the like warning. Care is willed to be had by the commanders of the strong places for fear of surprises."[59]

58. For Lenten stoppages, see Appendix 1.
59. James I, *Correspondence with Sir Robert Cecil and others in England*, ed. John Bruce (Westminster: The Camden Society, 1861), p. 73.

This preparation became international in scope, according to the notebooks of another contemporary, Roger Wilbraham, who maintained a journal sporadically from 1593 to 1616: "Since the first fear of her Majesty's indisposition, the Lords [of the privy council] hath ordered the Navy to be in readiness against foreign attempts, and divers parts of the kingdom had admonition. So had the sheriffs, lieutenants, and deputy lieutenants, [and] justices of the peace throughout the kingdom. . . . And stay [was] made of all shipping."[60] Given these concerns, the March 19 prevention of plays, although a major event for Shakespeare and his fellows, was one of many items in the planned pattern of tightening civil control.

The queen died about a week later, and James was proclaimed king on March 24, 1603, with surprisingly little disturbance in London and throughout the rest of England. But Shakespeare and his fellows probably did not resume acting, surely not even at the end of Lent, on Easter, April 24. The queen was dead, but she had not yet been buried and would not be until April 28 (*Hatfield*, 15:56). The nation was in official mourning and the new king had not yet arrived in London.

After the queen's funeral, however, the London players must have been active for several days, since, a week later, on Thursday, May 5, Philip Henslowe made a diary notation that "we left off play now at the king's coming." Henslowe's account books and his association with his son-in-law Edward Alleyn were confined to the affairs of a company other than Shakespeare's, the Lord Admiral's Servants, but all the players in London were subject to the same civil regulations. Henslow reflected the *anticipation* of the king's coming, as if something like decorum actually required theater closings prior to James's arrival. The king was not in London on this date, but outside the city at Theobalds swearing in a privy council at the residence of Sir Robert Cecil. He would not be in the city for several days, but only at the end of that time would the actors be allowed to resume play; another entry by Henslowe the following Monday notes Alleyn and his acting company "beginning to play again by the King's license."[61]

Almost simultaneously with King James, bubonic plague had been

60. See Roger Wilbraham, *Journal*, ed. H. S. Scott, in *Camden Miscellany* 10 (London: Royal Historical Society, 1904), p. 54. One such warning went to the earl of Shrewsbury for Derbyshire on March 16 from the privy council; see *Mss of the Duke of Rutland*, ed. 4 vols. (London: HMC, 1888) 1:388.
61. *Henslowe's Diary*, ed. R. A. Foakes and R. T. Rickert (Cambridge: Cambridge University Press, 1961), pp. 209, 225. Hereafter cited as *Diary*.

making its progress from the wharves of London to the rest of the city. The great plague of 1603 was slowly gaining its foothold. When the new king had paused at the border town of Berwick on April 8, 1603, preparing for his celebratory progress southward, eight plague deaths had been reported in the London parish of Stepney near the docks,[62] and the parish of Whitechapel had also begun recording such fatalities. By Thursday, May 12, three days after Henslowe had noted crown permission to resume acting, the authorities listed eighteen deaths in the preceding week. As Venetian ambassador Girolamo Carlo Scaramelli saw it on this same date, "two weeks ago the plague suddenly broke out here."[63]

Scaramelli continued to watch the situation closely. On May 20 he wrote Venice voicing apprehensions that might well have been the concerns of the London authorities themselves.

> The plague progresses. In nine infected parishes last week thirty-six died of plague and one hundred and twelve of other illnesses. As the day is nineteen hours long here and the season unusually hot, there is dread of the disease spreading, especially as no steps have been taken as yet, except to kill the dogs and mark the houses by fastening upon them a great printed paper with these words "Lord, have mercy upon us. (*SPV*, 10:42)

The Venetian ambassador's worries accord significantly with the warning sounded in the new patent for Shakespeare and his fellows issued May 19. At that point, deaths from plague, by the evidence of the weekly bill of mortality, were only at eighteen for the preceeding week, a relatively low incidence for plague outbreaks of the time. The patent creating the King's Servants at this very time nevertheless read: "And the said comedies, tragedies, histories interludes, morals, pastorals, stage plays, and such like to show and exercise publicly to their best commodity when the infection of plague shall decrease" (*MSC*, 1.3:264–265). Present in all three documents constituting the conventional stages of the warrant for the patenting of the new King's Servants, this reference to the plague is significant. It is an unambiguous instance, important for an understanding of

62. See L. Bradley, "The Geographical Spread of Plague," in *The Plague Reconsidered*, Slack, ed., pp. 127–132.

63. *SPV*, 10:33. Plague deaths (not counting the outer parishes), according to the annual report for 1603, proceeded as follows: 4 for April 14; 8 for April 21; 10 for April 28; 11 for May 5; 18 for May 19; see the annual bill reproduced in Wilson, *Plague in Shakespeare's London*, facing p. 114.

future years, about the city and crown attitudes toward the closing of theaters. Although the authorities had no way of knowing that here was the beginning of a very severe visitation of plague that would last for almost a year, they obviously closed the playhouses when weekly plague mortality was still less than twenty deaths.[64]

Shakespeare and his fellows were to have only a very brief period of playing after Lent ended on Easter. Plague worsened later that May, and King James himself seems to have become concerned. He was accustomed to more stringent approaches to plague control in Scotland.[65] London plague measures seem, by comparison, to have been mild (the Venetian ambassador appears to have thought so). Perhaps because of James's Scottish background in these matters, or because of increased concern by the English privy council, control over public assembly in London at this time was tightened further by a proclamation from the palace at Greenwich on Sunday, May 29, commanding all the nobles and gentry from out of town to depart for their homes until the coronation on July 25:

> For that we find the sickness already somewhat forward within our city of London which by concourse of people abiding there is very like to be increased, and importeth us, as well for our people's sake as for the safety of our own person (who for the most part live in places near the said city) to prevent by all provident means. (*Proclamations*, 1:21–22)

In late May and June, the weekly deathrate from plague rose from 30 to 43 to 59 and then to 72 for the week ending June 22. The deathrate for the next week more than doubled to 158, on July 14

---

64. That this figure is considerably lower than the one arrived at by the few scholars who have discussed the criteria for plague closings in these times, see n. 57 above.

65. In 1585, for example, the city fathers of Edinburgh ordered that all persons concealing the presence of plague in a household be put to death. Furthermore, those ill from plague in Edinburgh were sent away from town and resettled in specially built huts on the moor. Later, in 1597, the Edinburgh authorities prohibited all trade or other dealings between people of the capital city and those of any nearby infected towns; again, violation of this ordinance was punishable by death. In that same year, when the Scottish town of Leith became badly infected, a ditch was dug across the road between Leith and Edinburgh to facilitate the isolation of the city from its plagued neighbor; See Shrewsbury, *History of Plague*, pp. 260–263. Shrewsbury has implied that James himself tended to flee immediately any town where plague came, but I find little evidence of any abnormal plague phobia in James. When plague came to Scotland in August 1597, Cecil's agent in Scotland spoke of the general fear (including his own) but did not single out the king; see *Calendar of State Papers Relating to Scotland*, 13 vols., ed. J. D. Mackie (Edinburgh: HMSO, 1952) 13.1:81–83, 87.

plague fatalities in London alone rose to 424 for one week, and on July 21 they were 917 for one week. The numbers climaxed during the last week of the coming August with 3,035 plague deaths (outparishes now being counted) within seven days. Even four months later, in December 1603, 96 persons per week were still dying of bubonic plague.

Through all this, the attention of the court, and of England in general, stayed turned toward the coronation, which was not in fact delayed by plague, as scholars have averred.[66] As the "sickness" became more of a factor, however, the coronation planning had to accommodate it. There could be no curtailing the elaborateness of the crucial coronation ceremony that transferred power from dead monarch to living king and so vouched for the constancy of regnal order, but neither need there be large numbers of common spectators. No procession through the city, no pageants where the various guilds would have carpentered and peopled elaborate formal structures of welcome and praise to the new sovereign. All that would have to wait for almost a year.

Now tickets of admission were issued and only to persons officially attached to the court. These tickets allowed the bearer to witness the coronation ceremony itself, a ceremony to which no ordinary dwellers of plague-stricken London were to be admitted. To this end, a strong body of guards was placed at all the London gates to keep people from trying to travel from the city limits to Westminster Abbey. Documents also suggest that, in order to guard the river banks, the southern boundary of the city, from public access to Westminster, Scottish severity was invoked. Boatmen who conveyed persons trying to circumvent the guards on land would be punished by death (*SPV*, 10:75).

Precautions were also taken after the coronation. A proclamation issued four days later commanded all those not living in London to return to their own towns, especially justices of the peace and other local officials (*STC* 8329). Given these restrictions, Shakespeare and his fellows could, at that point, have had small hope for a summer playing season. Even if the theaters opened—a very slim possibility—the coronation crowds of July were gone. And on August 8, the commercially important Bartholomew Fair, another provider of good

66. Scaramelli (*SPV*, 10:27) erroneously spoke of postponement and is perhaps the source of later misapprehensions on the subject. The date was fixed by April 18 to take place on the new king's name-day (St. James's day, July 25) and never changed; see *Hatfield*, 15:49, 52.

audiences for plays, would be cancelled as were any other fairs within fifty miles of London (*Annals*, sig. 3Z8).

As the sickness worsened (2,713 plague deaths reported on August 18 for the seven days ending with August 17), the crown decreed a weekly day of prayer to be held each Wednesday, marked by sermons of repentance, collection and distribution of charity to the poor, and fasting—these Wednesdays to be observed until the plague ceased (*Annals*, sig. 3Z6).

The king and queen had early left the London locale for the palaces far from the city. Making a progress during August, they then tried to come up to Woodstock near Oxford in September, but plague was already in the town and they finally decided to remove west to Winchester "where will be a standing court unless the sickness drive them thence." The Michaelmas law term, when the courts were again open for litigation and which should have begun in London on October 6, was adjourned until November 12 at Winchester.[67]

The court itself moved through Winchester to Salisbury, specifically to Wilton, the young earl of Pembroke's great house several miles west of the city. As early as October 23, royal documents began to be dated from here. A fact not generally realized is that, from October to December 1603, the government of England was situated far to the west of London, in that part of the country for which Southampton served as the main seaport.[68] Plague had effectively forced all essential crown activity away from London, and all city businessmen—including the actors whose theaters were closed—had to adjust accordingly.

What was the situation for Shakespeare and his fellows, whose financial year certainly depended on the months when outdoor playhouses were at their most pleasant? June, July, August, and September had come and gone with no profit to be had from the Globe playhouse. Dramatic historians regularly assume that Jacobean acting companies in times of plague toured the provinces,[69] but in many plague visitations, especially during this one of 1603, such traveling would have been more difficult than one might assume because

---

67. Edmund Lodge, *Illustrations of British History*, 3 vols., (London, 1838), 3:36, 57. Plague indeed did come to Winchester by October 3.

68. See Howard Vallance Jones, ed., "The Journal of Levinus Munck," *English Historical Review* 68 (1953), 234–258. For the location of the court at these times, see p. 247.

69. For example, Chambers, *Elizabethan Stage*, 1:331–332, and Wickham, *Early English Stages*, 2:115.

plague was not now confined to London. During October most of Kent all the way down to Dover was infected, and this soon became the case in the Oxford area as well, even though some of these regions had sustained tours of professional actors when London had been forbidden to them in the past.[70]

Nevertheless, Shakespeare and his fellows do surface here and there, although the exact dates are not always easy to ascertain. Such records are more deceptive than is apparent from the statements of Chambers, and of Schoenbaum, who follows Chambers. Towns did not have the same fiscal year, nor did most towns date exactly; instead, they merely noted an event in their records, often without specifying a particular month and day.

The records of the city of Bath are a pertinent case in point. Of the three provincial documents tracing the King's Servants during 1603, this city's offers the most specific information, but even this record is ambiguous. Bath paid Shakespeare's company on an unspecified date within the one-year interval October 1602 to October 1603. On the basis of this vague reference, Halliwell-Phillipps argued that the King's Servants were already in Bath during the celebration of James's "accession."[71] But the sequence of entries for the Bath fiscal year October 15, 1602 to October 14, 1603, as recorded by Halliwell-Phillipps himself, is difficult:

[1]   item, given to a fencer that did play before the shot with the sword at the proclaiming of our dread and sovereign king, ij.s. vj.d.

[2]   item, given to the musicians at the same time, iii.s. iiij.d.

[3]   item, paid for five gallons of claret wine given the shot upon the King's holiday, xiij.s. iiij.d.

[4]   item, paid for a pound and half of sugar at the same time, ij.s. iij.d.

---

70. See H. E. Salter, *Oxford Council Acts: 1583–1626*, ed. J. Carter (Oxford: Oxford University Press, 1928), pp. 384–386. Although there has been relatively little sustained study of how plague was handled in the provinces, Creighton, *History of Epidemics*, and Shrewsbury, *History of Plague*, are helpful.

71. See J. O. Halliwell-Phillipps, *Shakespeare's Tours* (Brighton, 1887), pp. 13–14. Both he and Murray (n. 76 below) erroneously transcribe the dating period in question as "1602–4" but see Robert Alexander, "Corrections of Bath Dramatic Records 1568–1620 in Printed Lists," *Records of Early English Drama Newsletter* 10 (1985), 2–7. For Murray's and Halliwell-Phillipps's "1604" read: October 16, 1602, to October 14, 1603. For Murray's unreliability, see also David Galloway, "Records of Early English Drama in the Provinces," in *The Elizabethan Theatre*, vol. 7, ed. G. R. Hibbard (University of Waterloo: Archon Books, 1977), pp. 82–110.

[5] item, given to the musicians at the same time, v.s.

[6] item, given to the king's players, xxx.s.

[7] item, paid for two gallons of beer given to the shot upon the king's holiday, viij.d.

[8] paid for a glass that was lost at the same time, ij.d.

[9] paid more for cakes given to the shot at the same tyme, v.s.

The "proclaiming" (items 1 and 2) would have taken place when messengers arrived in Bath to order the legal proclamation of James as king: some time after March 24 or 25.[72] But it would have been impossible for the "king's players" as such to have been paid at this time because there were no king's players until Shakespeare and his fellows became the King's Servants on May 19, almost two months after James was proclaimed. It was the "King's holiday" (items 3–9) of the Bath record that would most likely have found Shakespeare and his fellows on tour, for this was probably July 25, 1603, the day of the coronation in plague-stricken London.[73] Although the public in London, we have seen, was not allowed to participate, coronation celebrations (without the sovereign, of course) most certainly took place elsewhere throughout England, and Bath itself was not visited by plague until the following year, in May 1604.[74] So the "king's

72. Sir Thomas Tresham's proclamation of James's accession in Northamptonshire illustrates such activity as an event (although in this case it was hostilely received); see *MSS. in Various Collections*, 8 vols., (London: HMC, 1904), 3:117–123.

73. In my view, this series of entries refers to two separate occasions as follows. The first several items refer to the time of the proclamation and the attendant celebration (1, 2). The next seven items (3–9) I take to represent a single occasion different from the proclamation celebration. Generally, the "King's holiday" would refer to Accession Day, always celebrated at court not with plays but with the old-fashioned medieval tournament termed in the records "tilting." But even though the Bath record spans October 1602–October 1603, it is only James's first Accession Day—a "King's [not a queen's] holiday"—that could have been celebrated within this interval: on March 24, 1603. Shakespeare and his fellows were then in London (see above) and would not yet have been traveling—nor (as above) were they yet "the King's players." But because there are two "King's holiday" listings between 1602 and 1603, the only occasion other than the proclamation before October 1603 is the July 25, 1603, coronation. Plague was then in London and the theaters were closed as per the new patent for the King's Servants which allowed them to act only after the pestilence had decreased. They were thus probably touring and authorized to use the King's name. See *Records of Early English Drama: Norwich: 1540–1642*, ed. David Galloway (Toronto: University of Toronto Press, 1984), pp. 123, 346–347, for similar Coronation Day and Accession Day payments.

74. Shrewsbury, *History of Plague*, p. 278.

players" were touring well to the west of London during July, for this part of the country was then free from disease.

The town of Coventry also seems to record payment to the "king's players" for 1603. Its fiscal year was November 28, 1602 to November 27, 1603, and a similar record exists for Shrewsbury (Dec. 1602 to Nov. 1603). Since the "king's players," as they were termed in the Coventry record, or the "King's Majesty's players," as they were termed in the Shrewsbury records, could only have existed after May 19, 1603 (when they were so created), both towns must have seen Shakespeare and his fellows between June and November, 1603.

Both Shrewsbury and Coventry were farther west and north of where Shakespeare and his fellows may usually have toured: no record has yet been found of the company in those towns prior to 1603. Furthermore, the company had not been in Bath for the previous six years. But the area outlined by Shrewsbury-Coventry-Bath is a coherent geographical grouping. The triangle they form has Bath and Coventry making a baseline west to east while Shrewsbury is the apex, a hundred miles north of Bath. On a diagonal line running east to west up to Shrewsbury from London, Coventry is the nearest edge of the triangle to London, ninety miles away.

In normal times Coventry accommodated the visits of some six to nine provincial companies during the course of a year, but during this plague summer and fall of 1603 the number was augmented by visits from the three London companies—King's, as well as Nottingham's and Worcester's Servants.[75] And once Coventry had been played, the famous old drama town must have served as a point of divergence for the troupes barred by plague from London. In addition to being in Coventry, for instance, the Servants of the Earl of Nottingham were in Leicester and in York to the north, at about the time Shakespeare and his fellows went to Shrewsbury in the west. It is as if territories in this year's financial emergency had been carved out.[76]

Whatever touring there was outside of London, to make money now that the London playhouses were inaccessible, this effort seems

75. In the chamberlains' and wardens' account book of Coventry, on p. 358, we find an entry for October 27, 1603; on p. 364, an entry for November 17; on p. 366, fifteen entries of payments to as many acting companies, including the King's Servants. All these companies cannot have played in Coventry between November 17 and November 27, so the entries must be retrospective and cumulative for the fiscal year. For all these records, see *Records of Early English Drama: Coventry*, ed. R. W. Ingram (Toronto: University of Toronto Press, 1981), p. 362.

76. See J. T. Murray, *English Dramatic Companies*, 2 vols., (London: Russell and Russell, 1910), 2:308; 392; 413.

to have ended when the players began to anticipate (wrongly) that autumn and cooler weather would bring an end to plague in London. Even as the royal family was leaving Winchester to clear the area for the treason trials there, removing to Salisbury and Wilton, Joan Alleyn, the stepdaughter of Philip Henslowe and wife of Edward Alleyn, was in London writing optimistically to her husband on October 21.

> My entire and well-beloved sweetheart, still it joys me—and long, I pray God, may I joy—to hear of your welfare, as you of ours. Almighty God be thanked, my own self (yourself) and my mother and whole house are in good health; and about us the sickness doth cease, and likely more and more, by God's help, to cease. All the companies be come home, and well, for aught we know, but that Brown of the Boar's Head is dead, and died very poor. He went not into the country at all. And all of your own company [Nottingham's Servants] are well at their own houses.[77]

Joan Alleyn's account is not quite accurate. On September 16, a proclamation had adjourned Michaelmas term until the fourth return—about October 28—and that notice had probably suggested to the touring city companies that late October was the time they could reasonably expect the delayed beginning of the London season finally to take place. But just three days before Joan Alleyn wrote, the proclamation of October 18 (*STC* 8335) had further delayed the beginning of Michaelmas term and also transferred to Winchester all law-court proceedings that would ordinarily take place in London. Perhaps, in the London area of middle-class affluence surrounding the houses of the Henslowes and the Alleyns, plague was thinning out. But when Mrs. Alleyn wrote her letter, the weekly London figure for October 14–20—a figure that would have been published on Thursday, October 28—was 642 deaths from plague, down 500 deaths from the week before but still a fearful number. Mrs. Alleyn's letter may have been sincerely meant, but, from the viewpoint, say, of the city or crown authorities, it was overly sanguine.

Nonetheless, the companies that had come back to London with mistaken expectations must have seen no great point in going out again. Few towns close by, in Kent, say, were now free from plague. To the west, between July and January 1603, 3,000 people died of plague in Bristol, and to the east, Norwich was bad and becoming

77. Greg, ed., *Henslowe Papers*, pp. 59–61.

worse. Elsewhere—in Northampton and Chester, for example—the situation was not much better.[78] One had to travel far indeed to find a province in which plague had not already struck. For all practical purposes, the city companies had nowhere to earn money at this time to supplement what they might have been able to pick up on the road during the summer. From the Bath entries, for example, it seems clear that companies did not establish prolonged residence in a given provincial town but were in the undesirable financial situation of traveling onward after only one performance; otherwise, as at Bath (item 6), even if they lingered longer, they had earned only 30 shillings for the length of the stay.

Where were Shakespeare and his fellows this same October? Documents suggest that they were in London—that despite the absence of the court and the change in locale of term time to Winchester, at least two companies, the King's Servants and those of the earl of Nottingham, elected not to tour, or to try to find plague-free spots, but to wait. Despite London's primacy at the moment as a plague center, and as if unwilling to miss a day should the playhouses be allowed to open, the actors remained close at hand, unaware that plague in London would persist through December.

There are grounds for assuming that Shakespeare had lodgings then near the Bear Garden in Surrey—that is, near the theater district that contained the Globe—and whether he had yet moved to the house of Christopher Mountjoy in the northwest part of the city between St. Paul's and Cripplegate is difficult to tell. The evidence from the famous lawsuit in which the poet testified merely establishes him in that household by November, 1604—a year later.[79] But Shakespeare might not have wished to be too close to the theater district in Southwark in the autumn of 1603, because this was one of the sections of the city hit first and hardest by plague.[80] Indeed, the spectacular mortality in St. Olave's could itself have precipitated his move across the river to the north to the Mountjoy household.

While Shakespeare and his fellows waited for the plague to end

---

78. See Creighton, *History of Epidemics*, 1:496–498; Mullett, *Bubonic Plague and England*, pp. 107–108; and Shrewsbury, *History of Plague*, pp. 270 ff. Regarding Norwich, see Galloway, *Norwich*, p. 120, for August, 1603.

79. See E. K. Chambers, *William Shakespeare*, 2 vols. (Oxford: Clarendon Press, 1931), 2:87–95.

80. Between May 7 and October 13, 2,640 of James Balmford's parishioners in St. Olave's had died of plague; see James Balmford, *A Short Dialogue Concerning the Plague's Infection*, as quoted by Creighton, *History of Epidemics*, 1:478–479. See also F. Herring, *Modest Defense*, sig. B.

in the autumn of 1603, were the companies themselves locked out of their own theater buildings lest they rehearse and draw crowds? There is no way of knowing, but what may be relevant is that, either for residential or professional purposes, Shakespeare and his fellows were now in the close vicinity of the present or future property of Augustine Phillips, one of Shakespeare's fellows. In his will a year and a half later (May 13, 1605), Phillips was to leave silver bowls worth £5 each to John Hemmings, Richard Burbage, and William Sly, his fellows among the King's Servants, and 30-shilling gold pieces to William Shakespeare and Henry Condell. Thus Phillips seems to have felt close to his colleagues.[81] Some time before 1604, Phillips had acquired a house and land in Surrey, in an area south of the Thames and west of Southwark, near Richmond Palace in the town of Mortlake—or, as it was known just as often in Shakespeare's time, Morclacke. A respectable enough suburb to contain the residence of the famous astrologer-astronomer John Dee, whom Queen Elizabeth had visited, Mortlake was relatively removed from London and plague in 1603. Phillips's house, if he owned it by then, would thus have been a convenient place in which to assemble, rehearse, or plan while waiting to see what was to come of the autumn season.[82] Even if the entire company was not all housed with Phillips, waiting in Mortlake at other lodgings with Phillips' house as a kind of headquarters might have seemed the best policy at this slow and doubtful time. The fact is, in any event, that in the record of payment made to the company for their performance noted at Wilton on December 2 of this autumn, the chamber account cites a compensation paid "for the pains and expenses" of the company in "coming from Mortlake" to the temporary site of the court far to the west at Wilton. Presumably, then, it was not for a performance in the provinces that Shakespeare and his fellows eventually left their London base in the autumn, but for that evening at Wilton which was the first known performance of the King's Servants at court in the early Stuart period.

Shakespeare's company was probably not summoned all that way

81. Shakespeare left £1.6.8 apiece to Burbage, Hemmings, and Condell in his own will for friendship rings.

82. The relevant texts lead us in a circle. There is no indication of when Phillips acquired his Mortlake holding before his 1604 will; see Edwin Nungezer, *A Dictionary of Actors* (New Haven: Yale University Press, 1929), s.v. "Phillips." The payment of Shakespeare and his fellows in December 1603 for coming to Wilton from Mortlake may be an indication of when Phillips owned a house there—or it may not be.

to Wilton merely to give one performance. At that time (before December 2), the master of the revels must have assumed that plague in London would prevent the court's return to London for Christmas and planned the holiday season for Wilton. But this Assumption proved wrong: plague receded and Christmas revels were held at Hampton Court. Shakespeare and his fellows had to accommodate themselves to the change in plans. Queen Anna left for Hampton Court only five days after payment was made to the King's Servants for their December 2 performance. It seems highly possible, then, that Shakespeare and his fellows were caught in this shift of royal plans.

The London mood was now optimistic. Christmas was coming and cold weather had set in. According to Scaramelli, the Venetian secretary in London, "no one ever mentions the plague any more." Further, he wrote, "the city is so full of people that it is hard to believe that about sixty thousand deaths [sic] have taken place" (*SPV*, 10:12b).

Although, as noted in Chapter 2, Shakespeare and his fellows were summoned now to Hampton Court where they performed several plays, the plague of 1603 was not finished as far as they were concerned. Although the plague bill for December 8 listed only 55 deaths for the week in London, that figure would almost double to reach 96 for a week during the middle of December. The last set of published weekly statistics for this great plague reported the week ending Thursday, December 22, and these figures listed 74 plague deaths in the previous seven-day period. Later figures sporadically surface in private comments and reports for the rest of the winter, indicating that plague deaths would not fall to significantly low levels (from the official viewpoint) for at least another month (*SPV*, 10:132).

On December 23, the day after the last official plague mortality report, Robert Cecil wrote a letter to the master of the horse, the earl of Worcester, that indicates the attitude of the privy council of England about plague prospects. "It is intended," wrote Cecil, "that the Parliament shall begin in March if the sickness stay [arrests itself]." Sir Thomas Edmonds, also at court, reported to his master, the earl of Shrewsbury, on the same day and seems to confirm Cecil's pessimism about the outlook for the forthcoming months: "It is projected that about the 20th of March a Parliament shall be called, if the sickness will give leave, whereof some doubt is made.[83]

83. Edmund Lodge. *Illustrations*, 3:83, 85.

In the middle of January there was another setback. Some plague-exposed bedding escaped the quarantined houses in London—in violation, of course, of the plague orders on the subject. Nicolo Molino, writing to Venice on January 19, reported that the date for the opening of Parliament had not yet even been announced. He explained why: "The plague has shown signs of increasing again, owing to the carelessness with which the bedding and clothes of persons who died of the disease are being used by the living" (*SPV*, 10:130). Throughout these difficulties, the London authorities apparently continued to enforce the plague orders with great rigor.[84]

Finally, on March 19, 1604, King James did convene Parliament. Some intimations of the length of time in which emergency measures for the plague must have continued may be gathered from his Parliamentary address: "It did no sooner please God to lighten his hand, and relent the violence of his devouring Angel against the poor people of this City, but as soon did I resolve to call this Parliament."[85]

There is nothing to indicate that, in this atmosphere of official attitudes toward plague, the playhouses in London had been allowed to reopen in the meantime. Rather, it seems as if Shakespeare's company's special friend (see Chapter 2) interceded again, for Shakespeare and his fellows were compensated by a payment in February 1604 that was not shared by their competitors:

> To Richard Burbage, one of his Majesty's comedians, upon the Council's warrant dated at Hampton Court viii *die Februarii* 1603 [1604] for the maintenance and relief of himself and the rest of his company being prohibited to present any plays publicly in or near London by reason of great peril that might grow through the extraordinary concourse and assembly of people to a new increase of the plague till it shall please God to settle the city in a more perfect health:
> by way of his Majesty's free gift   £ xxx (*MSC*, 6:39)

This award of £30, equal to the one the company received for traveling to Wilton, raised the income from Christmas plays to a gross of £150 out of which the trips to Wilton and Hampton Court, as well as salaries and upkeep of the Globe, had to be paid. The other two companies were not as fortunate, although they too had suffered from plague conditions, and it seems clear that some friend

---

84. For the activity of the London authorities, see the *Journals*, vol. 26 fol. 141b, quoted by Wilson in *Plague in Shakespeare's London*, p. 115 n.3.

85. Speech delivered March 19, 1604; see James I, *Political Works*, ed. C. H. McIlwain (Cambridge: Harvard University Press, 1918), p. 269.

in a high place made this payment possible. The same friend, however, was obviously unable to open the public theater where the big
money was to be made. The payment's date (February 4) and its
remark about the continued presence of plague attests to the continued paralysis of the London theater. Finally, however, the long
period of theatrical closing that had in effect begun on the eve of
Elizabeth's death came to an end—when, on April 9, 1604, the privy
council of England offered good and bad news: playing was now to
be allowed, but conditions concerning future plague closings were
also established, conditions that would have a significant effect on
Shakespeare's production and the shape of his professional career.
The privy council warrant is preserved among the papers of Edward
Alleyn and is worth quoting extensively:

> Whereas the King's Majesty's Players have given [His] Highness good
> service in their quality of playing and forasmuch likewise as they are
> at all times to be employed in that service whensoever they shall be
> commanded, we think it therefore fit, the time of Lent being now
> past, that your Lordships [the lord mayor of London and the justices
> of the peace in Middlesex and Surrey] do permit and suffer the three
> companies of players to the King, Queen, and Prince publicly to ex-
> ercise their plays in their several and usual houses ... without any let
> or interruption in respect of any former Letters of Prohibition here-
> tofore written by us to your Lordships. Except there shall happen
> weekly to die of the plague above the number of thirty within the
> City of London and the liberties thereof. At which time we think it
> fit they shall cease and forbear any further publicly to play until the
> sickness be again decreased to the said number.[86]

Among the six nobles signing the warrant were the lord chamberlain, the earl of Nottingham, and the earl of Worcester—the master of the master of the revels plus two expatrons of dramatic
companies. Of passing note is that the king himself was not involved
in these permissions and that the members of the privy council do
not seem to have been swayed by any favoritism for drama over
what they perceived as the safety of the city. Despite the standard
of thirty deaths per week, which emerges here for the first time, the
council would always feel free to close playhouses when there
seemed danger of plague, however small the weekly deathrate might
be.

Shakespeare and his fellows had thus been idle for slightly more

---

86. For the text, see Greg, ed., *Henslowe Papers*, pp. 61–62.

than a calendar year beginning almost with James's accession, losing income that can only be guessed at. Furthermore, because of the nature of the disease, their activity in the provinces during plague was severely restricted. As best they could, companies took advantage of the windows of time in which money could be made before plague reached out to claim new areas and new victims. But records for 1603—fuller than most—suggest that playing in the provinces was a highly imperfect solution to the problems caused by the closing of the public theaters in London.

A more viable alternative seems indicated by the performance at Wilton. Very often the court was the only acting environment accessible to Shakespeare and his fellows and to other companies as well during long stretches in which they were barred from the Globe. At the same time, however, these appearances at court could hardly hope to compensate financially for extended closings of their playhouses. Even in the best of times, the King's Servants rarely gave more than fifteen plays at court for a gross of £150 over a span extending from All Saints' Day to Shrove Tuesday, a period of approximately four months. Extended playhouse closings, in 1603 but also for the next six years, became a real problem. They are a constant factor throughout Shakespeare's continued creative production, the subject of the chapters to follow.

4

Shakespeare after the First Stuart Plague: 1604–1606

It is now time to consider how the highly disruptive situation in which the London theaters found themselves during 1603 and in the beginning of 1604 affected Shakespeare's creative effort. Certainly, as a member of his company he would constantly have been involved in the everyday mechanics of its survival and he may have been extremely busy.[1] The company's tour in the provinces during the summer of 1603, its journey to Wilton, its presence in the same month at Hampton Court and later for other performances during the holidays, its presence in London during James's delayed 1604 coronation procession, and its spell of service at Somerset House in the summer of 1604 have all been noted in Chapter 2. But how did these generally difficult circumstances affect Shakespeare's writing? Did he maintain a creative flow regardless of external disruptions, or is it possible that his dramaturgy depended on the immediate availability of the Globe playhouse, on ready access to a place where his scripts might immediately be realized?

Because the early Stuart years are a period difficult to gauge in Shakespeare's life, the answer to this question depends on the exploration of several contradictory indications from documents avail-

---

1. That he was active in the details of company business is suggested in 1595 when he was one of the three persons collecting payment at Whitehall in March for plays given in December; *MSC*, 6:29.

able—and not available—for these times. Part of the difficulty lies in the unusual dearth of two kinds of basic documents well known to scholars and copiously connected with Shakespeare's plays before the death of Queen Elizabeth. These are, first, the published quartos of the dramatist's plays, texts that bear dates on the title pages. For the period 1603–1616, only two of his presumably new plays, *King Lear* and *Pericles*, were published and thus offer dates on printed title pages. What remain, instead, are a second, equally misleading kind of Shakespearean production record.

Of the known allusions to Shakespeare's plays, by far the most frequent are those entries by publishers into the stationers' register by the printers in London. Listing titles, dates, and often dramatic provenance, these entries are the most specific (though by no means definitive) time indications available for Shakespeare's work before the appearance of the 1623 Folio. But the circumstances of theatrical commerce, as helpful as they are, suggest that such entries most probably (but not always) were made after a new play had already been performed. Notwithstanding this assumption, students of the London printing trade continue to puzzle over the precise circumstances of individual play publication in a time before authorial copyright and in a business in which any playing company might logically wish to resist printings of scripts that could be taken up by competing companies or even by readers. No play had to be listed in the stationers' register at all if it was not going to be printed. Nor was every play intended or released for print.

Accordingly, an entry in the stationers' register could come long after a first performance—or never. To take but one example, *Twelfth Night* was seen in performance on February 2, 1602, but it was never entered in the Stationers' register during Shakespeare's lifetime and never appeared in print until the First Folio of 1623. More immediately bearing on Shakespeare's Stuart period, *Hamlet*, published in its "good quarto" in 1604, after James's accession, was first entered in the stationers' register in July 1602, yet it was known to Gabriel Harvey before February 1601.[2]

Thus, if the final stationers' register allusion before King James's accession was to a hitherto-unsurfaced Shakespeare drama on February 7, 1603 (an entry in the stationers' register by James Roberts for *Troilus and Cressida*), the performance of this particular play

2. For the latest recension of the argument, see *Hamlet*, Arden edition, ed. Harold Jenkins (London: Methuen, 1982), pp. 1–13.

could still have been considerably earlier. Consequently, there is no way of calculating the gap in time between *Troilus and Cressida* and any new plays performed after King James's accession—or even of knowing whether *Troilus and Cressida* was the last play before the beginning of Shakespeare's Jacobean production which is the subject of this book. Further, for the plays thought to have been written in Shakespeare's Stuart period, the stationers' register offers only *King Lear, Pericles,* and *Antony and Cleopatra;* and the first two of these cases simply expand on already available information— *King Lear* and *Pericles* appeared in print with dates on their title pages.

Given these difficulties, we must reach beyond quartos and stationers' register entries to various texts that include not only records of plague in London—these establish important parameters for Shakespeare's Stuart career—but crown records of disbursement and other political and social documents of the period. At the same time, given presently privileged lines of discussion, it is necessary to reconsider such dating tools as topical allusion (e.g., the Gunpowder Plot and *Macbeth*) and progressive stylistic change (e.g., metrical tests). These methods have too often been determiners of the presently accepted set of dates for plays in Shakespeare's Stuart canon even though, as I suggest in this chapter (and in Appendix 4 on metrical tests), they have little validity.

Ultimately, I try to show that the availability of the Globe playhouse was an extremely significant factor in Shakespeare's writing— that when the Globe was closed, Shakespeare's production slowed markedly or stopped. To this effect I present, in this chapter, two chronological sequences for the four years surrounding James's accession to the throne. The first period, 1602–4, witnesses the performance of no more than two new Shakespearean plays; in the second, 1605–6, as many as three of Shakespeare's major dramas may have been produced.

I

To begin, it should be borne in mind that contemporary notations first refer to Jacobean plays by William Shakespeare not one year but almost two years after King James came to the throne of England. *Othello* and, soon after, *Measure for Measure* appear in the record of court performances for the All Saints' Day and Christmas revels of the winter of 1604–5. After this, no reference to the performance of any other new Shakespearean play would appear for almost twenty-four months.

Were these recorded performances of *Othello* and *Measure for Measure* landmark events—the *first* productions of these plays? If so, there may have been a gap in Shakespeare's output, a hiatus extending to a time even before James's accession in March 1603— back to whenever *Troilus and Cressida* was first produced before its Stationers' Register entry in February 1603. If, however, *Othello* and *Measure for Measure* were not now new—if they had already been presented on the public stage prior to the court performance dates of late autumn 1604—then when might they have first appeared at the Globe?

The year 1603 can probably be eliminated from consideration. The death of Queen Elizabeth (and Lent) and then plague dominated these twelve months, keeping the playhouses closed even through Lent 1604. And *Othello* and *Measure for Measure* would not have been shown at court during that first Stuart Christmas season of 1603. Why? Because they would not then have been performed during the succeeding Christmas holidays of 1604. The King's Servants (and the master of the revels) could scarcely have wished a repetition of the former year's offerings. For example, *A Midsummer Night's Dream*, which very probably was presented at court during James's first Christmas, did not appear in the succeeding Christmas court season of 1604–5, for which we possess a rare listing of plays shown.[3]

But if *Othello* and *Measure for Measure* were new to court for Christmas 1604–5 (and not performed in the 1603–4 holidays), they must have been performed at the Globe between Christmas seasons, sometime in 1604 after the plague ended. When? In April 1604, the privy council had at long last allowed the resumption of play. Easter had been celebrated on April 8, so the rest of April presumably saw theatrical activity at the Globe, forbidden since the few days of May 1603—perhaps even the first production of *Othello* and *Measure for Measure*.

If, however, the players did not perform these two plays in April, *Measure for Measure* and *Othello* could not have been introduced

3. In the payment for court performances in James's first Christmas season, no play titles appear in the records, but Dudley Carleton wrote John Chamberlain from court that on January 1, 1604, "we had a play of Robin Goodefellow"; E. K. Chambers, *The Elizabethan Stage*, 4 vols. (Oxford: Clarendon Press, 1923), 3:279. The playing company paid for that evening was the King's Servants; *MSC*, 6.38.

at the public theater later than this. For by May a general anxiety about infection was again arising. True, the privy council letter's proviso mandated theater closing only when deaths rose to thirty, and weekly deaths were only at 19 and 20 during late April, not rising to 34 per week until the middle of May, after which they sank again. But plague, in the late spring and summer of 1604, was everywhere in England *except* London. Indeed, barely a month after playing had resumed in April 1604, on Wednesday, May 2, Nicolo Molino, the Venetian resident in London, concluded his report to the doge and the senate with the observation that "the week before last [April 19?] ten, in the last, nineteen, deaths from plague. Alarm is felt at the approach of the warm season." Then, on the following Wednesday, May 9, Molino wrote: "Last week 20 deaths from plague. They fear that this week the number will be much greater." On May 17, 24 plague deaths were reported, and then, for the week after that, the limit of thirty was crossed with a report of 34 on May 24. "A further rise is expected," Molino wrote five days later: "Everyone is beginning to look out for a house in the country" (*SPV*, 10:150–155).

A spell of abnormal cold in the middle of June caused plague deaths to sink again below thirty, and the report for July 5–12, as indicated by a surviving brief (see Appendix 2), lists only three plague deaths in the city and five in the liberties. On the other hand, after Nicolo Molino had expressed his first misgivings on May 2, he continued to keep a record of plague figures until the following October 23, 1604. He probably did so because, during the summer of 1604, although London itself was the healthiest place in the kingdom, the rest of England was still experiencing severe plague, and it seemed only a matter of time before London itself would again be heavily infected.

It is probable that this threat of plague in the late summer of 1604 caused London officials alternately to cancel and then to go ahead with Bartholomew Fair on August 27, as Molino reported to his Venetian master. The fair was a major trade event, important to the economy of the city and its outlying areas as an occasion for heavy business activity in buying and selling of goods and animals brought in from all over England. Yet, as previously observed, the dangers of allowing wool, linens, and clothing to circulate during plague were well known. What to do, when most of England was heavily infested, even though London was not? The decision, finally, was to go ahead with the fair, a conclusion that seems to have been vindicated since plague deaths remained at twenty and below for each of the following weeks (*SPV*, 10:182, 190).

But if the authorities in August were undecided about allowing such a commercially important event as the annual Bartholomew Fair, they can scarcely have been as tolerant of stage playing, which in the circumstances would have had few redeeming commercial virtues. With plague deaths in the twenties, though that was well below thirty per week, the city authorities or the privy council need not have been as tolerant of the drama. Thus the possibility of public playing from May 1604 through September 1604 seems dubious.

Documentary indications of the activities of Shakespeare and his fellows at this time are, as usual, sparse, but they did not play at the Globe for the greater part of August. They *may* have been out of London, in Oxford, between May 7 and June 16.[4] If this is so, then the company had obviously decided that the London situation was, for the moment, untenable. From August 9 through August 27, 1604, however, the constable of Castile was in England, residing at Somerset House, and, as previously observed, Shakespeare and his fellows were attending him as grooms of the chamber. Not only was the Globe certainly dark then, but the Fortune too, for the Queen's Servants were grooms of the chamber at Durham House during the same period. Whether the Servants of the Prince (the old Admiral's Servants) therefore had the London theatrical scene to themselves depends on whether or not the authorities had shut the theaters in the weeks before Bartholomew Fair.

Life is never so tidy as one would like to sketch it in historical narrative, and, in the case of 1604 in London, one faces a conceptually confused period of openings and closings. Because of the high incidence of plague all over the country, the authorities might have feared that the sickness could break out again in London at any time. Cold it may have become in June, for a little while, but this cold had soon disappeared with the onset of summer, and certainly the June frost did not stave off plague throughout the rest of the country.

4. See Chambers, *Elizabethan Stage*, 2:211; cf. H. E. Salter, *Oxford Council Acts 1583–1626*, ed. J. Carter (Oxford: Oxford University Press, 1928), p. 386. J. O. Halliwell-Phillipps, *Shakespeare's Tours* (Brighton, 1887), p. 33, thinks the record refers to late May or early June but is not certain, while J. T. Murray, *English Dramatic Companies: 1558–1642*, 2 vols. (London: Russell and Russell, 1910), 2:378 n. 5, opts against this time. The Oxford council's fiscal year was Michaelmas to Michaelmas. For the July plague bill in London, see "Sackville MSS." in *Cranfield Papers*, 2 vols, ed. A. P. Newton et al. (London, HMC: 1940–66), 1:64.

I believe it most likely that the authorities kept the theaters closed until they could evaluate the risk taken with Bartholomew Fair, and that they probably opened the playhouses at Michaelmas in late September. If this was the case, then *Othello* and *Measure for Measure* might very well have seen their debuts at the Globe in the autumn, sometime before November 1, when *Othello* itself came to court.

This spotty outlook for theater openings and closings must be considered in conjunction with information deriving from sets of documents for the Christmas season of 1604–5. One set is the court warrants for payment to the actors, the nights of playing being stipulated. The other set comprises two texts, the audit office accounts and an abstract of a revels office list naming the plays that were performed on the nights for which the court payment records exist. These latter two documents have long served as the basis of the dates of the court performances of *Othello* and *Measure for Measure*. Further, they represent one of only three such lists for Shakespeare's entire professional lifetime (the others being for 1611–12 and 1612–13)—a fact not sufficiently appreciated in Shakespearean criticism. This early and rare instance not only offers a production date for *Othello* and *Measure for Measure* but also yields an important picture of a crucial moment in Shakespeare's progress through his canon.

To understand this moment fully, it is important to consider what this 1604 court payment record does *not* tell about the canon—what Shakespearean plays are not accounted for by scholars prior to this listing. Here are the as yet unsurfaced plays, in alphabetical order— those that had not been mentioned in any known contemporary document by about October 1604:

All's Well that Ends Well	Measure for Measure
Antony and Cleopatra	Othello
Coriolanus	Pericles
Cymbeline	Tempest
Henry VIII	Timon of Athens
King Lear	Two Noble Kinsmen(?)
Macbeth	Winter's Tale

There are thus thirteen or fourteen plays to account for between the appearance of the 1604–5 list and June 1613, when a performance

of Shakespeare's last unchallenged play, *Henry VIII*, would mark
the burning of the Globe.

What Shakespearean plays can be found that antedate this list,
say, within two years or so? (1) *Merry Wives of Windsor* was entered
in the stationers' register on January 18, 1602; (2) *Twelfth Night* was
described with identifying accuracy in Manningham's *Diary* for Candlemas, February 2, 1602; (3) *Hamlet*, whatever the disputed dates
of the early printed quartos (Q1 1603; Q2 1604) had been entered as
"it was lately acted by the Lord Chamberlain his Servants" on July
26, 1602; and (4) *Troilus and Cressida*, as previously noted, was in
the stationers' register on February, 7, 1603, a month or so before
Queen Elizabeth died. Thus the last known play to have been recorded was *Troilus and Cressida*, which seems to have been preceded
in early 1602 by a cluster of *Hamlet, Twelfth Night*, and *Merry Wives
of Windsor*.

No one knows just what James's court had seen in the Christmas
season of 1603–4 (except for *A Midsummer Night's Dream*), but we
do know about the 1604–5 Christmas season. The following table
is the first extant list from the pipe office declared accounts of holiday plays presented by Shakespeare and his fellows for that second
Stuart Christmas season, the season when one first hears of *Othello*
and *Measure for Measure*.[5] One might guess that the absence of
Twelfth Night and *Hamlet* from the 1604–5 list, together with that
of other well-known plays (*Henry IV, As You Like It*), and even the
absence of *Troilus and Cressida* can be accounted for by their having
been presented at court during the first Stuart Christmas season.
Since the King's Servants were paid for one play at Wilton, for six
at Hampton Court, and for two at Whitehall during those first holidays, they might easily have shown as many as five of Shakespeare's
plays, particularly if the 1604–5 list is any indication of the Shakespearean proportion of the company's offerings. Thus, that *Hamlet,
Troilus and Cressida*, and *Twelfth Night*, or *As You Like It* and
Much Ado about Nothing—both of which surfaced as early as 1600—
may have been offered in the first holiday season of 1603 may help
explain the selections in the 1604–5 list: they represent a reaching
back into the repertoire. Indeed, the interesting and crucial feature

5. See Chambers, *Elizabethan Stage*, 4:138–139, for the authenticity of this list,
and E. K. Chambers, *William Shakespeare*, 2 vols., (Oxford: Clarendon Press, 1931)
2:331–332, for a reproduction of it. See also *MSC*, 13:7–9, for a later edition of it by
W. R. Streitberger. Also presented, by different companies, were *How to Learn a
Woman to Woo* (new?) on December 30 and Chapman's *All Fools* (new?) on January
1.

Court Playing Date (1604–5)	First Known Date	Play
November 1	new	*Othello*
November 4	1602	*Merry Wives of Windsor*
December 26	new	*Measure for Measure*
December 28	1598	*Comedy of Errors*
January 1–6	1598	*Love's Labor's Lost*
January 7	1600	*Henry V*
January 8	1599	*Every Man out of His Humor*
February 2	1598	*Every Man in His Humor*
February 3		(play ready but not called for)
February 10	1598	*Merchant of Venice*
February 11	?	*Spanish Maze*
February 12	1598	*Merchant of Venice*

of this same list—the fact that so many of the plays belonged to the old repertoire—is what it implies about Shakespeare's rate of production.

From the record, one can suspect that Shakespeare was perfectly capable of turning out work rather quickly—from 1592 to 1602 he produced perhaps twenty-seven plays, about two per year. Using this as some sort of rough norm, and taking July 26, 1602, as the latest possible date of *Hamlet* (actually, its date of entry into the stationers' register), Shakespeare thus had nothing new appear (except perhaps *Troilus and Cressida*) until November 1, 1604. And from the last possible date for *Troilus and Cressida* (February 1603), a month before Queen Elizabeth's death, to a year afterward, Shakespeare may have written no new plays at all. For, to repeat, if *Othello* or *Measure for Measure* had been played at court as early as Christmas 1603–4, then probably neither would have been presented (as both indeed were) in James's second court season of 1604–5. And if *Measure for Measure* and *Othello* had already been written by James's first Christmas (but not performed), then, conversely, Shakespeare wrote nothing more for all of the year (1604) afterward.

In other words, by November 1604, in the twenty-one months since February 1603 (*Troilus and Cressida*), or in the twenty-eight months since *Hamlet* was printed, Shakespeare had produced only two plays: *Measure for Measure* and *Othello*—"only," of course, being a word appropriate to the unusual case of a Shakespeare. The two plays are certainly achievement enough for a span of two years and four months; yet the process of producing them falls below the prior Shakespearean rate: an average of two plays per year.

Thus, these various texts suggest various scenarios for this period. In one, Shakespeare wrote *Othello* and *Measure for Measure* quickly, before King James came to the throne in March 1603, and then wrote nothing more for several years. In a second alternative, Shakespeare wrote nothing after late 1602 until playing was permitted in the spring of 1604, more than a year after James's accession to the throne. Or possibly Shakespeare wrote sparsely during the period embraced by the twenty-one months between February 1603, when *Troilus and Cressida* was entered, and November 1604, when *Othello* was performed. Finally, Shakespeare may have written nothing after *Troilus and Cressida* until, say, the end of King James's first holiday court season that ended with Lent 1604; then he wrote, quickly, *Othello* and *Measure for Measure*. No matter what the specific scenario, the one obvious explanation for the limited Shakespearean output is twelve successive months of theater closings from plague: April 1603 to April 1604.

The Christmas season of 1604–5 produced a second document that accords with the implications of the playlist just looked at. This text is a letter to the first secretary, Robert Cecil, now Viscount Cranborne, written by Sir Walter Cope early in January 1605; that is, during the same holiday season that yielded *Othello* and *Measure for Measure*. Knighted in April 1603, in honor of the accession, Cope was now serving Cecil as the chamberlain of the exchequer. His career would eventually be successful enough that he could in 1612 house and entertain King James during a progress. Even in 1604–5, when the document in question is dated, Cope seems to have been operating as Cecil's administrative assistant. For example, on Cecil's orders Cope had searched Lord Cobham's house in Blackfriars for incriminating papers incidental to the Bye and Maine Plots of the summer of 1603, seized Cobham's servant there, and reported the results to Cecil. At another time in the same year, Cope had drafted a position paper for Cecil detailing arguments for and against the idea of three estates of government. (*Hatfield*, 15:274, 368). In his letter of January 1605, Cope wrote Cecil:

> I have sent and been all this morning hunting for players, jugglers, and such kind of creatures, but find them hard to find. Wherefore, leaving notes for them to seek me, Burbage is come and says there is no new play that the queen has not seen; but they have revived an old one called *Love's Labor Lost*, which for wit and mirth he says will please her exceedingly. And this is appointed to be played tomorrow night at my Lord of Southampton's, unless you send a writ to remove

the *corpus cum causa*, to your house in Strand. Burbage is my messenger ready attending your pleasure.[6]

The letter that Richard or Cuthbert Burbage, both major stockholders in Shakespeare's troupe, was told to carry to Cecil's suite at the palace suggested to C. C. Stopes some sort of competition between Cecil and the earl of Southampton for the services of Shakespeare and his fellows.[7] But this reading, I think, once more derives from the inflated notion of Shakespeare's personal court popularity discussed in Chapter 2. The truth is that Robert Cecil had many overlapping responsibilities to the crown. He was certainly powerful enough to commandeer any play he wanted, yet, as the lord high steward of the queen's court (one of his many roles) he would have been officially concerned with the proper entertainment of the queen. A lord high steward might, as the operative head of the household accounts, at times serve as overseer of the queen's royal entertainment when this fell outside the purview of her lord chamberlain, Sir Robert Sidney. Cecil, as secretary to the king, was probably the most powerful individual in the kingdom under James. This point is relevant because, after January 8, 1605, the queen would have been the chief royal person at court, King James having left Whitehall for Royston on that day. Cecil would thus have been responsible for a queen who was reigning, at least socially, during the king's absence. Furthermore, one of the queen's brothers, the duke of Holstein, was visiting from Denmark and required entertainment appropriate to the family of a friendly Danish sovereign, for another brother of the queen was the king of Denmark.[8] Thus Sir Walter Cope could hardly have thought that his master, Cecil,

6. *Hatfield*, 16:415. The persistence of Burbage as the court contact for the King's Servants (he received the plague reward for the company in the holidays of 1603–4) is significant, considering the manner in which the earl of Pembroke responded to his death.

7. See Charlotte C. Stopes, *The Life of Henry, Third Earl of Southampton* (Cambridge: Cambridge University Press, 1922), pp. 288–289 n. 2. See Chambers, *Elizabethan Stage*, 4:136–141, for discussions regarding this letter. Because the king actually left Hampton Court on January 9, the entertainments in question had to occur between January 9 and 15 (see *Carleton*, pp. 53–55); but cf. Chambers, ibid. Cope's letter is actually endorsed "1604," and this has occasioned some further discussion, but many contemporary writers (such as Philip Henslowe in his famous diary) retained the old year in their post-December datings through to Lady Day (March 15) and sometimes beyond.

8. *SPD*, 8:186; *Hatfield*, 17:9; *SPV*, 10:212. The Venetian secretary, Molino, said that the king left for Royston on January 9.

wanted to snatch *Love's Labor's Lost* from the earl of Southampton's entertainment of the queen simply to be competitive, despite the fact that Cecil could easily have done so. In such a case Cecil would only have put off, not solved, an immediate problem, for he was ultimately responsible for the decorum of the royal situation in any place during James's absence.

In a letter written before January 15, 1605, Dudley Carleton, another courtier, places the two "competing" dinners for us within the general perspective of the problems of royal entertainment rather than of private emulation:

> It seems we shall have Christmas all the year and therefore I shall never be out of matter. The last night's revels were kept at my Lord of Cranborne's [Cecil] where the Queen with the Duke of Holstein [her brother] and a great part of the court were feasted, and the like [queen, Holstein, and greater part of court] two nights before at my Lord of Southampton's. (Chambers, *Elizabethan Stage* 4:139–140)

Whether *Love's Labor's Lost* was performed at Cranborne's or at Southampton's, it is clear that what was important at this time was the entertainment of the queen and her younger brother. Thus the document once again reinforces a sense that Shakespeare and his fellows had the status not of close associates to the court but of occasional servants. Yet the document's primary importance lies elsewhere. Cope's letter has a definite bearing on our sense of the order of Shakespeare's dramatic production. Queen Anna cannot have seen all the plays *ever* performed by the King's Servants by 1605, or even all of the plays Shakespeare himself had written. But she had apparently seen all the plays the company had performed at court in the two years since James had come to the throne. In fact, during the first season of the reign, a year before, she had seen a total of eighteen plays by all companies in addition to the plays of the present season a year later.[9] The actors, in fact, appear to have been telling Sir Walter Cope that, if his master Cecil wanted a new play for the queen right now, Cope had better know that they had only one reworked (Shakespearean) comedy. And so the players seem in as much a dilemma as Cope—two royal (queenly) engagements, one "new" play.

9. See L. Barroll, "A New History for Shakespeare and His Time," *Shakespeare Quarterly* (1988), 441–464, esp. p. 459.

The dilemma, however it was solved, is crucial to an estimate of Shakespeare's Stuart career. In January 1605, *Othello* and *Measure for Measure* seem to have been William Shakespeare's only new dramas since 1602—or, to stretch a point, since 1603 (counting the February 7, 1603, entry of *Troilus and Cressida* in the stationers' register). This is how the situation remained, it seems, up through Lent 1605, for after the revival of *Love's Labor's Lost* in January 1605 the only other Shakespearean play to be performed before the king at court that winter (see the 1604–5 list) was another revival, *Merchant of Venice* (also 1598), given twice during Shrovetide in early February. What has appeared, then, is a significant hiatus: an identifiable period of two months—January and February 1605—when, with high probability, one can distinguish between what Shakespearean plays had already been produced and what plays remained to be produced, to be performed for the first time—what was past and what was future.[10]

What, then, was the next new Shakespearean play the King's Servants would produce after January 1605? To answer this question is to review the reopening of the public playhouses in 1605 and to examine additional indicators suggesting the appearance of new Shakespearean work.

II

When Lent ended in 1605, there seems no reason why playing could not have resumed on the Bankside. A bill of mortality showed 21 (miscounted as 19) plague deaths for the previous week (before Easter),[11] but the London council and the lord mayor do not seem to have been unduly disturbed after Easter. In May a physician visiting from Germany managed to impress King James so much with his credentials as an expert on plague that the king had the privy council write the lord mayor to put this physician on a retainer and let him try his skill. The lord mayor wrote back: "Thanks be to God

---

10. I stressed this point in an earlier study of the problem, L. Barroll, "The Chronology of Shakespeare's Jacobean Plays and the Dating of *Antony and Cleopatra*," in *Essays on Shakespeare*, ed. Gordon Ross Smith (University Park: Pennsylvania State University Press, 1965), pp. 115–162. It has been reiterated in Stanley Wells et al., *William Shakespeare: A Textual Companion* (Oxford: Clarendon Press, 1987), p. 93.

11. For the bill, see "Sackville MSS," in *Cranfield Papers*, ed. Newton, 1:104.

we have no use at this time of any such skill, nor any means to make trial of it, for there has not died of late of the sickness within the City or Liberties above two or three a week at the most, and those have been dead or past all remedy before it was known what sickness they had" (*Hatfield*, 17:206). It was such low levels of concern that permitted the playhouses to proceed normally.

So, as spring ripened into the summer of 1605, the city heard bells peal and saw bonfires glow for the first birth of a royal offspring in England (the short-lived Princess Mary) since the time of Henry VIII, and Shakespeare and his fellows no doubt played at the Globe, presenting any new plays Shakespeare had written since Cope's letter in January.

As the summer of 1605 began, however, a bill of mortality showed two plague deaths in the liberty of Westminster for the week ending July 5 (*Hatfield*, 17:307). There had been other rumblings. Late in June, the Midsummer Fair in Chester had been canceled because of plague. Now, late in July, the crown, perhaps using plague only as an excuse to prorogue Parliament from its expected opening in September, issued a proclamation:

> Whereas at the rising of the late session of our Parliament, we pro-
> rogued the same until the third day of October now next ensuing: we
> have since considered... that the concourse of people, which follow-
> eth the assembly coming from all parts of the realm, in many whereof
> there may yet remain some dregs of the late Contagion, may be an
> occasion to revive it in that place, where our most abode is. And
> therefore we have thought it fit to prorogue it further for one month's
> space. (*Proclamations*, 1:117–118)

It is possible that the true purpose of this prorogation, a purpose hinted at in the correspondence of the lord chancellor and more clearly suggested by the Venetian ambassador, was that "the King desires to weed out certain turbulent and seditious spirits, who right willingly thwart all his Majesty's schemes, the chief of which are first, to obtain a subsidy to pay off the debts contracted by these bonds under the Privy Seal... and secondly, to effect the Union of England and Scotland. The King will not summon Parliament until he is sure of carrying his two points."[12] Thus the question whether the playhouses were closed later in the summer is, again, difficult to answer. To use plague as an excuse for proroguing Parliament in

12. See *Hatfield*, 17:340, and *SPV*, 10:270 (Sept. 4, 1605).

late July and then not to close the theaters might seem unsubtle, if the aim was political; if the aim was hygienic, it is hard to see how Parliament, but not theaters, would be suspended. The theaters were probably closed in August 1605, since plague did demonstrably become the main issue in September.

Sometime before Michaelmas (September 30), the mayor of Hertford wrote Robert Cecil requesting that Michaelmas term be held in Hertford for it was obvious, he argued, that the term had to be held somewhere other than London. The plague was raging there, he observed, and in Westminster (*Hatfield*, 24:29). Indeed, on Saturday, October 5, 1605, came the official letter from the privy council of England to the lord mayor and the justices of the peace for Middlesex and Surrey. The order was "to forbid stage plays and to take order that the infected be kept in their houses, etc." (*MSC*, 1.4/5:371–372).

Since this order for the closing of the theaters would not be lifted until December 15, 1605, two months later, it is again important to note some of the weekly plague death figures for this interval. They again suggest that thirty plague deaths per week must not be taken literally as indicators of theater closings in these times. The lord mayor and the aldermen, and the privy council of England, were much more interested in trends than in mere numbers. John Chamberlain wrote of the "sudden rising of the sickness to thirty a week," presumably at the time of the October 3 report. Plays were forbidden the following Saturday, but then he observed that "the abating of some few this week makes all hold on" (Saturday, October 12) as deaths declined to 20 or 22.[13] Yet the playhouses were not allowed to open. From October 10 to October 24, 1605—as the the closing order promulgated by the privy council remained in force—the number of plague deaths in London was *below* thirty.

On October 24, Chamberlain wrote: "The sickness keeps still much at a stay. There died this week 160 in all, whereof 22 of the plague" (*Chamberlain*, 2:212). Shakespeare and his fellows had not waited for plague death figures to unravel themselves. Four days after the order against playing had been promulgated, they were to be found in Oxford where they were paid for playing on October 9 (although plague had been there since September 1).[14] Indeed, the

13. *Chamberlain*, 1:209, 212, and *SPV*, 10:281. The Venetian ambassador wrote that the sickness was not plague at all, but smallpox. If so, this did not make the authorities relax their restrictions.

14. Chambers, *Elizabethan Stage*, 2:212, and Salter, *Oxford Acts*, p. 390.

company may have stayed in the provinces for several months, since the theaters in London were not to be allowed to reopen until December 15.

But the reason for the long break in fall 1605 derived from something more than plague. The last official plague death figure during this period was, as noted, 22 for October 24 (cited by Chamberlain), and no subsequent figures are available up to the new year. This lack of figures does not, however, negate the possibility that plague kept the theaters closed. Quite the contrary: on October 28, Philip Gawdy had been showing his nephew around London but had not been able to take him to the playhouses for, he wrote, the plays "are all put down."[15] After November 5, however, political events may have reaffirmed theater closings.

November 5, 1605, was the occasion of the Gunpowder Plot. This effort to blow up the royal family and all the peerage at once at the ceremonial first meeting of Parliament naturally produced official consternation, not the least result of which was the closing of all the seaports, the measure previously invoked on the death of Queen Elizabeth. Indeed, the ports were not reopened until November 18, since this was a method of keeping conspirators from escaping and fresh subversives from infiltrating (*Hatfield*, 17:492–493). The relevance to drama is that in just such conditions, after the queen had died, the playhouses had been closed, and I suspect that it was the Gunpowder Plot, as much as prolonged plague, that kept the theaters from reopening in December 1605 until the fifteenth, when a privy council order gave permission.

All aspects of the conspiracy itself were treated with the utmost seriousness. The early months of 1606 reverberated with the aftershocks of the event. The authorities were continually finding second and third tiers of accomplices, not intimately connected with the original plot, who were willing to shelter fugitives believed to have attempted killing king, queen, prince, and most of the important peerage. For example, when two of the last uncaptured conspirators, Robert Winter and Steven Littleton, were seized while trying to escape the country, they were being hidden by Littleton's cousin in Hagley, Worcestershire, as part of his large household composed of at least ten tenants (*Hatfield*, 18:11–12, 34–35). As a consequence, it seemed necessary to imprison not only the two conspirators but also the cousin of one of them and three other Hagley citizens. These

15. See Philip Gawdy, *Letters*, ed. I. H. Jeayes (London: Roxburghe Club, 1906), p. 160.

latter three were actually hanged for conspiracy, while the cousin, Humphrey Littleton, was spared after he offered a written deposition describing what he knew of a Jesuit underground network and accusing five additional persons.

As far as domestic stability was concerned, then, the question of the plot's authenticity was moot. The worrisome phenomenon was the apparently large number of sympathizers. In Stratford-upon-Avon, for example, twenty-four jurors met on February 26 to initiate proceedings against certain persons believed to be Gunpowder co-conspirators (*SPD*, 8:293), one of the jurors being July Shaw, a friend and subscribing witness to Shakespeare's will. Elsewhere, in Staffordshire, two other men were executed for aiding the fugitive conspirators (*Hatfield*, 18:34–35).

In terms of public knowledge, the eight "principal traitors" (Salisbury's phrase) were executed as early as January 29 and 31, 1606, in two groups. Thus the sensation might have ended, but, in the interim, on January 30 the crown had the great good fortune of capturing Henry Garnet, the secret provincial of the entire Jesuit order in England. It is this event, finally, that brings up the matter of equivocation that many scholars have thought to be important in establishing the date of *Macbeth*, and thus arises the first indication (be it true or false) of the existence of a Shakespearean play since the Christmas season of the previous year.[16]

In the spring before the Gunpowder Plot, the interval from Easter at the end of March 1605 until September 1605, the public playhouses of London *may* have been open to show any new play Shakespeare might have written, but in September, definitely, plague and then the Gunpowder Plot had closed the theaters until December 15, 1605. Was a new Shakespearean play shown before the Gunpowder Plot, in the spring-summer interval that seems to have been tainted with plague? There is no way to know. Traditional approaches to dating *Macbeth* obscure rather than contribute to the resolution of this issue, and for this reason the methodology of those approaches requires comment.

III

Traditional critical thinking places the date of *Macbeth*'s composition between 1605 and 1607, tying this play to a nexus of historical

16. For general discussion of the date of *Macbeth*, see J. M. Nosworthy, *Shakespeare's Occasional Plays* (London: Edward Arnold, 1965), chap. 1.

events. Not only the Gunpowder Plot, but the notion of the appropriateness of a complimentary "Scottish" play for King James, especially during the visit of King Christian of Denmark (August 1606), become relevant considerations. But there is confusion regarding whether *Macbeth* was written before or after *King Lear*, the first known performance of which was on December 26, 1606. Many scholars, to evade this dilemma, take their cue from Chambers to argue that Shakespeare's stylistic development puts *King Lear* before *Macbeth*.[17]

This matter of stylistics, the theory of a metrical development in Shakespeare's verse as an indicator of the order of his plays is relied on heavily by the editors of the Oxford Old Spelling Shakespeare. I consign this topic to Appendix 4, in which some of the statistical problems underlying such methods are considered, so that space may be devoted here to another traditional misconception: the quasi-historical notion of topicality. Specifically, it is important to ask whether the notion of topical allusion can be used to argue persuasively (as stylistics cannot be) that, after indications of *Othello* and *Measure for Measure* in 1604–5, the next play Shakespeare was to write was indeed *Macbeth*. Associating the Scottish play with the Gunpowder Plot, as so many critics have done, obviously places the tragedy in the temporal vicinity of November 1605, a calendar year after the first known appearance of *Othello*. Can, then, topicality lend itself to a plausible narrative to make this claim seem true?

The topicality of *Macbeth* to the Gunpowder Plot has primarily been related to the theme of equivocation. The porter at the gate peoples his imaginary Hell with an "equivocator that could swear in both the scales against either scale; who committed treason enough for God's sake, yet could not equivocate to Heaven (2.3.8–11.)" Given that the porter is speaking of equivocation, relating this speech to the Gunpowder Plot in purpose and in time becomes a procedure riddled with inconsistencies.

If, for example, *Macbeth* indeed contains a topical allusion to the Gunpowder Plot, a specific date for the play is by no means assured. *Macbeth* could have been written several years earlier than the Gunpowder Plot and then updated with an allusion to get a rise out of the audience—this updated version being now preserved for the rest of time in the only known text of the play, that in the 1623 First Folio.

17. See Chambers, *William Shakespeare*, 1:273–274, and Wells et al., *Shakespeare*, p. 128.

Beyond this textual question lies a somewhat more theoretical dilemma for those who deal in topical allusions: the problem of circularity. To advert for the moment to *King Lear*, a play seemingly close in time to *Macbeth* and also traditionally discussed in terms of topical allusions, the character Gloucester, wondering why the court and his own family seem to be disintegrating, attributes the disturbing events in the 1608 quarto to "these late eclipses of the sun and moon." His words have traditionally been construed as an allusion to eclipses that took place in the real world. After searching for and finding such an eclipse, critics have then used it as a basis for dating the composition of *King Lear* (see Chapter 5). But such a date is accurate only if Gloucester is alluding to actual eclipses that took place prior to the play and were visible in the England of Shakespeare's audience. If *King Lear* had actually been written prior to such an eclipse, then, of course, there would be no chronological relationship whatsoever between actual eclipses and the date of *King Lear*. Searching for historical eclipses as a way of dating the composition of *King Lear* therefore, begs the question. Another way of putting it is to observe that dating King *Lear* via an eclipse is to *assume* that the eclipse talk in the play refers to a real event. But this need no more be the case than that the eye-gouging of the earl of Gloucester refer to the actual eye-gouging of some earl in the court of James I—or that eclipses occurred just before Q2 *Hamlet* when Horatio speaks of how the "moist star was sick almost to doomsday with eclipse" and that the "like precurse" have "heaven and earth together demonstrated to our countrymen."

Similar conceptual difficulties, beyond the problem of text, surround the traditional practice of dating *Macbeth* by adverting to equivocation. Equivocation in *Macbeth*, that is, need not be a topical allusion to the Gunpowder Plot at all. In fact, as we see below, the writings of Shakespeare reveal talk of equivocation as early as 1604.

In the analysis that follows, I consider the historical material commonly used to date *Macbeth* because the tradition is particularly long-standing, based on a line of reasoning inscribed by E. K. Chambers and Kenneth Muir, who themselves combined stylistic evidence with the so-called topical allusions to equivocation to establish the production of *Macbeth* around January or February 1606. I suggest that such historical topicality causes difficulties not only for the dating of *Macbeth* but for a sense of the temporal relationship between *Macbeth*, *King Lear*, and even *Antony and Cleopatra*.

Tradition has viewed the porter's association of equivocation with treason specifically as a reference to Father Garnet. Chambers in fact argued that equivocation was a popular topic in 1606 earlier than March because of a book by the earl of Salisbury. According to William James, the dean of Durham Cathedral, who was writing him on February 5, 1606, Cecil's book was being "greedily read," presumably at some point before this date.[18] Chambers concludes from this evidence that Shakespeare's *Macbeth* most probably was composed very early in 1606.[19]

One might first ask how weighty the relevance of this book by Cecil to the date of *Macbeth* could be. In a letter written by Sir John Ferne to Robert Cecil on January 16, 1606, the day after the archbishop of York had died, there is another reference to Dean James. Stating his view that the crown should appoint to York's seat a successor who would be more severe with Catholics than his predecessor, Ferne suggests a candidate: the present bishop of Durham. Who, then, should replace the bishop of Durham if he were translated to York? It so happens, wrote Ferne, that Dean William James would be an excellent choice. He is learned, grave, "a stout oppugner of papists," and even courageous enough to visit and search the houses of known Catholics, apprehending "the most insolent of them." He is, Ferne concluded, "an excellent magistrate in that country" (*Hatfield*, 18:22).

Ferne was not the only advocate for William James's candidacy. During this same January 1606, Robert Cecil also heard about York's death from Lord Sheffield, who himself recommended the bishop of Durham as successor at York and suggested further that then Dean William James would be a suitable candidate for Durham's post (*SPD*, 12:469–470; *Hatfield*, 18:37–38). At the same time, Dean James himself was corresponding with Cecil, contributing directly to the cause of his own career and mentioning the death of the archbishop of York.[20] In other words, the dean had a rather pronounced (and successful) promotional campaign in progress.[21]

---

18. The book had also been read by Prince Henry, in print or in manuscript, by January 23; see *Hatfield*, 18:29.

19. See Chambers, *William Shakespeare*, 1:474–475.

20. On December 9, 1605, James wrote Cecil complaining about the evil behavior of recusants in Durham (*SPD*, 8:269), and on January 19, 1606 (several days after the Ferne letter of recommendation), he wrote again, reporting that he had committed to jail in Durham "a base houswife, a recusant" for speeches she had made at some time before the Gunpowder Plot (*SPD*, 8:281).

21. See *Hatfield*, 18:270. Indeed, in February Cecil received several more self-ingratiating missives. On February 7, Dean James sent Cecil a copy of a scurrilous

It is within this context, I think, that one must view the February 5 report about Cecil's book described by Chambers—the report noting that the comments on equivocation were being greedily read. The report, ostensibly about the arrest of a priest, John Sicklemore, who had, it seems, equivocated under interrogation, was one of the February missives from the self-promoting Dean James (*SPD*, 8:286). And because Dean James would still be writing Cecil on April 30 regarding the bishopric of Durham, the objectivity (or accuracy) of his remark about Cecil's book is open to question (*Hatfield*, 18:125).

The nature of Cecil's publication itself casts doubt on an equivocation benchmark for dating Shakespeare's *Macbeth*. Cecil's book, *An Answer to Certain Scandalous Papers* (*STC* 4895), was a small quarto printed in several issues between January and February 1606, at a time when scandalous papers, according to Cecil, were spreading reports around England that because of the Gunpowder Plot there was going to be a general persecution of all Catholics. Cecil's book, the only one he ever wrote, was in effect an informal crown public position paper issued to avert the panic these rumors might be causing. There was, as previously observed, some substance to feed the rumors with witchhunts in progress for the abettors to the act of concealing Gunpowder fugitives, as well as for *their* concealers. Widespread social disruption was always a possibility if the momentum of such activity increased.[22] For this reason the continual thrust of Cecil's book is reassurance: he makes the point again and again that loyal Catholics have nothing to fear. The "scandalous" rumors and papers being circulated about imminent persecution of Catholics are simply not true.

It is during the course of this argument that Cecil alludes to equivocation in a short aside (sig. C3), adducing St. Augustine as against the concept, but it is unreasonable to assume that eager readers fastened on this phrase. For, in January 1606, Cecil's treatise was not the place to go to learn anything new or to read anything detailed

---

letter signed "Jesus Christ," commenting on it as a "damnable libel." The next day, James came out into the open by again writing to Cecil, this time specifically requesting the bishopric of Durham for himself in the event there was an upcoming vacancy. Ultimately, these efforts were successful. On September 1, at Robert Cecil's recommendation, King James signed the authorization for Dean William James's elevation as bishop of Durham.

22. See, for example, *SPD*, 8:283 (January 25, 1606), which reports the execution of six of Percy's followers, and *Hatfield*, 18:138, a letter from the bishop of Bristol as late as May 15, 1606.

on the subject of equivocation. If, as Dean James observed, Cecil's book was indeed being greedily read, James could only be speaking of the far north, Durham, where he lived, and not of London, where Shakespeare's plays were being performed.

Talk of equivocation was nothing new early in 1606. It had generally been associated with Catholics and especially with Jesuits in contemporary writings in England since 1595—Shakespeare refers to equivocation as early as 1604, in the second quarto of *Hamlet* (V.i.149).[23] So commonplace was the concept, in fact, that one of the Jesuits under suspicion in connection with the Gunpowder Plot, John Gerard, when interrogated on January 23 promised to avoid equivocation in his answers (*SPD*, 8:282). Garnet himself had long been associated with equivocation; the authorities were concerned about his *Book of Equivocation*, written in 1598 and as yet unpublished. After Garnet's capture in January 1606, he was interrogated about the book; Sir Edward Coke had found two hidden copies of the manuscript as early as December 6, 1605. On February 13, 1606, Garnet admitted to his interrogators that he was preparing the manuscript for the press. Thus equivocation was a subject associable with Father Garnet by the authorities much earlier than 1606.[24]

Nonetheless, one must agree with Kenneth Muir about one event that could have made equivocation a cause célèbre—not immediately after Father Garnet's capture in January, but later, during his trial. The London frame of mind two weeks after the capture is best described by the Venetian ambassador to England—himself, of course, a Catholic—in a report to Venice. Garnet, wrote the ambassador, "will not be executed in public, for he is a man of moving eloquence and vast learning, and they are afraid that his constancy and the power of his speech may produce just the reverse of what they desire. Indeed, some other outbreak is so confidently expected that on the smallest rumor in the city one hears of reports and deeds which indicate a deep-rooted suspicion and mistrust of the Catholics" (*SPV*, 10:321).

The trial did not, in fact, take place until March 28, 1606; in the meantime, Shakespeare and his fellows presumably performed at their public theater up to Ash Wednesday, March 5, 1606, when Lent would have terminated their playing until Easter. During this period,

---

23. See Philip Caraman, *Henry Garnet and the Gunpowder Plot* (London: Longman, 1964), pp. 254–255.
24. See *SPD*, 8:288; Caraman, *Henry Garnet*, pp. 254–255.

there was still no strong reason to allude in a play to jesuitical equivocation. Indeed, a patriotic flashpoint was ignited to burn in quite a different direction through a rather bizarre series of events seven or eight days before the trial. On March 22, 1606, a rumor somehow got started that King James had been assassinated. He was on a hunting trip and, as his group passed through one of the outlying villages near London, their hunting intersected with local activity. At this moment, the constables of the village were chasing a man for some minor offense. The fugitive grabbed a horse and was now galloping hard, sword drawn, to escape his pursuers, who were crying after him "traitor!" Then, according to a contemporary description,

> the people of the village joined in the hue and cry thinking that he [the fugitive] must have attacked the King who had passed through a while before. The crowd grew from village to village, and also the rumor, until persons set off at full speed from London to tell the Queen and [privy] Council that the King was dead; this news was immediately confirmed by newcomers and was believed by the Court. The Council instantly took all necessary steps at the palace and summoned an extraordinary meeting. The news spread to the City and the uproar was amazing. Every one flew to arms, the shops were shut ... and had not the contradiction arrived some terrible accident would have happened to us all. (*SPV*, 10:333)

Meanwhile, outside that same village, King James and his party knew nothing of all this and were returning to court in a leisurely fashion when the king's party encountered people who described the uproar. James immediately sent a messenger to court with the news that he was safe, but he also decided to return to the village and show himself in person. The villagers, who were now running to look at the place where the king had been killed, found James and fell on their knees with tears of joy. But their hysterical and confused behavior in turn caused James to think that perhaps some crucial event in London was ultimately causing all this fuss, so he quickly sent another messenger to the queen and the court to let them know that he was not only safe but also moving swiftly toward London with his entourage. On arriving at London, he entered to popular acclamation. Fireworks were set off and bells were rung.

All this happened on the same day, Saturday, and that evening a proclamation was hastily issued accusing the enemies of the state of starting the pernicious rumor of James's death. Assembly was banned (acting was already presumably suspended for Lent) in an attempt to abolish what could clearly have become dangerous and general disorder, and the ban was still in effect five days later, on March 27, the very eve of Father Garnet's trial.[25] There was, then, a series of very disrupting events that would certainly have distracted Londoners from the Gunpowder scandal prior to Garnet's trial in late March.

A vast crowd had witnessed the earlier trial of the eight Gunpowder conspirators in January, but no visitors from court were noted there. In contrast, the trial of the provincial of all the secret Jesuits in England appears to have been intended as a showcase. King James was present, partially concealed behind a screen of wickerwood, and he stayed there, apparently, for the whole of the eleven hours, from eight in the morning to seven in the evening. Among the commissioners for the trial were the most politically powerful earls in the country.[26] There were also ladies present—among them Arabella Stuart, the king's first cousin; the countess of Suffolk; Audrey Walsingham; and Sir James Hay's new wife (for whose wedding Ben Jonson had written his well-known masque).

In the middle of this spectacular trial Father Garnet was given the opportunity to speak, and part of his speech included a long, startling defense of the concept of equivocation. This caused a sensation. The Venetian ambassador wrote his government that Garnet's disquisition on equivocation shocked the court officials and especially the king, "who is particularly versed in such matters." Furthermore, the Venetian ambassador wrote, Garnet's speech caused a real outcry against Catholicism. The incident was also discussed by Sir John Chamberlain in a letter to Winwood and was covered at some length in the published account of the trial, *A True and Perfect Relation*, which, with a 1606 imprint, could not have been issued until after May 3, since it also includes an account of Garnet's (May 3) execution.[27]

So, if equivocation and Father Garnet are to be connected especially with *Macbeth*, I must agree with Cunningham and Muir that it was the public declaration by Father Garnet himself at his spec-

25. *Chamberlain*, 1:218, and Sir Ralph Winwood, *Memorials of Affairs of State*, 3 vols., ed. Edmund Sawyer (London, 1725), 2:204–205.

26. Winwood, *Memorials*, 2:205–206. These were the earl of Nottingham (the lord admiral), the earl of Suffolk (the lord chamberlain), the earl of Worcester (master of the horse), the earl of Northampton, and Robert Cecil, earl of Salisbury.

27. See *SPV*, 10:337; Winwood, *Memorials*, 2:206; and *A True and Perfect Relation of the Proceedings* (London, 1606), sigs. T2 and V4ᵛ ff. (STC 11618).

tacular trial on March 28 that was the beginning of a period in which topical allusion in drama would have evoked optimal audience response.[28] Indeed, Father Garnet's execution date was deliberately chosen to occur two days after May Day to avoid exaggerating the perennial danger of May Day riots.

Because Easter came on April 20 in 1606, and because Father Garnet was executed on Saturday, May 3, there was, in fact, a two-week period between Garnet's trial and the execution in which the equivocation allusion might have been extremely topical, and in which playing was permitted in the public theaters. Moreover, on May 2, the day before Father Garnet's execution, Dudley Carleton, a constant source of gossip at court, wrote a letter to a friend in which he mentioned Garnet's situation and played on the word "equivocation" no fewer than three times, indicating, if not an overly refined sense of verbal variety, a least a temporary obsession that contemporaries may have shared (*Carleton*, pp. 80–81).

It is only from this kind of resonance that topical allusion can have viability in the dating of plays. If it is a matter of trying to establish a terminus a quo for Shakespeare's *Macbeth* by way of the porter's allusion to an equivocator who commits treason, the most favorable moments for audience recognition seem to have been not early 1606 but any time after Father Garnet's (March 28) trial and after Lent, when playing at the theaters had resumed: from Monday, April 21, 1606, to some undetermined point after Garnet's execution on May 3, 1606. That, of course, is the sticking point. Any effort to establish a hypothetical terminus ad quem must take into account events that transpired after the May 3 execution, events that might have contributed to a quick deterioration of equivocation as a timely allusion.

The Republic of Venice, for example, had been in controversy with Pope Paul V since April of this year over the question of his ecclesiastical jurisdiction (*SPV*, 10:339). The pope had actually issued an edict against Venice, recalled his nuncio, and dismissed the Venetian ambassador to Rome by May 2 (the day before Father Garnet's execution). When the papal action was known, English opinion was, as one might expect, decidedly in Venice's favor. The issue could be seen as cut from the same cloth as the Gunpowder Plot: papal

28. See *Macbeth*, Arden edition, ed. Henry Cunningham (London: Methuen, 1912), p. xxxi, and *Macbeth*, Arden edition, ed. Kenneth Muir (London: Methuen, 1951), pp. xvi–xxi.

interference in the internal affairs of a sovereign state (*SPV*, 10:349). And so, on May 21, the Venetian ambassador in London, Zorzi Giustinian, reported to the doge that in London "great and small express indignation and use such language that if it reached the ears of him [the pope] who is thus unwarrantably annoying the Republic, it would most certainly cause him to desist" (*SPV*, 10:353–354).

In this atmosphere, the execution of Father Garnet being almost a month in the past, Parliament instituted a new oath of allegiance to be required of all English subjects, the oath being specifically formulated to counteract the claims of the pope of power to depose any monarch whatsoever (*SPV*, 10:363). On June 4, King James lectured the Venetian ambassador on the evils of the Catholic church and of the Jesuits. Giustinian reassured James that the Jesuits had, in fact, been expelled from the Venetian republic.

Outside the palace, the Venetian business was said to be, in fact, the sole topic of conversation at the English court. "Indeed," wrote Giustinian to the doge, "I can hardly protect myself from the continual offers of men and of ships made me by great and small alike, English and Scotch" (*SPV*, 10:361). Meanwhile, the doge had written a formal protest to the pope on the entire matter and by June 18, 1606, it had been translated and printed in London and was being read everywhere (*STC*, 19482). On this same day, a proclamation was promulgated in London and throughout England that all Jesuits and Catholic priests had to leave England and Scotland by August 1, 1606, on pain of death (*STC* 8393).

By July 5, a week before the long-planned visit of the king of Denmark, and two months after Father Garnet's execution, still another event could have blunted the salience of equivocation in the public mind. A new plot against the life of King James came to public attention. It was alleged that a Captain William Newce, an English Catholic, had been approached by the brother of one of the English Gunpowder conspirators; the two were later joined, it was said, by an Irish Catholic servant of the Spanish ambassador to England. After requiring Captain Newce to take a mighty oath not to reveal what they were going to tell him, the conspirators urged him in a plan to assassinate King James while he was hunting. They would all escape by means of good pistols and swift horses. The payoff would be 200,000 crowns (£50,000).

Captain Newce, so went the report, did not seem as enthusiastic as the two proposers had assumed he would be, and so, when they bade the captain good-bye, they offered him sweets, as was the custom. The sweets were poisoned. Captain Newce consumed several of them on the spot and took the rest home to give to his two little daughters, who died after they ate the gifts. The father himself became very ill and, feeling near death, made a confession of the plot from his bed. This confession reached the privy council of England.

It was then July 16, 1606, the day after the king of Denmark had arrived in England. The crown immediately sent for the Spanish ambassador to appear before the privy council. The envoy complied but denied all knowledge of the affair. While the ambassador was in attendance upon the privy council, however, the royal bodyguard, carrying no weapons or badges of office, hurried to the ambassador's lodgings in London and searched them. The Irish servant and the brother of the Gunpowder plotter were taken and brought to the palace, where they were personally interrogated by King James at some length. During these events, and even before then, feeling had been running high against Spain. The Spanish ambassador had actually been insulted within the pale of the royal palace on his way to his audience with the king, and the privy council was entertaining a proposal to break the recently signed Peace of 1604 with Spain.

During August, this purported assassination plot ultimately proved to be a fabrication—so wrote Robert Cecil in a letter that month—not embroidering upon his bare statement; but as late as July 19 Cecil had been writing at length and seriously about the affair to Sir Ralph Winwood, who was out of the country, and as late as August 1 the matter was still being talked about in higher court circles.[29] The point is that the excitement generated by these affairs in the wake of the execution of Father Garnet might easily have made stale the specific topic of equivocation, even though the Newce affair perpetuated the atmosphere of suspicion originally generated by the Gunpowder Plot eight months before.

In view of these matters, the relevance of Father Garnet's trial to the date of *Macbeth* is problematic. Topical allusions, one would think, strike a timely and responsive chord, but equivocation seems, during the summer of 1606, to have been muted by more clamorous topics: Rome's way with Venice, the Newce plot, the visit of the king of Denmark. To argue that, nevertheless, thoughts about equivocation lingered with Shakespeare is merely to agree to an indefinite extension of a terminus ad quem for *Macbeth*. For, if the concept

29. See *SPV*, 10:375 n., 388; *Hatfield*, 18:197; and Winwood, *Memorials*, 2:246–247.

lingered on as interesting for several months, despite other intervening political sensations, who is to say when the subject ever
died—or that it was dead to Shakespeare even in 1611, the first year
in which a performance of *Macbeth* is actually reported by Simon
Forman?

All these considerations are further complicated by another event
following Father Garnet's May execution: once again, the onset of
plague. Beginning in June 1606, there would be no public presentations of plays in London for seven or eight months, and thus no
performances of *Macbeth* at the Globe. As early as February 10,
1606, long before the Garnet trial, someone was buried in Richmond
after a five-day sickness (*Hatfield*, 18:48). Sir David Foulis, an official
reporting to Cecil, had become suspicious and investigated this sudden death, which was in a locale ordinarily suburban (in the modern
sense) and relatively safe. The cause proved to be plague. Several
weeks later 9 plague deaths were reported for March 7–13, 14 plague
deaths for March 14–20, and 17 for March 21–27, a definite upward
trend.

During the second week of April 1606, as Lent was coming to an
end, plague deaths rose to 27—and then dropped to 12. "The sickness
is well abated to twelve this last week," wrote Dudley Carleton to
John Chamberlain (*Carleton*, p. 78) on April 17, three days before
Easter, showing by his remark that there was some concern about
these figures. The numbers dropped to 11 after Easter, rose again to
17 in the May Day report just before Father Garnet's execution, and
then for the last weeks of spring the figures were 13, 13, 14, 9, 16,
19, 15, 24—erratic enough to be confusing, consistent enough to
hint at a trend.

It is uncertain how the London authorities reacted to these figures.
F. P. Wilson argues that after March 1606 the officials "quickly and
vigorously enforced the plague orders," which presumably included
the closing of playhouses, but Wilson's sources in fact seem to suggest April as the enforcement date.[30] It is difficult to tell whether,

---

30. Wilson's reference here, *The Plague in Shakespeare's London* (London: Oxford
University Press, 1983), p. 119 and n. 1, is to the Corporation of London records: the
Repertories, vol. 27, fol. 191, and the *Journals*, vol. 27, fols. 35b, 72, 74b. Fol. 187[b]
of the *Repertories*, however, starts the recording year in April 1606, and fol. 192
contains an April 9, 1606 entry. Therefore his *Repertory* references are really to April.
As for the *Journals*, three of Wilson's references are to July 1606, and fol. 35b is not
necessarily pertinent to specific dating: item 7 in this list of public works to be
undertaken is a burial place, but a connection with plague is not explicit.

as Wilson implies, there was no theater activity in the spring because of plague, or whether, as I think, there was an even chance that the theaters were open after Lent and through June 1606 as weekly death figures continued to seesaw between 15 and 25. In all events, it is important to remember that those two specific playing prohibitions from plague that we noted in previous chapters were both promulgated when plague deaths were in the low twenties.[31]

Whatever the case, plague definitely settled in during July 1606, with a weekly plague death figure of 33 reported for July 10, just before the arrival of the king of Denmark. The death figures rose thereafter continually, through sixty and seventy per week during Denmark's visit, up to eighty per week in August, and mounting to 116 per week in the beginning of September. By the third of the month, Sir Thomas Lake, one of the king's attendants and the inditer of his letters, communicated to Cecil from Ivychurch where the king was hunting that James was grieved with the growing sickness in London lest it delay the reconvening of Parliament and the continuation of the effort to effect union between England and Scotland. Meanwhile, the powerful earl of Mar, a member of James's closest inner council, had fallen ill of a burning fever and was extremely sick (*Hatfield*, 18:272). In plague time, such fevers were always alarming.

Salisbury must have moved quickly in response to James's political concerns about the continuation of plague, and the episode is another important counterweight to any assumption that city officials were always puritanically eager to use plague as an excuse for closing the theaters whereas the crown kept them open. On the same day, September 3, the lord mayor of London described Cecil in a letter as "conceiving a great fault" in the lord mayor's "not taking meet care in repressing the contagion of the plague within this city." The lord mayor made the following response, which bears on the playing season of the previous spring after the Lent of 1606: "Upon the increase of the sickness in the beginning of the year I directed precepts at sundry times to my brethren the Aldermen for the putting in execution sundry orders within their several wards, whereof some are in print one of which printed I send herewith."[32]

31. One recalls that any privy council order closing the theaters because of plague is now irretrievable because of the destruction of the records for these years; see Chapter 3, n. 3.

32. *Hatfield*, 18:273. Whatever the lord mayor sent with this message has not survived.

The mayor went on coolly to indicate to Cecil that the provost marshal personally inspected the city every day to see that the plague orders were being carried out. In addition, the lord mayor indicated that the city would execute Cecil's command that red crosses be painted on every infected door. Indeed, he would see to it that these red crosses "be laid in oil to the intent that they may not easily be put out."

Nevertheless, plague was rumored at Windsor several days later, and the king, who had been heading in that direction, wrote to both Cecil and the earl of Suffolk, the lord chamberlain, that he did not want the queen (at Hampton Court at the time) to come to Windsor. "For if in this seasonable weather the contagion spread, his Majesty judges it to be a sign that the infection is strong" (*Hatfield*, 18:274; *SPV*, 10:409).

The king wrote to Cecil again on September 7, 1606, and indicated that the lord mayor of London should be queried once a week to account for his execution of the orders of the privy council concerning the plague. "Many of these prescriptions," wrote Sir Thomas Lake, relaying the king's views to Cecil, "his Highness finds to be agreeable to the orders of Scotland, and thinks that in penning of them your lordships [the privy council] have called to mind his speeches about like matters" (*Hatfield*, 18:276). These orders do not survive, but judging from Scottish plague measures the English orders might well have been severe. The Scots tended, as previously mentioned, to execute people for infringements and also to quarantine the infected in zones outside Edinburgh. What is significant at this time is the level of concern. The king and privy council were no strangers to plague, but clearly they here exhibit more worry than usual as well as some dissatisfaction with the efficacy of previous measures. None of this could have been good news for the playhouses.

Michaelmas term, 1606, was delayed until the fourth return on the "mense Michaelis" (October 27), and a proclamation of September 23 ordering this postponement explained that plague was "so dispersed in divers of the best and most open streets of the said cities [London and adjoining suburbs] as to give just cause to doubt [fear] that the contagion thereof, by great resort of people, might be further spread, as well in the city as in other parts of the realm" (*Proclamations*, 1:148–151). Thus it is no surprise to find Shakespeare and his fellows at Dover on August 30, 1606, after their short stint at court before the two kings, and to note the Prince's Servants and the Queen's Servants at Ipswich in September and October 1606 (*MSC*, 23:282; *MSC* 7:49).

In early October, John Chamberlain expressed dismay when the plague figures jumped from 87 for one week to 141 for the next (*Chamberlain*, 1:234). The death figures stayed above one hundred through October. On All Saints' Day, November 1, a proclamation forbade anyone from London, Westminster, or the outlying districts to come to Whitehall—where the king, as traditional since the beginning of the reign, was now in residence—or to any place where the king, queen, or prince might be, until further notice. Certain persons were allowed in—bishops, judges, the privy council, principal city magistrates, and household servants and others connected with the provisioning of the court—as long as they had not had plague in their houses for at least six weeks. Indeed, a royal servant had died of plague at Hampton Court in early October. Again, these measures are more stringent than those observed earlier, and presumably common players were not among the exceptions (*SPV*, 10:416). Accordingly, there seem to have been no All Saints' performances at court.

Although Parliament began meeting on November 18, 1606, the weekly plague death figures for the month were 68, 41, 28, and 22. So I do not think that the theaters reopened. As late as December 9, the keeper of Newgate Prison was allowed funds for the relief of prisoners as long as the infection continued.[33] The weekly death figures were at 45 according to the December 4 report, then 38, 28, and 38 again for the last week in December. Thus it is not likely that public acting would have been possible during any of this time— and even through to Lent, 1607. Weekly figures in January were 26, 16, 14, 28, and in February, 33 and 20 for the two weeks before Lent beginning February 18, 1607. In sum, public performances ceased in London at least by June or July of 1606, and the only opportunities Shakespeare and his fellows had to play at all beyond July and for the rest of 1606 would have been at court.

To return, then to *Macbeth*, if one insists on using equivocation as a way of dating the play, then it has to have been acted just after Father Garnet's Lenten trial; that is, following the Easter resumption of play and before plague, beginning in June or July, forbade public acting for the remainder of 1606. This situation, then, might seem to strengthen the view that *Macbeth* was especially written for a

---

33. See Wilson, *Plague in Shakespeare's London*, p. 119.

court performance in the summer of 1606 before King James. Certainly the Scottish scenario and the compliment to the Stuart house in the procession of the kings watched by Macbeth warrant such speculation. Indeed, it is for this reason alone that H. N. Paul suggested the king of Denmark's visit as a plausible occasion for a performance of *Macbeth*.[34] The time considerations are, briefly, as follows.

During the king of Denmark's visit, Shakespeare and his fellows were paid for three undated performances. One was at Hampton Court which, however, the king of Denmark visited for only one night: Thursday, August 7. The other two payments were for performances at Greenwich, the specific days being more difficult to ascertain because the royal party was at Greenwich often, undoubtedly to visit Queen Anna, who was recovering from childbirth. The king of Denmark had in fact arrived two weeks before Queen Anna had completed the forty days before her churching; thus she was inaccessible except very privately until she was finally churched on Sunday, August 3 (*Annals*, sig. 4E5). The rather fatuous chronicler of *England's Farewell to the King of Denmark* noted that before the churching the queen "had not been partaker of any of their kingly sports," and, it is interesting to note, Shakespeare and his fellows were to be found at Oxford (on tour because of London plague) as late as July 28, even though the king of Denmark had been in England for over a week.[35] So it seems that players were not to be summoned until the queen herself was able to attend court entertainments. Promising dates for the two Greenwich performances by Shakespeare and his fellows, then, span Sunday through Tuesday, August 3–5, immediately after the queen's Sunday churching there. After that the royal party would be absent from Greenwich until August 8, the king of Denmark's last evening at that palace.[36]

34. H. N. Paul, *The Royal Play of Macbeth* (New York, Macmillan, 1950), pp. 317–331.

35. See Salter, *Oxford Acts*, p. 393

36. On the following day the group was at Windsor, where the king of Denmark was formally installed at the Chapel of St. George as a Knight of the Garter. That evening the group was at Hampton Court, where Shakespeare and his fellows presented a play (*MSC*, 6:44), probably in celebration of Denmark's installation. The next evening was spent by the royal party at Greenwich again. This day was the final opportunity for the King's Servants to have performed at that palace, for on Saturday the royal party traveled to Rochester, where they spent their last two nights before Denmark's departure from England; see John Nichols, *The Progresses . . . of James the First*, 4 vols. (London: J. B. Nichols, 1828), 2:80–85.

According to H. N. Paul, for reasons unconnected to the activities of Queen Anna, the most appropriate date for a court performance of *Macbeth* among the three alternatives is Tuesday, August 5, the anniversary of the Gowry Plot. This was a day King James always observed in thanksgiving and formal celebration, although he never included plays as part of the ceremonies. But the king of Denmark's presence warranted the kind of formal revelry that plays seem to have represented, and although the morning of "Gowry Day" was spent in religious services, in the afternoon Edward Alleyn and Philip Henslowe arrived, bringing bulls and bears for the baiting, a conventional entertainment also extended to foreign dignitaries. This activity was followed by a running at tilt, the lords and other courtiers being "most gallantly mounted and richly armed."[37] In the evening, according to the same contemporary chronicler, there was "delightful sport," and the celebratory atmosphere might well have called for a play.[38]

On the morning after "Gowry Day" at Greenwich, Wednesday, August 6, masters of the sword and of other weapons were assembled in the palace yard at the cost of £100 (as opposed to the £10 paid Shakespeare and his fellows for each of their three performances) to show their skill so that the king of Denmark might see the manner of English combat. In the afternoon the royal party set off on a tour of the other palaces, spending the evening at Richmond. So ended the playing opportunities of that summer at court for Shakespeare and his fellows.

To recapitulate, the use of topical allusion in determining when Shakespeare wrote *Macbeth* creates more problems than it solves. To use topical allusion as a criterion, we must delineate one period during 1605–6 in which *Macbeth* might have been first produced. If one then takes the topic of equivocation as a tool for dating *Macbeth*, Father Garnet's trial on March 28 in Lent becomes the optimal moment for the sensationalizing of equivocation. Thus, since Easter came on April 20 in 1606, Shakespeare's *Macbeth* could have played at a public theater between April 21 and June or July. But then the public theaters were closed for the rest of the year because of plague. So, after spring, with equivocation still as benchmark, there were

37. See Nichols, *James the First*, 2:80, and *MSC*, 6:45–46.

38. This was certainly the case on a comparable occasion in 1611 when the anniversary of the king's deliverance from the Gunpowder Plot was celebrated at the palace. After a similar day, there was, that evening, a play; see *MSC*, 6:52, and Chapter 5.

only three possibilities for a first performance of *Macbeth* in the London area during the remainder of the summer, all of them at court before the king of Denmark in August.

Thus, the equivocation argument regarding the date of *Macbeth*, based on a theory of topical allusions and on another traditional view, the idea of the play as congratulatory of King James, cannot coexist. The significance of topical allusions as a means of dating plays has always been their immediate contemporary relevance, their topicality. But if a *Macbeth* reference to Father Garnet's equivocation was relevant in August 1606, three months after the impact of his trial and despite intervening events of competitive interest, then how does such topical allusion finally help to date the play? Conversely, if *Macbeth* was indeed written as a courtly compliment to James on a state occasion, and if it also contains an allusion to equivocation because the Garnet matter was still interesting to Shakespeare and presumably to others, does not the allusion actually mislead? Plays at court came only at Christmas and Shrovetide, or, in 1606, in August. Further, if *Macbeth* was performed *first* at a public theater—in that window of time allowed by plague in late spring—and *then* at court in August, one can hardly argue that Shakespeare conceived of the play as a compliment to James for, say, a "Gowry Day" occasion he had no way of foreseeing would call for this play.[39] One can only claim *Macbeth* for the evening of the Gowry anniversary through observing that by an interesting coincidence Shakespeare happened to have a play ready that seemed a perfect fit for the circumstances.

These unexceptionable-seeming conclusions have, however, crucial implications for any theory of Shakespeare's rate of production. By opting for either of these alternatives, one offers important assumptions about the order of *Macbeth* within the tragedies in general. On the one hand, an equivocation-generated public performance date of *Macbeth* in spring 1606 closes the hypothetical gap between *Macbeth* and *King Lear* by four months. On the other, a *Macbeth* debut in August significantly places the two tragedies within the same half year. For it has not been realized that the annual court holiday performances during the remainder of 1606 (public theaters remaining closed) were so extraordinarily restricted by

39. The nature of royal ceremonial movements, not to mention the king of Denmark's decision to depart England earlier than he had planned, and the ever-present possibility of cancellations would make it difficult for Shakespeare to pick a particular play for a particular occasion.

plague that plays before King James did not even begin at the end of October on All Hallows', as was customary, or even in early December. There were no palace plays at all until the day after Christmas. On December 26, the first play of the holidays was finally allowed at court, at Whitehall. This was *King Lear*.

Macbeth then collides with *King Lear*. Dating by "equivocation" squeezes *Macbeth* into several spring weeks of 1606 before the onset of plague. A choice whereby *Macbeth* debuts during the August visit of the king of Denmark theoretically dismisses the equivocation issue, but there is no indication that *Macbeth* was first performed when the king of Denmark visited. It could well have been performed at court in the same Christmas season as *King Lear*, while the public playhouses were still closed. In the absence of other performance indications for *Macbeth*, and with the elimination of topical allusion, *Macbeth* precedes *King Lear* only by virtue of stylistic distinctions, highly flawed and dubious criteria, although they continue to be considered important (see Appendix 4).

In the end, the dating of *Macbeth* defies final resolution and the methodologies commonly used for the task are seriously flawed, subject to the schematics of a narrative urging the consistent and definable development of Shakespeare as a playwright and the steadiness of his dramatic production. But these developmental assumptions or expectations are challenged by many historical texts, particularly those containing plague figures. Such texts suggest that Shakespearean production was not a symmetrically implemented plan but behavior greatly influenced by opportunities for playing. Such opportunities, the same documents suggest, were erratic, subject to the vicissitudes of the time, to the availability of playhouses or to plans for royal revelry. One must conclude, then, that Shakespeare's pattern of production looks as uneven as his company's pattern of performance.

Finally, placing *Macbeth* any time in 1606, by whatever method, ironically complicates rather than reinforces the traditional view of Shakespeare's production. A traditionally dated *Macbeth* requires the rethinking of its relation not only to *King Lear*, but, as I discuss in Chapter 5, to *Antony and Cleopatra* as well. One must also position *Antony and Cleopatra* with *King Lear* in the same plague-delayed 1606 Christmas season, suggesting a significant increase in Shakespeare's rate of production in comparison to the period observed in the beginning of this chapter, the period from 1602 to 1605.

If *Macbeth* indeed belongs to the same year as these other two tragedies, particularly to the second half of the same year, then here is a concentrated efflorescence of creative power as strong or stronger than any other in Shakespeare's career, a surge that was the product not necessarily of an inner spiritual tempo but of the social circumstances that surrounded him.

5

1606: Social Confusion and Creative Concentration

I have suggested that any attempt to establish the date of the first performance of *Macbeth* via traditional maneuvers centered on the notion of topical allusion raises rather untraditional questions about the order of Shakespeare's Stuart canon and in particular about the relationship of *Macbeth* to *King Lear*. In the present chapter the dimensions of the problem increase when we consider the difficulties also inherent in the hitherto accepted dating of another tragedy, *Antony and Cleopatra*. These difficulties add up to the possibility that *King Lear*, *Antony and Cleopatra*, and *Macbeth* may all have first appeared, not only in the same year, but even in the same two-month holiday season at court, December–February 1606–7.

This suggestion of a 1606–7 date for the first performances of all three Shakespearean plays is, however, not crucial to the scope of this study in its search for the tempo of Shakespeare's production and his attitude toward it in his Stuart decade. I am concerned only with identifying in Shakespeare a general unwillingness to write plays when the public theaters were closed. In the process, a relevant problem is the method of evolving a plausible description of this tempo, but there is, in the end, no need to claim one particular narrative as absolute historical truth. Nevertheless, this offering of the *Macbeth/King Lear/Antony and Cleopatra* scenario, though unconventional, is in theory as viable a model of Shakespeare's artistic development as presently privileged accounts. Traditional standards of verification can lay equal claim to relevance, but they cannot appropriate hegemony.

To pursue the matter of *Antony and Cleopatra*, it is time to consider *King Lear*'s chronological relationship to the Roman play. *King Lear*, usually dated by eclipse allusions and by "style," is often seen as preceding *Macbeth*; and *Macbeth*, with its allusion to Caesar cowing Antony's spirit, as anticipating Shakespeare's composition of *Antony and Cleopatra*. The time frame conventionally suggested for this sequence extends from 1606 to 1608, the year *Antony and Cleopatra* appeared in the stationers' register. Any challenge to this canonized order takes issue, ultimately, with prevailing critical senses of how and at what rate Shakespeare approached the heart of his major tragic production.

In the case of *King Lear*, of course, there are early records, a quarto of the play that carries the date 1608 on the title page, and a preceding entry in the stationers' register on November 26, 1607, which reads: "Entered for their copy under the hands of Sir George Buck, Knight, and the Wardens a book called Master William Shakespeare his history of King Lear as it was played before the King's Majesty at Whitehall upon St. Stephen's night at Christmas last by his Majesty's Servants playing usually at the Globe on the Bankside."[1] St. Stephen's Day is December 26. Thus, though there is no royal court record of the title of any play performed by Shakespeare's company before the king between 1606 and 1611, the wording of this stationers' entry indicates the Christmas season prior to November 1607 when *King Lear* was entered, so the reference is obviously to December 26, 1606, a matter not under any dispute.

But, as indicated in the preceding chapter, plague had closed the playhouses throughout the late spring of 1606, the entire summer, and even the autumn. Indeed, the king had not come to London for the usual All Saints' Day celebration on November 1 and November 2 when, during the first ten years of James's reign, plays were performed in all but the most difficult circumstances (all having to do with plague). Indeed, no holiday plays by any city company were presented before the king in autumn or winter 1606 until that St. Stephen's Day—much later in December than holiday court playing usually began. Thus, with the public playhouses being closed by plague, the first play to have been produced by *any* city company either in the public playhouses or at court since the August enter-

1. Register C. fol. 161ᵛ modernized spelling.

tainment of the king of Denmark was, in fact, *King Lear*; this situation has not generally been recognized.

Was *King Lear* then new on St. Stephen's Day, 1606? Most probably new to the court. The tragedy could not have been performed at court during the king of Denmark's visit, for Shakespeare and his fellows (or the master of the revels, responsible for court entertainment) would hardly have inaugurated the long delayed Christmas season with a play King James had seen as recently as four months earlier.[2] By the same token, *King Lear* would not have been shown during the previous (1605–6) Christmas season, for one can assume that a performance of the same play before the king would not be featured in two successive Christmas seasons.

If these assumptions seem valid, then there are difficult alternatives in trying to estimate the date of the first production of *King Lear*. It either saw its debut at court on December 26, 1606, or, if it was first presented at the public playhouse, it was at a time too late for performance at court in Christmas 1605–6; if the play had been new and already in existence by Christmas 1605, it would have been presented then at court and thus not presented again in December 1606.

In these circumstances, the first time after the Christmas holidays of 1605–6 when public plays were possible was the spring of 1606, at such a time when the absence of Lent or of plague allowed playing. Easter was April 20, 1606.

But, it might be objected, with *King Lear* already in production in this spring, would not the tragedy have been an ideal choice for the king of Denmark's visit in August? It would indeed seem so. On the other hand, given that *King Lear* would almost certainly not be presented at court twice within a four-month period (August–December), one must assume that Shakespeare and his fellows chose not to perform it during the visit of the king of Denmark even if the tragedy was ready. The king of Denmark saw only three of the King's Servants' plays. Thus, one must argue that *King Lear* had its debut either at court on Christmas 1606 or in public between April and June 1606 before plague returned to London.[3]

2. See Chapter 6, section IV, for an example of this principle of nonrepetition in the case of *Winter's Tale*.

3. The playing dates for the King's Servants during the holiday season 1605–6 are not known; payment was in a lump sum on March 25, 1606 (in the middle of Lent). The Prince's Servants came to court on Shrove Monday and Shrove Tuesday (*MSC*, 6:43), so Shakespeare's company did not. If indeed there is a topical allusion to the

It is immediately obvious that this time frame for *King Lear* co-incides with that discussed in the previous chapter for *Macbeth*. To insist on a 1606 date for *Macbeth* is to crowd that play closely together with *King Lear*. Thus one of the traditional placements of the Scottish play, a performance before the king of Denmark in August 1606, would also imply that between the Christmases of 1605 and of 1606 Shakespeare produced both *Macbeth* and *King Lear*. The other traditional argument, associating *Macbeth* with the Gun-powder Plot and thus first putting the Scottish play in the public theater some time after the trial of Father Garnet in May 1606 (but before the plague closings of June or July), also overlaps with a plau-sible period for the debut of *King Lear*. From either of these tradi-tional perspectives, then, *Macbeth* becomes very closely implicated with *King Lear*. That both in turn become chronologically associated with Shakespeare's *Antony and Cleopatra* is the subject of this chapter.

I

On May 20, 1608, a publisher's twin entry in the stationers' register mentioned both *Antony and Cleopatra* and *Pericles* ("the book of Pericles Prince of Tyre"). No quarto of *Antony and Cleopatra* was printed at that time, but the notice establishes a terminal point for Shakespeare's Roman play. Any initial point, however, can only be suggested after a resumption of the long chronicle of plague which must so often be applied to this discussion of Shakespeare's Stuart production.

For the last week of December 1606, after *King Lear* was produced at court, plague deaths stood at 38. Thus the theaters were probably still closed. January showed some improvement, deaths dropping to

---

eclipse of October 2, 1605, in *King Lear*, as many scholars assume, it is important to note that playhouses were closed because of plague three days after the eclipse and not allowed to reopen until December 15, 1605 (*MSC*, 1.4/5:371–372). If first acted in the last fifteen days of December 1605, *King Lear* was not then brought to court because it would appear there the *following* Christmas. Thus the 1608 text of *King Lear* could easily have had its first production (from the viewpoint of the eclipse motif) during the early part of 1606, a time proposed for *Macbeth* (see below). Actually there seem to have been two eclipses of the sun. The first, October 2, 1605, was reported by Tycho Brahe and by Kepler; it ended over London at 2:21 P.M. The second took place on February 15, 1607; see A. G. Pingré, *Annales Celestes du Dix-Septième Siecle* (Paris: Academie des Sciences, 1901), pp. 19–21.

26, 16, and 14; nonetheless, such numbers were unusually high for this time of year and in the following two weeks the toll rose to 28, and to 33, then dropped to 20, the figure contained in the plague death report published February 12, 1607, the Thursday before Lent. I do not think that Shakespeare and his fellows played at the Globe in January or early February, nor from the beginning of Lent, February 18, to Easter, April 5.

The players may have seized on the end of Lent as an excuse to begin acting again, for on April 12, the Sunday after Easter, even though the Thursday report had cited only 23 plague deaths the lord mayor of London wrote to the earl of Suffolk, the lord chamberlain, who, as previously noted, was the master of the master of the revels: "Whereas it pleaseth God that the infection of sickness is for these two or three weeks of late somewhat increase[d] in the skirts and confines of this city and by the untimely heat of the season may spread further than can hereafter be easily prevented, my humble desire is that your Lordship for the preventing of so great a danger will vouchsafe your honorable favor . . . in restraining such common stage plays as are daily showed."[4]

E. K. Chambers remarked on this instance that the mayor was "unjustified as yet by the plague bill" in asking for this restraint of plays.[5] But Chambers was inclined to be overly arithmetic with what was for the Londoners of Shakespeare's time an important issue of public health, and to assume, as always, a proto–Cavalier-Puritan struggle over the Renaissance theater. According to this scenario, the city officials would exaggerate the danger of plague in order to suppress the hated plays, while an aristocratic privy council judiciously resisted this bigotry. But another way of looking at the matter is to remember that the city fathers might, in fact, have been concerned that restraints of playing would affect the livelihoods of many of their middle-class constituents, including the shopkeepers around the playhouses as well as the thousands of watermen who plied the Thames bringing audiences back and forth across the river. To this effect, all during Lent, the lowest plague death figures had been 13, the highest 33, and in those several weeks prior to the lord mayor's letter to the privy council the weekly sequence in plague

---

4. See *MSC*, 1.1:87–88. The weekly plague deaths during Lent up to Maundy Thursday, when the last bill of mortality would have come out before Easter, were 14, 20, 30, 33, 22, 13, 23.

5. E. K. Chambers, *The Elizabethan Stage*, 4 vols. (Oxford: Clarendon Press, 1923), 4:350.

deaths had been 13, 23, 27. The twenties, as previously mentioned, had seemed reason enough to the authorities, on at least two occasions, for closing the theaters.

The lord mayor's present concern was in the end justified, for weekly deaths would rise from 23 to 27 for the April 16 report, drop to 26, and then show a sudden rise on the Thursday, April 30 report to 43. But it was not only the city that was concerned about these figures. The extremely powerful earl of Salisbury, Robert Cecil, first secretary, found plague in his own household in May, so he forbade his son to come to London (*Hatfield*, 19:97). Elsewhere, on April 22, Zorzi Giustinian, the Venetian ambassador, wrote: "At this beginning of summer, the plague begins to give signs of spreading. The King and Court will leave immediately, and I, as do the Ambassadors, will endeavor to take up my abode in the country, as near as possible to the place where the King lodges" (*SPV*, 10:494)—this despite the fact that at the beginning of June 1607, as William Shakespeare presumably left London for Stratford-upon-Avon for the marriage of his daughter to Dr. John Hall, London plague death figures would be even lower than they had been in May, when they had fallen to an average of fifteen per week.

But eventually the predictions proved accurate. Toward the end of June 1607, and rather quickly in July, plague deaths mounted again, being reported at 33 on July 9 and reaching 77 at the end of July when the king began his summer progress (*Hatfield*, 19:191). So even if the privy council had ignored the lord mayor's April letter and allowed the playhouses to remain open, public acting certainly would have been forbidden by July or August, 1607, as the weekly plague deaths moved steadily up from 33 to 105.

September 1607 was no better; great strides were made by the plague and there was a general sense that London was in for another autumn siege of it. On August 14 the Queen's Servants were in Oxford and on September 7, Shakespeare and his fellows. In the city, the opening of Parliament was delayed.[6]

As in the autumn of the previous year, plague continued through October, rising to 177 deaths in one week. In November a proclamation forbade all but necessary persons from coming to court as a step to prevent further infection (*SPD*, 8:378). It was perhaps for this reason that, for the second consecutive year on the All Saints' and

---

6. See *SPV*, 11:36; *L'Isle*, 3:412; *Hatfield*, 19:258; J. O. Halliwell-Phillipps, *Shakespeare's Tours* (Brighton, 1887), p. 33.

All Souls' holidays of November 1–2 no plays were presented at court—the third such All Saints' omission for plague in four years. It was not until November 19, finally, that there was a court performance in the palace at Whitehall (it was the Prince's Servants, rather than Shakespeare and his fellows, who acted before the king and the prince on that Thursday; *MSC*, 6:45–46). In the city, the latest plague bill showed 55 deaths for the preceding week, and the playhouses presumably remained closed.[7]

Matters seemed to take a turn for the better in December 1607, as plague began dwindling away, but apparently this late autumn and early winter would mount yet another challenge to the public playhouses. December started very cold. The temperature fell uncharacteristically to freezing on December 8, so that although plague deaths were down to 7 by the middle of the month, the outdoor playhouses could not have been bearable in conditions that were to produce thick ice on the Thames by December 31:

> The eight of December began a hard frost which continued seven days and then thawed gently five days' space, and the two and twentieth of the same month the frost began again very violently, so as within four days many persons did walk halfway over the Thames upon the ice, and by the thirtieth of December the multitude at every ebb, and half flood passed over the Thames in divers places. And although the violence of the frost abated now and then, yet it held from the third of January [1608] unto the fifteenth of the same.[8]

At court during this Christmas season of 1607, Shakespeare and his fellows presented some thirteen plays between Christmas and the following February. "All the holidays there were plays," but apparently they were "with so little concourse of strangers that they say they wanted company," so one imagines that the restriction of access to court because of plague was still in effect although the remark could merely have meant that the weather prevented *foreign* visitors from traveling across to England (*Chamberlain*, 1:251).

During early January 1608, public playing must still have been difficult or impossible because of the freeze. The weather continued very cold "in a very strange manner" through the end of January 1608, and toward the end of the month the river ice had damaged

7. See F. P. Wilson, *The Plague in Shakespeare's London* (London: Oxford University Press, 1983), pp. 192–199, and Appendix 5 of this book.
8. See *Annals*, sig. 4F2–4F2ᵛ, and cf. *SPV*, 11:82.

wooden structures, so menacing London Bridge, in fact, that the merchants had evacuated all the shops on it.[9] References to the ice were still being made as late as February 4, and even on February 28 the weather was described as very cold.[10]

To repeat, playing on the Bankside in these conditions must have been extremely difficult, if not impossible. Certainly customers wishing to cross the river to Southwark would have had a rather hazardous time of it. The open-air playhouses would themselves have been virtually uninhabitable unless the Jacobean audiences of early 1608 were much hardier than those to be found in any modern North American city when block ice fills the rivers. These were not usual English weather conditions, and I think they conjoined with the earlier incidence of plague to keep the public theaters closed during most of 1607 and into the new year of 1608, in the spring of which the script of *Anthony and Cleopatra* was first recorded in the stationers' register.

II

This chronicle of plague and freezing temperatures offers a context within which to view the materials that have been traditionally used to date the appearance of *Antony and Cleopatra*. The most prominent such text is a closet drama by Samuel Daniel, *Cleopatra*, first written in 1594. Daniel continually revised all his printed material, and *Cleopatra*, having been reprinted more than six times in various collections of his works, was no exception; it was revised for a 1607 collection of his poems. To R. H. Case, and later to E. K. Chambers, this 1607 revision of *Cleopatra* demonstrated that Shakespeare's *Antony and Cleopatra* was an intervening influence.[11] Here is the traditional chronological sequence: 1594, Daniel's *Cleopatra*; 1605, 1606, or 1607, Shakespeare's *Antony and Cleopatra*; 1607, Daniel's revised *Cleopatra*. In other words, commentary has argued Shakespeare's Roman play as written one, two, or three years before the Daniel revision.

9. For these matters, see Thomas Birch, *The Court and Times of James I*, 2 vols. (London, 1849), 1:71: Edmund Lodge, *Illustrations of British History*, 3 vols. (London, 1838), 3:224–225; and *Chamberlain*, 1:253.

10. See *SPV*, 11:96; *Hatfield*, 20:38.

11. William Shakespeare, *Antony and Cleopatra*, Arden edition, ed. R. H. Case (London: Methuen, 1907), pp. viii-ix; E. K. Chambers, *William Shakespeare* (Oxford: Clarendon Press, 1930), 1.476–478.

All the material in Daniel that Chambers attributes to Shakespeare's influence, however, either can be found in Plutarch's *Life of Marcus Antonius*—Shakespeare's and Daniel's common and sole source for the events of the Cleopatra story—or need not have originated in Shakespeare. Certainly Daniel added new material about Charmian and Iras—Plutarchan characters greatly developed for humor by Shakespeare—but Daniel treats them quite differently, offering a separate scene in which the two women soberly consider their futures.[12]

Further, from 1594 until whenever Shakespeare wrote his own Roman play, Plutarch's Cleopatra story from the *Life* of Antonius seems to have been the preserve of the countess of Pembroke and of Samuel Daniel, along with another member of her circle, Samuel Brandon. (Brandon wrote a Senecan tragedy in 1598 about Antony's rejected wife entitled *The Virtuous Octavia*, which told the story from her point of view.) Because of this coterie familiarity with the material, it is risky, I think, to attribute changes in Daniel's Cleopatra—changes often originating in Plutarch—solely to Shakespeare's influence. At the same time, since Daniel was constantly revising—the bibliography of his extant texts is extremely complex—it is difficult to assert that he would only revise his *Cleopatra* once again because of the influence of Shakespeare.

Yet a minor but highly significant (and unremarked upon) instance argues strongly for Shakespeare's influence. Shakespeare changes the sequence around Antony's learning that Cleopatra has "killed" herself. In Plutarch's work, Antonius, resolving to commit suicide, asks his servant Eros to slay him. But Plutarch's Eros is so unwilling to perform the deed that he kills himself instead, the marginal gloss in the North translation reading, "Eros, Antonius' servant, slew himself." When Shakespeare adapted this incident, he repeated a technique used with the Plutarchan characters Scarrus and a scarred soldier; the melding of two characters from his Plutarchan source to create one stage figure. Here Shakespeare first constructed his

12. Chambers also cites Daniel's new character Dircetas as a Shakespearean derivation. In both Daniel and Shakespeare, a Dircetas takes Antony's bloodied sword to show Caesar after Antony's death, but Dircetas has this role in Plutarch as well. Further, the dowager countess of Pembroke, one of Daniel's patronesses in the 1590s, had also developed Dircetas as messenger of Antony's death in her translation of Robert Garnier's *Marc Antoine*, which appeared in 1592 even before Daniel dedicated his own *Cleopatra* in 1594 as a compliment to the countess and a complement to her work. In the 1607 version of his play, in fact, Daniel wrote a greatly enlarged dedication to the countess, indicating her continuing influence on his career.

Eros from Plutarch's Eros, whom Antonius long before had caused to swear to kill him in extremity but who, in the end, slew himself rather than kill his master: call him suicide helper *A*. Then Shakespeare reached back through the earlier portion of Plutarch's *Life* to the lengthily related Parthian expedition which shows the Romans in a harassed and deadly retreat. Antonius, reduced to desperation, calls for his man, "one Rhamnus, one of his slaves *enfranchised* that was of his guard, and made him give him his faith that he would thrust his sword through him when he [Antonius] would bid him."[13]

It is this new Plutarchan figure (call him suicide helper *B*) that surfaces when Shakespeare's Antony tells Eros (Plutarch's suicide helper *A*) to kill him. First Shakespeare's Antony says to Eros:

> Thou art sworn, Eros
> That when the exigent should come, which
> Now is come indeed: when I should see behind me
> The inevitable prosecution of
> Disgrace and horror, that on my command,
> Thou then wouldst kill me.

Shakespeare's Eros demurs, saying:

> The gods withhold me
> Shall I do that which all the Parthian darts
> Though enemy, lost aim and could not?

Antony replies:

> Draw that thy honest sword, which thou hast worn
> Most useful for thy country.

Eros:

> Oh, sir, pardon me.

Antony:

> When I did *make thee free*, swor'st thou not then
> To do this when I bade thee? [emphasis added] (4.14.62–82)

13. Plutarch, *Lives*, 6 vols., ed. George Wyndham (London, 1896), 6:51.

Shakespeare has obviously turned his Eros into someone freed—enfranchised—who wears a sword which he has borne most useful to his country. His Eros has in effect taken on the characteristics of Plutarch's suicide helper *B*—Rhamnus from the Plutarchan Parthian expedition; Shakespeare's Eros refers to Parthia. And the manumission (from Plutarch's Rhamnus) has become so significant in Shakespeare that it is part of the structure of Antony's effort to persuade Eros—a persuasion, indeed, telling enough to force Eros either to honor Antony's plea or to kill himself to avoid the debt.[14]

In this context, Samuel Daniel's addition of Antony's suicide to his 1607 revision of Cleopatra becomes significant. In this 1607 quarto, when Antony's suicide is reported by Dircetas, Daniel's hero says to Eros:

> Come, Eros, do this service for thy lord,
> The best and greatest pleasure thou canst do.
> Employ this weapon here. Come, make this sword,
> That won me honor now to save it too. (sig. 68)

The account continues:

> Eros, his late enfranchis'd servant takes
> The sword, as if he would have done the deed.

Enfranchised? Eros? Neither the countess of Pembroke's *Antonius* nor Plutarch's *Life* of Antonius, as previously observed, has Eros a freedman, or enfranchised.[15] In Plutarch, the marginal gloss specifically describes Eros merely as Antonius's servant. If Daniel's Eros is enfranchised, why does his Antonius then say, in his speech: "must both a woman and a slave/ The start before me in this glory

---

14. In this connection, Shakespeare may also have been recalling a sequence he used in *Julius Caesar*. An episode in Plutarch's *Life* of Caesar describes, in North's words, how Cassius "got into a tent where nobody was and took Pindarus with him, one of his freed bondsmen whom he reserved ever for such a pinch since the cursed battle of the Parthians where Crassus was slain (though he [Cassius] not withstanding escaped that overthrow). But then casting his cloak over his head and holding out his bare neck unto Pindarus, he gave him his head to be stricken off" (Plutarch, *Lives*, 6:266). Shakespeare altered this sequence, again using the motif of slave freeing to set up a return favor as a moral requirement from the person freed.

15. "Now he had a man of his called Eros, whom he loved and trusted much, and whom he had long before caused to swear unto him that he should kill him when he did command him: and then he willed him to keep his promise"; Plutarch, *Lives*, 6:79.

have?" (sig. G8ᵛ) True, the word "slave" may be an aristocratically derogatory figure of speech (however inappropriate here) for someone in a lower class. But even if the term "slave" is figurative, there seems little point in Daniel making Eros a freedman since this freeing is not used as persuasion. Further, no one (except Shakespeare) ever said Eros was free. Indeed, Lady Pembroke's version is more consistent on this minute point than Daniel's, for her translation merely reports the Plutarchan information that Eros had once sworn to kill Antonius when asked.

The exceedingly minor nature of the Daniel lapse from Plutarch is the telling point. It is as if Daniel, in no way concerned about Eros as a character, simply assumed Shakespeare's version to be factual (i.e., from Plutarch).

Daniel's revision first appeared in a volume entitled *Certain Small Works . . . Now Again by Him Corrected and Augmented*. The book bears "1607" on the title page and was printed by John Windet, who dated in the new style.[16] December 31, 1607, was the last day of the year—in Windet's terms (as opposed to March 25 in the old style)— on which one of his books could have been dated 1607. When, then, could Daniel have seen Shakespeare's *Antony and Cleopatra* in time to prepare a new version of his own play that would appear in print no later than the last day of 1607?

In reckoning this, plague again becomes a factor. For much of 1607, the public playhouses had been closed from plague. In addition, because of the plague, the royal family had not admitted extraneous outsiders and there had been no plays for the All Saints' interval at the end of October. Moreover, although other companies had played at court in November 1607, there is no record of Shakespeare's own group there until St. Stephen's Day, December 26. Thus, if Daniel saw *Antony and Cleopatra* between April and December, 1607, his earliest opportunity would presumably have been at court on December 26. But then he would hardly have found time to revise and

16. Windet printed *STC* 4473, Latin poems in memory of Sir Philip Sidney. Alexander Neville, compiler of the book, dated his preface in the old style, February 16, 1586, for Sidney died in the previous fall of 1586. Specifying the present date on the title page as also February 16 (the day of Sidney's funeral), Windet nevertheless puts the new style "1587" as the publication date. See also Windet's title page for *STC* 20905 (stationers' register, January 15, 1605/06). This reads "1606," but litigation against Windet's printing of this title took place at the court of the stationers as early as February 17, that is, well before Lady Day when old style dating might change from 1605 to 1606. For the court case, see W. A. Jackson, *Records of the Court of the Stationers' Company. 1602–1640* (London: Bibliographical Society, 1957), p. 17.

print with Windet by the end of the year 1607. This is especially so because the play formed part of a collection printed in 1605 and now updated by revisions and by the inclusion of two pieces that had previously been published in 1606 and were "corrected and augmented" for the 1607 printing in question.[17] Further, this 1607 revision went through two issues before the end of the calendar year.[18]

There could, of course, have been public performances of *Antony and Cleopatra* at the Globe earlier—at the end of Lent eight months earlier in 1607. Easter had occurred on April 5. On April 12, however, as previously observed, the city administration had written the lord chamberlain requesting that he restrain plays, and correspondence indicated a general expectation of a siege of plague. Certainly by the middle of July 1607, when the weekly plague death figure in London was 51, the siege was on. Thus Daniel's access to a Globe performance of *Antony and Cleopatra* in 1607 would have been extremely limited.

The players might well have played illegally here and there. They played during plague in the week after Easter 1607, else the lord mayor would not have asked the lord chamberlain to close the theaters. Daniel could have seen Shakespeare's play at this time or during other brief intervals. But if, as seems likely, Samuel Daniel did not see Shakespeare's Roman play at the Globe in late spring, then an earlier date for the first performance of the play must be conjectured.

Prior to Lent, in January and February 1607, plague had kept the public theaters shut. Presumably, then, to see any plays in the late autumn or early winter of 1606–7, the spectator, unable to go to the public playhouse, would have to see them at court during the Christmas season. But, as previously mentioned, this was the same holiday season in which *King Lear* was presented and which may also have seen *Macbeth*. Because the placing of *Antony and Cleopatra* at court in this same period has profound implications for theories concerning the order and rate of production of Shakespeare's tragedies, it is important to view this possibility quite carefully.

A dating of *Antony and Cleopatra* based on a possible relation to Barnabe Barnes's *Devil's Charter*, first argued in 1906 by R. H. Case, has even more significance than critics have hitherto attributed to

17. These additions were *The Queen's Arcadia* (first presented in August 1605) and the funeral elegy to the earl of Devonshire, who died on April 3, 1606.

18. See W. W. Greg, *A Bibliography of English Printed Drama before the Restoration* (London: The Bibliographical Society, 1939–62), 4 vols, 1:218–219.

it.[19] Barnes's play was published late in 1607; the entry was in the stationers' register for October 16, 1607, and "1607" is on the title page of the quarto. The register entry states that the work was "played before his Majesty," and the title page contends that it was performed at court "upon Candlemas Night last, by his Majesty's Servants." Quite obviously, as traditional commentary has observed, this bespeaks a performance on February 2, 1607, when, indeed, the King's Servants were paid for presenting a play (*MSC*, 6:45).

E. K. Chambers, Case, and M. R. Ridley, editor of the new Arden edition *Antony and Cleopatra*, thought that Barnes's *Devil's Charter* borrowed from Shakespeare's *Antony and Cleopatra* and thus postdated it. Barnes, using the *History* of Francesco Guicciardini as a source for his story, read a passing allusion there to Prince Astor of Faenza, who, with his bastard brother, was secretly put to death after "some had satisfied their vile unnatural lust on him."[20] This motif is carried into *Devil's Charter* as Pope Alexander arranges for the death of two "Faventine" princes. In one scene, the princely prisoners complain about the homosexual demands made on them and invoke the Destroyer of Sodom for deliverance from this soul-slaying prostitution. In a later scene, after unknowingly drinking wine that has been drugged by the pope, they "lay themselves upon a bed" and after "one strain of music" fall asleep (sig. I3). The pope enters in his cassock and nightcap. Making many references to Morpheus, god of sleep, while the boys murmur through their dreams about paradise, he draws out of his boxes aspics, saying:

> Come out here now, you Cleopatra's birds,
> Fed fat and plump with proud Egyptian slime
> Of seven-mouth'd Nylus, but now turn'd lean:
>
> *He putteth to either of their breasts an aspic.*
>
> Take your repast upon these princely paps.
> Now Ptolomy's wife is highly magnified,
> Ensigning [teaching] these fair princely twins their death.
> And you my lovely boys, competitors,
> With Cleopatra share in death and fate.
>
>   ⋮
>
> What now proud worms. How tastes yon princes' blood?

19. Shakespeare, *Antony and Cleopatra*, Arden edition, pp. viii-ix.
20. Francesco Guicciardini, *The History*, tr. Geoffrey Fenton (London, 1599), sig. R6ᵛ-S.

The slaves be plump and round. Into your nests.
Is there no token of the serpents' draught?
All clear and safe. Well, now, fair boys, goodnight.

The pope leaves. Various characters come on stage to exclaim over the sight of the "princely boys" on the bed until the bodies are finally carried out (sig. I4ᵛ).

Clearly Barnes, however familiar he may have been with Guicciardini, was not too conversant with (or did not choose to follow) Plutarch, other recent versions of the Cleopatra story, or even natural history as understood in his day. For the author of *Devil's Charter* made rather literal use of what in Shakespeare's tragedy is only Cleopatra's metaphor—the idea of asps nursing at her breast. Barnes's asps are originally plump, then starved lean so they will hungrily suck their "draught" until they are plump and round again. When Barnes weirdly turned his asps into vampire bats, he may thus have been recalling Shakespeare's coup de theatre, for Cleopatra's asps would seem to provide a more suitable inspiration for Barnes than the relevant passage in Plutarch's *Life* of Antonius, which describes asps that kill quickly (but not at Cleopatra's breast) with a poison that puts one to sleep. Finally, Barnes's emphasis on the sleep motif (including the god Morpheus) is close, I think, to Shakespeare's use of the sleep motif in Cleopatra's appearance after her death when she "looks like sleep."[21]

Another similarity between the two plays (one not previously observed) is the presence in *Devil's Charter* of Lucretia Borgia, beautiful and strong-minded, who murders her husband on stage. She is given a Cleopatra-like scene alone in her boudoir where, in a speech of forty lines, she reminisces about how the marquis of Mantua

---

21. I previously made this point in L. Barroll, "The Chronology of Shakespeare's Jacobean Plays and the Dating of *Antony and Cleopatra*," in *Essays on Shakespeare*, ed. Gordon Ross Smith (University Park: Pennsylvania State University Press, 1965), pp. 148–150, but Stanley Wells et al., *William Shakespeare: A Textual Companion* (Oxford: Clarendon Press, 1987), cite George Peele's *Edward I* (Qq. in 1593, 1599) in which "a woman is murdered by an 'Adder' described as her 'Babe' at 'her breast', she being described as its 'nurse'." Barnes's own treatment, Wells et al. argue, resembles Peele's more closely than it does Shakespeare's. But even granting an unlikely surge in the popularity of *Edward I* in 1606–8, eight to ten years after the last quarto of the play was published, Barnes differs significantly from Peele by terming his serpents "Cleopatra's birds" while Peele's evil queen Elinore seems to have neglected this facet of her classical education, avoiding all associations of her "adder" with matters Egyptian or Cleopatran. See *Edward I*, ed. W. W. Greg (Oxford: Oxford University Press, 1911), Malone Society Reprints, Vol. 11, lines 2317ff.

gazed upon the whiteness of her brow, how the duke of Bourbon begged her on his knees for a lock of her hair for which he paid six thousand crowns, and how the prince of Salerno doted on her (fully described) eyes and mouth. It is difficult not to recall Cleopatra's well-known reminiscences of her own lovers in Shakespeare's play.

The real problem with the Barnes material, a matter not noted by commentators, is that when the play was printed in quarto (somewhat grandly divided into acts and scenes) it was, according to a front matter remark by Barnes, rather extensively augmented and revised. While having little effect on the question of Shakespeare's influence, the remark does pose a problem in dating first productions. Theoretically, Barnes's Candlemas performance might not have contained any Shakespearean touches at all, since the plot about the princes is a very minor episode in the play, nor is Lucretia's narcissism indispensable to the action. In such a case, Barnes might not have seen Shakespeare's *Antony and Cleopatra* until long after February 1607. Nonetheless, the Barnes play must be considered among the totality of texts concerning the dating of a first possible performance of Shakespeare's *Antony and Cleopatra*, particularly in conjunction with Daniel's *Cleopatra*.

Both the Daniel and the Barnes plays suggest a similar time frame for Shakespeare's *Antony and Cleopatra:* a performance no later than the Christmas holidays of December and January 1606–7. Because Barnes's play with "Shakespearean" material in it appears at the latest in its printed form by the end of 1607, his seeing Shakespeare's *Antony and Cleopatra* is subject to all the plague-dictated parameters applicable to Daniel; that is, if Barnes used Shakespeare material only for the *printed* version of his play, he almost certainly could not have first seen *Antony and Cleopatra* after April 1607, when plague began closing the theaters. But if the Barnes text published in 1607 represents his whole play as presented back in February 1607, at court, then a holiday performance of *Antony and Cleopatra* at court becomes at least as strong a possibility in the case of Barnes's relationship to Shakespeare as it does in the case of Daniel's. Both authors, by virtue of the circumstances of their writing, suggest a viewing period that puts a performance of *Antony and Cleopatra* in the holiday season of 1606–7.

The implications are obvious. The holiday season of 1606–7 seems also to have been associated with *Macbeth* and *King Lear*. Did this same period then see the debut not of two but of three new Shakespearean tragedies?

III

In Chapter 4 and the present chapter I have been viewing texts that suggest a reordering of the commonly accepted arrangement of several Shakespearean tragedies. Traditional modes of assessing Shakespeare's artistic development have long suggested a bias—probably unconscious—to fit surviving documents to a somewhat rigid preconception of human behavior, ordering Shakespeare's writings into a pattern that satisfies certain unvoiced theories of artistic creation. The pattern according to which Shakespeare produced tragedies—his "tragic period"—has been the instance in point through Chapters 4 and 5. I have, in effect, been offering a revisionist view of Shakespeare's career from 1603 to 1607 which presents his rate of production as erratic and uneven. Not spaced in an orderly progression, it seems, rather, to be clustered. There were, for instance, two intervals within which Shakespeare was producing plays. The first period revolves around the November–February 1604–5 season at court, when *Othello* and *Measure for Measure* were first performed. From the early end of that first period stretches back a span of time, plague-filled and restless with the succession, in which *Othello* and *Measure for Measure* might have been first performed at the Globe (if they were). On the other end, just after these new plays were performed at court, and marked with a letter from Cope (January 11, 1605) telling Cecil that the King's Servants had no new plays, stretch ahead the two new years—1605 and 1606—leading to the present moment in this overview.

At this moment, the Christmas season of 1606, several documents and indications seem to converge. Plague and Lent closed the playhouses from the Easter (1606) following the Gunpowder Plot to the next Easter, a period of about a year. But thrusting through the gray sameness of the playhouse closing all during that summer and autumn of 1606 appear, as it were, two peaks. The smaller peak represents the group of performances given in August 1606 at court by Shakespeare and his fellows for the visit to England of the king of Denmark. The larger peak represents the delayed holiday season of 1606–7 inaugurated by *King Lear* on December 26, the first play to be performed for the court Christmas season by any London company.

I have essayed a more detailed map of this incomplete landscape by fixing on smaller regions. Many scholars writing on the probable date of Shakespeare's *Macbeth* have attempted to locate it by recourse to the equivocation allusion, placing the play close to the Gunpowder Plot. But it was Father Garnet's trial in April 1606, five months after the Gunpowder Plot, that gave the topic of equivocation popular notoriety. And Father Garnet's trial occurred in Lent 1606, while theaters were closed. After Lent the public theaters may have been open between Easter and June or July, but then plague took hold and closed playhouses even through the following Christmas, when *King Lear* actually inaugurated the 1606 holiday season at court. So if critics adhere to the relevance of equivocation as a topical allusion in *Macbeth*, then this drama in some way falls together with *King Lear*. The earliest time *Macbeth* could have been performed after Father Garnet's trial was in that window allowed by the plague in the spring, or in August (at court), or in December (at court). Was *Macbeth* then performed by August 1606, and was *King Lear* being written during late summer?

These questions are vexing enough, but they become more so as the traditional approach to dating *Antony and Cleopatra* comes into play. Twentieth-century critics writing about the date of this tragedy see Samuel Daniel's revised closet drama *Cleopatra* as affected by Shakespeare's tragedy. If it was, then *Antony and Cleopatra* itself must have been produced before the first of the two issues of Daniel's revised *Cleopatra* (dated 1607). Thus it is unlikely that Shakespeare's Roman play was initially presented at court as late as the Christmas season of 1607–8.

Because all critics since R. H. Case agree that Barnabe Barnes's *Devil's Charter* also shows influence by Shakespeare's Roman play, *Antony and Cleopatra* thus assumes a place where are collocated, by the implications not only of new narrative but of traditional chronology, both the first performance of *King Lear* and possibly that of *Macbeth*. This collocation presents a challenge. Critics, I think, must either reinterpret most of the available documents, both new and traditional, by which these three plays have been dated, or they must deal with the strong probability that all three plays appeared in very close succession, possibly in one court season. This latter probability, conjoined with the picture drawn in Chapter 4 from the documents of December and January 1604–5, argues that Shakespeare may have composed his major tragedies of the Stuart period in a far different manner from that sketched in traditional biographies.

Because *Hamlet* was written before 1603, one deals, when speaking of Shakespeare's major tragedies (excluding *Coriolanus* and *Timon of Athens*), with only four early Stuart years. One of these was the plague-filled first year of James's reign, when the only permissible performances were at court at the end of 1603. There survive no titles for the plays presented before the king in that first year, but the second year, including the holiday season of November–December 1604, saw the performances of *Othello* and *Measure for Measure*. At that point, according to Sir Walter Cope on January 14, 1605, Shakespeare's company had nothing new to offer the court beyond these two plays that the queen had already seen. Then come one hundred weeks that separate this date from the probable debuts of *King Lear*, *Macbeth*, and *Antony and Cleopatra* in 1606–7, one hundred weeks of which forty closed the playhouses from plague and cold. This leaves a period of sixty weeks—slightly longer than a year—in which three new Shakespearean tragedies may have been first performed on the stage. If such is the case, then contrary to traditional critical belief William Shakespeare's tragic period—as far as the first performance of the tragedies was concerned—was indeed a short one. In January 1605 there was nothing new. In the latter part of 1606—perhaps in the last month of that year—three major tragedies suddenly made their debuts.

Further, it appears that Shakespeare's rate of composition had a direct relationship to the King's Servants' opportunities for playing, to the unrelenting epidemics of plague, and to the more or less predictable relief afforded all the major theatrical companies during the Christmas seasons at court. It may even be that if plague had *not* been a major factor in Shakespeare's so-called tragic period—and ironically enough, plague was soon to abate for the remainder of Shakespeare's career—his production would have been more copious. If Shakespeare could produce *King Lear*, *Macbeth*, and *Antony and Cleopatra* in a period of sixty weeks, and it seems likely that he did, and if he produced two-thirds of his entire canon from 1591 to 1602, then it is clear that, for whatever reason, he was not, during much of the first Stuart decade, producing in a manner consistent with the capabilities suggested by these two well-separated periods of his career.

6

The Problem of the
Later Shakespeare

Shakespeare's Stuart period was, until 1611 (the date of *Tempest*), seldom free from the confusion of overfrequent playhouse closings. Not only were the first seven years of James's reign heavily plague-ridden, but political emergencies such as the Gunpower Plot and sudden punitive closings played their part. These latter occasions, though infrequent, when operating in conjunction with the frequent return of bubonic plague, made for an incredibly patchwork series of playing seasons during Shakespeare's last ten years of production. Figure 1 offers a graphic review of this situation.

It may be difficult to grasp how chaotic these early years were for the commercial theater companies; the traditional picture of Stuart drama has often been that of a flourishing and uninterrupted enterprise. Plays, presumably, were there to be seen every afternoon for year after sunny year. But this conception of affairs, though current, can no longer rest unchallenged.[1] To an observer looking back from

---

1. The preliminary study, L. Barroll, "The Chronology of Shakespeare's Jacobean Plays and the Dating of *Antony and Cleopatra*," in *Essays on Shakespeare*, ed. Gordon Ross Smith (Pennsylvania State University Press, 1965), pp. 115–162, noticed in Stanley Wells, "The Year's Contributions to Shakesperian Study," *Shakespeare Survey* 20 (1967), 162–163, served Wells et al. as a basis for discussing the dates of Shakespeare's Jacobean plays, but the figures in Appendix 2 of the present work supersede my 1965 study. These figures should be used only as estimates of first productions, not as parameters of play composition.

FIGURE 1
Theatrical Conditions in London: 1603–1613. UPPER CASE = THEATERS CLOSED; lower case = theaters open.

	jan	feb	mar	apr	may	jun	jul	aug	sep	oct	nov	dec
1603	jan	feb	MAR	APR	may MAY	JUN	JUL	AUG	SEP	OCT	NOV	DEC
1604	JAN	FEB	MAR	APR apr	may MAY	JUN	JUL	AUG	SEP sep	oct	nov	dec
1605	jan	feb FEB	MAR	apr	may	jun	jul	aug	sep	OCT	NOV	DEC
1606	jan	feb	mar MAR	APR apr	may	jun JUN	JUL	AUG	SEP	OCT	NOV	DEC
1607	JAN	FEB	MAR	apr APR	MAY	JUN	JUL	AUG	SEP	OCT	NOV	DEC
1608	JAN	FEB	MAR	apr	may	jun	jul JUL	AUG	SEP	OCT	NOV	DEC
1609	JAN	FEB	MAR	APR	MAY	JUN	JUL	AUG	SEP	OCT	NOV	DEC
1610	JAN	feb	MAR	apr	may MAY	jun	JUL	AUG	SEP	OCT	NOV	dec
1611	jan	FEB	MAR mar	apr	may	jun	jul	aug	sep	oct	nov	dec
1612	jan	feb	MAR	APR apr	may	jun	jul	aug	sep	oct	nov NOV	DEC dec
1613	jan	feb FEB	MAR mar	apr	may	jun	JUL	AUG	SEP	OCT	NOV	DEC

Globe burns down June 29

1642, the previous thirty years might indeed have seemed to witness a placid flow of drama, broken briefly by the 1625 and 1636 plagues before the fruitful current continued. But if the observer had stood at the end of 1607, the previous four or five years of London public play performance would have seemed a broken landscape. Following the accession of James, one year of great plague in London was succeeded by a second, a widespread and severe assault throughout England, initially outside London for the most part, but imminently awaited—and received—in London itself. Then a series of five- and six-month outbreaks again struck the city, all repeatedly causing closings of the theaters. Turning around to look ahead at the immediate future, plague continued off and on for three years, until December 1610.

Some idea of the way these conditions were viewed at the time may be gathered from the playwright Thomas Dekker in one of several pamphlets he authored—presumably when his own playwrighting was curtailed by plague. In *Dead Term*, published in 1608 but entered in the stationers' register November 3, 1607, the "City of London" and "Westminster" compare their troubles. Glossed in the margin of the printed book as "London's Complaint about the Plague," London's lament to Westminster observes in 1607:

> Sickness hath dwelt a long time in thy [Westminster's] chambers, she doth now walk still in a ghostly and formidable shape up and down my streets. She (with her ill company) infecteth my sons and daughters and leads them daily into such dangers that (in hundreds at a time) do they lose their lives. *Five years* hath she been a troublesome guest unto me; I received her at first (though I loved not her company yet). I gave her good entertainment, and patiently endured her insulting over me and mine, because I knew she was a messenger sent from Above.
>
> But woe to me (infortunate City!) Woe unto us both (O my distressed neighbor,) shall we never shake hands with her and part? Shall our fair bodies never recover of this disease which so often and often hath run all over them, and doth now again begin to be as a plague unto us? ... Dead unto us both are our liveliest days, whilst this pestilent vapor hangs over our heads. Dead are our pleasures, for we do now take delight in nothing but mourning: dead are our houses of leisure, and those which are full of business.[2]

2. Thomas Dekker, *Non-Dramatic Works*, 4 vols., ed. A. B. Grosart (London, 1884–86), 4:77–78; emphasis added.

In the arguments of litigants, too, and in the provisos of contracts bearing on playhouses, plague had come to be taken for granted as a significant factor in the world of public drama. On May 9, 1609, for instance, Edward Kirkham noted his agreement to pay a fee of £10 per six-month period for his company of children to use a particular playhouse for their regular performances, but "if the said children should not play or make any shows the full time of six months in every year by reason of any prohibition or pestilence in the city," then the group would be required to pay only £0.16.8 per month for the months when they did play.³ Again, in February 1610, Robert Keysar, litigating about a former lease he had held from Shakespeare's associate, the famous actor Richard Burbage, on the Blackfriars playing space, claimed that he had gone to the trouble of keeping his playing company together two years to his "exceeding charge" in order to have his plays ready "upon the ceasing of the general sickness." Burbage and his associates, responding four days later, though disputing many details in Keysar's testimony agreed that he did have trouble keeping his company together by reason of "the plays ceasing in the City of London either through sickness or for some other cause" that forced the company to be "dispersed and driven each of them to provide for himself."⁴ In another instance Cuthbert Burbage, brother of the famous actor and also one of Shakespeare's associates, testified in 1612 that these former holders of the Blackfriars lease had found long before that no great "profit and commodity [could be] raised and made of and by the said playhouse as was hoped for and expected" even in the first year of James's reign by reason of the "great visitation of sickness in the cities of London and Westminster."⁵ As late as 1639, when the great plague visitation of 1625 would be a memory, John Shanks described a share in a playing company as one yielding profits which "are things very casual and subject to be discontinued and lost by sickness and divers other ways and to yield no profit at all" (*MSC*, 2.3:368).

Thomas Dekker also suggests the effect of plague on actors and dramatists in these times. In 1609 he again turned to pamphlet writing because plague again had closed the playhouses, and in *Work*

3. For the text, see H. N. Hillebrand, *The Child Actors* (Urbana: University of Illinois Press, 1926), p. 335.
4. See C. W. Wallace, *Shakespeare and His London Associates* (Lincoln: University of Nebraska Press, 1910), pp. 83, 97.
5. See F. G. Fleay, *A Chronicle History of the London Stage, 1559–1642* (London, 1890), p. 235.

for Armorers (printed in 1609) he made further observations about the plague worth quoting in full:

> Pleasure itself finds now no pleasure but in sighing and bewailing the miseries of the time. For (alack) what string is there now to be played upon whose tench can make us merry? Play-houses stand (like taverns that have cast out their masters) the doors locked up, the flags (like their bushes) taken down; or rather like houses lately infected, from whence the affrighted dwellers are fled, in hope to live better in the country. The players themselves did never work till now, their comedies are all turned to tragedies, their tragedies to nocturnals, and the best of them all are weary of playing in those nocturnal tragedies. Think you to delight yourselves by keeping company with our poets? *Proh Dolor!* Their muses are more sullen than old monkeys. Now that money is not stirring, they never plead cheerfully but in their term-times when the two-penny clients and penny stinkards swarm together to hear the Stagerites. Playing vacations are diseases now as common and as hurtful to them as the Foul Evil to a Northern Man or the Pox to a Frenchman. [*Nec dant proceres neque histriones*: marginal gloss]. . . .
>
> To walk every day into the fields is wearisome; to drink up the day and night in a tavern, loathsome, to be ever riding upon that beast with two heads (lechery) most damnable, and yet to be ever idle is detestable. What merry gale shall we then wish for? Unless it be to ferry over the Hellespont, and to cross from Sestos to Abydos, that is to say from London to the Bear Garden? The company of the Bears hold together still; they play their tragicomedies as lively as ever they did: the pied bull here keeps atossing and a roaring when the Red Bull dares not stir.[6]

The constant presence of such a situation disturbs traditionally positioned theories of a sequential and patterned course of Shakespeare's dramatic composition even after *King Lear* and *Antony and Cleopatra*. Plague was a stubborn and erratic phenomenon thwarting the imposition of a logical order on all Shakespeare's Stuart production. The scene directs the observer to imagine clusters of Shake-

6. Dekker, *Non-Dramatic Works*, 4:96–97. "Tench" is obscure and may signify the initial stretching or tuning of the string of a musical instrument. "*Nec dant proceres . . .*" I take as "neither the illustrious [audience] nor the [common] players remain." The reference to the relative immunity of bear gardens from plague closings is strange but valid and warrants investigation by scholars. Henslowe's *Diary* (p. 264) indicates his reception of moneys from this activity at a time when playhouses were presumably closed from plague. But the order for mourning the death of Prince Henry, not a matter of plague hygiene, specifically includes bear-baitings with plays (*MSC*, 1.1:88).

speare plays emerging in brief periods of intense productivity: a two-year hiatus, then *Othello* and *Measure for Measure* in 1604, sixteen to twenty-two months of further hiatus, then *Macbeth, Antony and Cleopatra,* and *King Lear* by the end of 1606.

If this narrative is at least plausible, then the remaining plays in Shakespeare's canon pose particular difficulties as one attempts to envision Shakespeare's mode of dramatic production. For three plays—*Coriolanus, Timon of Athens,* and *Two Noble Kinsmen*— there are no printing or performance records at all in Shakespeare's lifetime. Although traditionally ascribed to Shakespeare's "final period" on the basis of style and other kinds of "internal evidence," they could have been composed, strictly speaking, any time during Shakespeare's professional career. To include them, however tangentially, in this final chapter is to reinforce this supposition, but they form no integral part of my narrative.[7] I focus instead on those dramas for which there is some information during the period in which Shakespeare lived: *Pericles, Cymbeline, Winter's Tale, Tempest,* and *Henry VIII.*[8] Assuming that Shakespeare wrote *Pericles* and *Henry VIII,* I inquire into the rate at which he may have produced all five final plays. Thus my narrative begins after the 1606 Christmas season, when Shakespeare was forty-two, and proceeds to the destruction of the Globe playhouse by fire in 1613. This seven-year span was again marked pronouncedly by disruption: indeed, in Sections I and II I suggest that from 1606 to December 1610, when plague would cease for the remainder of Shakespeare's lifetime, the public playhouses were not likely to have been open for more than a total of nine months.

In this situation, once again, it would appear that Shakespeare responded only to performance opportunities. In Sections III and IV I contend that *Pericles* and *Cymbeline* were produced at the Globe between 1608 and 1610, prior to the cessation of plague (*Pericles* in

7. Because *Coriolanus,* like *Macbeth,* has inspired considerable debate over its date by reference to topical allusions, I briefly discuss this tragedy in Appendix 5.

8. Though Shakespeare's partial authorship of *Pericles* is still somewhat controversial, the arguments are too lengthy to rehearse here. The play is included in this study for those who assume that Shakespeare was the major author of the drama. For various views on this issue, see *Pericles,* Arden edition, ed. F. D. Hoeniger (London: Methuen, 1963), pp. lii–lxiii.

Although the play *Cardenio* was twice included in performance lists, there is no extant text of it (*MSC,* 6:55–56). *Cardenio* was entered in the stationers' register on September 9, 1653, by Moseley as "by Mr. Fletcher and Shakespeare"; see John Freehafer, "*Cardenio,* by Shakespeare and Fletcher," *PMLA* 84 (1969), 501–513.

1608, not in 1606 with *Antony and Cleopatra*, nor in 1607; *Cymbeline* in 1610, prior to Simon Forman's viewing in 1611). *Winter's Tale* and *Tempest* may both be dated in 1611, with *Winter's Tale* appearing at the Globe shortly after it reopened; but documents offer other information bearing on the place of both plays in Shakespeare's production.

In the end, one might be tempted to correlate performance opportunities with probable dates of first production for these four plays and assume, additionally, that Shakespeare worked in spates, that the plays assigned by tradition-oriented criticism to this same period—*Coriolanus* and *Timon of Athens*—fit into one or another of these windows of opportunity. But there is no way of exploring this notion. Nor is there a convincing theory, unless it be Shakespeare's retirement to Stratford, for the seeming hiatus between *Winter's Tale* and *Tempest* (1611) and *Henry VIII* (1613)—a plague-free period in which one might expect increased production. But the present narrative is not best served by attempting to pursue its own symmetry, having eschewed such structuring in other arguments about Shakespeare's canon. It is sufficient to suggest that Shakespeare's "final period" may be viewed as has the time that preceded it—in terms of the pressure points that were produced by playhouse closings. In this respect, the ending of Shakespeare's creative period deviates little from the general thrust of his entire Stuart career.

I

Before we follow the interaction of theatrical activity and plague between 1607 and 1610, let us briefly recall the plague situation from 1606 to 1608 (from Chapter 5, Section I). Plague deaths for the last week of December 1606 (when *King Lear* first surfaced) were at 38. In January and February of the new year, Shakespeare and his fellows were probably still unable to play at the Globe; they might have worked for a week after Easter before being restrained. Plays then were not possible from May through December 1607. In late December, infection subsided but then the weather became extremely cold, freezing the Thames over and such atypical temperatures probably inhibiting open-air performances. Contemporary references to this extreme cold continued through January 1608 and are to be found as late as February 28, Lent having already begun on Ash Wednesday, February 10.

To continue these annals from that point, Easter came on March 27, and though the playhouses were temporarily enjoined from opening as late as Easter Tuesday (the crown responded to ambassadorial complaint about a boys' company play), the matter was probably soon resolved.[9] So, between April and some time in July 1608, the playhouses were again briefly open. On July 14, however, there began a siege of plague which, though not as spectacular as those visitations of 1592 and 1603, was to prove the longest-lived of Shakespeare's career.

On July 14 the weekly plague deaths, which had been creeping upward, jumped from 16 to 26. "Our bill is shrewdly risen this week to 102 whereof 26 of the plague," wrote Sir John Chamberlain (*Chamberlain*, 1:262). The rise continued, and steeply, for the bill of mortality appearing on July 28 listed plague deaths for the week at 50. In August the weekly climb continued, 70, 79, 73, 123, and increased through early September. The weekly rate stood at 136 on the eighth, when William Shakespeare, his company idle, might well have been in Stratford-upon-Avon for the funeral of his mother.

Even the peerage, often safe from plague because of their standard of living, began to worry. Dudley Carleton now noted with concern that Parliament was to be postponed until the following February 1609, "in regard of the sickness though there be very good order taken, more than usual." The production of these new orders in 1608 and 1609 is in itself sufficient testimony to the perceived seriousness of the situation.[10]

On September 16, the countess of Bedford left the queen's circle at Hampton Court because one of the countess's own household had succumbed to the sickness. The queen herself had agreed to stand as godmother of the earl of Arundel's new child, but on September 20 the christening was put off for a week, "so as then for a night or two the Queen will be at London if the number of them that die of the plague do not increase" (*L'Isle*, 4:44). On September 22, the king, on his way from Theobalds back to Hampton Court,

9. See E. K. Chambers, *The Elizabethan Stage*, 4 vols. (Oxford: Clarendon Press, 1923), 2:53–55.

10. See *Carleton*, p. 106 and *L'Isle*, 4:44. The reference may have to do with the revision of the London plague orders to conform with the national program. In 1608 a revision (*STC* 16723) established a weekly tax on infected parishes, and in 1609 another (*STC* 9341) appointed six surgeons who were to divide the city among themselves. These standardized orders were reprinted in 1630, 1636, 1646, and 1665; see Paul Slack, *The Impact of Plague on Tudor and Stuart England* (London: Routledge and Kegan Paul, 1985), pp. 214–215.

rode through London without halting (*SPV*, 11:177). In October, Sir Robert Sidney felt alarm that his son-in-law had fallen ill and might have plague. Indeed, two other servants had died in the palace housing the queen, and so on October 23 she herself determined to remove to London. John Chamberlain noted on October 21 that the weekly bill had abated little; it listed one hundred twenty-seven deaths from plague.[11]

November 1608 held much the same story. Deaths during one week stood at 69 from plague, and on November 26 King James himself expressed anger that the lord chamberlain had not sent him the bill of sickness for the week (*SPD*, 8:470). Weekly plague deaths were still as high as 47 at the end of December, and 39 at the new year.[12] There were, however, "balls and comedies" all Christmas week at court, and Shakespeare's company presented twelve plays whose titles have not been recorded (*SPV*, 11:212). But they were the only plays by the King's Servants allowable in the entire London area for the previous five months, the playhouses having been closed since the middle of July.

On February 3, 1609, the Venetian ambassador observed that the plague death figures—56 for the previous week—were causing alarm about what the summer might bring (*SPV*, 11:232). Indeed the death numbers would shoot up to 90 for the reporting week ending February 9, causing John Chamberlain and other persons to comment with some concern.[13] Even when cold weather came, about a week after Lent had started (March 1), the death figures still stood at 32, rising yet again in several weeks, while the outbreak of two plague cases in Greenwich where King James had been in residence caused him to remove to Hampton Court. Easter, April 16, brought no solace for theater people either, since London was still being described as a "plaguey town" as worry continued with the latest weekly plague deaths at 93.[14]

That the situation was quite bad for professional actors is easily imagined, but it is also indicated by a document dated ten days later, on April 26, with the plague-figure listing 86 deaths. Paid now for the twelve plays at court over the holidays of 1608–9, Shakespeare and his fellows, by the same warrant, were also given an extra £40

---

11. See *L'Isle*, 4:53, 63, *I*, Chamberlain, 1.264.

12. See Birch, *James I*, 1:82.

13. *Chamberlain*, 1:283; Birch, *James I*, 1:89; *SPV*, 11:232; and *SPD*, 8:492.

14. See *Chamberlain*, 1:283; Birch, *James I*, 1:89–90, 96; and Sir Ralph Winwood, *Memorials of Affairs of State*, 3 vols., ed. Edmund Sawyer (London, 1725), 3:6.

(more than that 1603 fee for coming to Wilton from Mortlake). This money, the warrant reads, was "by way of his Majesty's reward for their private practice in the time of infection that thereby they might be enabled to perform their service before his Majesty in Christmas holidays [1608–] 1609." (*MSC*, 6:47)

John Hemmings, that member of Shakespeare's company who had annually collected the court moneys due the King's Servants since the beginning of James's reign, apparently made a separate trip to collect this £40. He had picked up payment at Whitehall for twelve plays on April 5 in Lent (*MSC*, 6:47), but twenty-one days later he collected this "reward," again at Whitehall, on a separate warrant. Again, no other company received a similar reward, so again one assumes some kind of intervention by someone at court. The king himself was at Theobalds on April 26.

The plague situation continued bad through the spring of 1609. In April, the bishop of Rochester was unwilling to come to court to see the king because he had been exposed to infection. He was still reluctant to approach James by the end of the month, and there seemed to have been a general feeling that a medical emergency existed. Plague deaths were at 92 in the first week of May. "The plague is unusually active," wrote Marc'Antonio Correre: "Those who have charge of the City are beginning to think of taking steps for the care of the sick and the safety of the sound. The other day the Earl of Salisbury asked me for details as to the steps which were taken in Venice in such circumstances."[15]

So the spring of 1609 was theatrically empty, as was the summer. In June, after term time had ended, the upper classes left the town. Plague dominated the city. July and August were plague-filled, but Bartholomew Fair was allowed to open on August 26 (even though plague deaths had been reported on the weekly bill at 150).[16] There was a food shortage in England, and the fair was thought necessary. The severity of the death toll from plague led to a delay in opening the law courts for Michaelmas term (210 plague deaths as of the September 21 report). A week later, September 29, another proclamation (*STC* 8440, 8441) put off the beginning of Parliament as the ambassador from Venice himself commented on "the fury of the plague." On October 12 he wrote, "The plague is not only active

---

15. See *SPV*, 11:273; see also *Hatfield*, 21:46, 50.

16. See Birch, *James I*, 1:100, and F. P. Wilson, *The Plague in Shakespeare's London* (London: Oxford University Press, 1963), p. 121.

here, but is spreading everywhere to such an extent that the Queen said they were safe nowhere. Last week she lost her groom of the robes." On October 19, the king's household at Royston—where he had gone early in October to spend a month hunting—was stricken. At about the same time, another of the attendants in the queen's household at Hampton Court died. Plague deaths in London stood at 131 for the week (*SPV*, 11:363, 365, 373–374).

Nevertheless, the annual influx of royalty and of the peerage for the All Saints' festivities of November 1 was not cancelled. By October 30, 1609, all were in place at Whitehall, plague deaths being still at 55. Did the actors play at court during All Saints'? Neither the Prince's Servants nor the Queen's Servants were paid for that celebration, and the payments to Shakespeare's company for this year are not itemized by dates. In previous years, with plague figures high at All Saints', the crown did not entertain players. As for the public theater opportunities, plague deaths in November averaged in the seventies and the theaters must have remained closed. Two deaths in the kitchen at Whitehall alarmed the royal family and made the queen think of removing to Hampton Court, the king himself being about to depart for Royston to resume hunting on December 11.[17]

It was now getting cold and, more important, dry, driving plague deaths down from 51 to 28 for the report of December 7, 1609 (*SPV*, 11:401). That the playhouses were permitted to open immediately is dubious. Putting oneself in the place of the London council, or of the privy council of England, for that matter, one might place this figure of 28 plague deaths in the frightening context of seventeen unabated months of plague—the longest continuous plague seizure of Shakespeare's professional lifetime. The question the authorities must have asked was, Do we permit public gatherings again, right now, on December 7, merely because plague deaths are suddenly down from 51 to 28 per week?

A more prudent course would have been to wait and see what the next weekly figures might bring. Deaths sank from 28 to 23, then held at 23 for the following week, and then rose to 39 for the week of December 28. The weekly reports after that were 32, 19, 31, and 17 to the end of January 1610. I suggest that the playhouses were kept closed all December and perhaps through January; for, as previously mentioned, the authorities knew what plague figures were

17. See *L'Isle*, 4:163, and *SPV*, 11:389, for plague matters.

typical (and undisturbing) for this time of year: 5–8 deaths per week, not 19 or 17.

For December 1609, at least, there is strong indication that there were no public plays; there survives another warrant (issued several months later, in Lent, in March 1610) for a royal plague gratuity to the King's Servants, "being restrained from public playing within the City of London in the time of infection during the space of six weeks in which time they practised privately for his Majesty's service" (*MSC*, 6:48).

In this situation, John Hemmings collected a bit less, £30, than in the previous year. The money came in a separate warrant dated March 10—eight days after the warrant paying the group for the holiday season's thirteen plays. The plague death figures had not been excessively high, but a guess that the companies did not play at the public playhouses in December 1609 is, it seems, borne out by the existence of this financial award to Shakespeare and his fellows.

The end of the first month of the new year 1610 may, however, have seen a reopening of the public playhouses. By February comes the (admittedly relative) statement that the city has not for a long time past been as free of plague "as it was all this winter" (*SPV*, 11:427). Plague deaths sank to 10 in the week of Ash Wednesday (February 21). In fact, a play had already been suppressed by February 9. When, then, were the theaters reopened? When had this suppressed play been acted, suggesting a time when Shakespeare could have had access to the Globe again?

On February 8, 1610, the king's English first cousin, Arabella Stuart, first lady at court after the queen and a possible claimant to the throne, complained in a letter that "in a certain comedy the playwright introduced an allusion to her person and the part played by the Prince of Moldavia." The play was suppressed. It must have been played sometime between December 29, 1609 (when Arabella was placed under guard for several days on the suspicion that she was planning to elope to France with Sir George Douglas) and February 8.[18]

---

18. Arabella's embarrassment at the hands of Moldavia had been established through a series of disclosures. On January 18, 1610, the Venetian ambassador (*SPV*, 11.414) told the doge that Sir George Douglas was not the object of romance with Arabella at all. His role, rather, had been to bear messages from Arabella to Stephen Bogdan, pretender to Moldavia, who had negotiated for marriage with Arabella months before. But King James had told Bogdan to return to the continent and secure

I have argued that most of January must have seen the theaters still closed. To repeat, Lady Arabella complained about the play on February 8, so the drama was probably produced in early February when plague death figures were at 21 and then 11. Thus I suggest that the playhouses were open again in early February 1610, Ash Wednesday, however, coming February 21.

Spring 1610, after Easter on April 8, must have seen normal playing at the Globe and at the other public and private playhouses in and around London. Indeed, Prince Lewis Frederick of Wurttemburg went to the Globe on Monday, April 30 to see *Othello*.[19] But the playing season this spring was again a short one, for after a three-month hiatus plague, incredibly, once again appeared on the scene, at the beginning of July. Yet the playhouses may have been closed even sooner—because of a far different and highly dramatic event that shook the court.

On May 4, 1610 (the playhouses were still presumably open), Henry IV, king of France, was assassinated. The event stunned the English court. King James had been away at Royston, his hunting lodge, but on hearing the news he rushed back to London. Because Henry IV was a Protestant king, there was fear of a similar attempt on James and so all known troublesome Catholics in England were immediately jailed (*SPV*, 11:501). The queen dismissed one of her ladies of the bedchamber who, though "gently reproved" for it a number of times before, had habitually carried a stiletto in her purse. An oath of allegiance was "voluntarily" taken by all whose duties placed them near the person of the king, and the oath was also required of all clerics, all lawyers and judges, and all students at Oxford, Cambridge, and the inns of court (*Annals*, sig. 4G3).

In this atmosphere the playhouses themselves may have been closed, for they had been shut immediately following the discovery

---

documentation for his claim to the princedom, and Bogdan had subsequently found this documentation something of a problem to obtain. Instead, by January 18, he was in Venice, and after unsuccessfully claiming to the British ambassador there that he was engaged to Arabella and was entitled to housing and honors he seems to have married someone else. Thus, by January 18, 1610, the time of the letter describing this situation, there was probably public matter for some playwright's merriment whether or not the story was true. See, for instance, *DNB*, article on Arabella Stuart which emphasizes her liaison with Seymour, her future husband, at this time. Whatever the case, the deed had apparently been done by February 8. See also *SPV*, 11:414–427.

19. See W. B. Rye, *England as Seen by Foreigners* (London, 1865), p. 61. The prince dated English style, since he placed 30 April on "Lundi."

of the Gunpowder Plot and also after Queen Elizabeth's death, when mourning was not unmixed with fear of civil disorder. Further, the court itself was ordered into official mourning for Henry IV, wearing full black, which was still the costume on May 24. It would continue to be so until May 30, the Wednesday after Whitsuntide, when the installation of another Henry as England's prince of Wales would presumably dissipate the clouds of woe, twenty-six days after the assassination.

Certainly the playhouses had been open on April 30; *Othello* had been performed then at the Globe. Henry IV was killed on May 4, but news of the event does not seem to have impacted the English court until May 7 (*SPV*, 11:485). If the playhouse were closed, it was probably for two weeks at the end of May. But all of June 1610 seems to favor open playhouses until July 5, when plague deaths in the city were reported at 38 for the previous week. Robert Cecil, earl of Salisbury, corresponding with the king via Sir Thomas Lake, wrote then:

> My Lord Chancellor and I and my Lord Privy Seal with some others have caused strict watch to be kept upon the infected houses in the City and suburbs, by laying in his Majesty's name a severe charge upon the Mayor and Aldermen who with the justices have been ordered to meet before this filthy Fair of St. Bartholomew [August 22], memorable for a massacre and continual origin of the plague.[20]

During August 1610, the weekly plague death figures rose from 47 to 99 at the end of the month, and September brought similar figures. Marc'Antonio Correre, the Venetian envoy, in fact determined to stay out of London for some weeks after a young man in his own suite died of plague. The royal family itself did not come close to the city, staying at Greenwich or Hampton Court until it grew colder (*SPV*, 12:41, 50–51). This was a wait of some weeks; the weekly plague deaths remained in the sixties and seventies through October 1610, with the queen deciding to stay out of town at Hampton Court until Christmas (*L'Isle*, 4:234). At the end of October, deaths from plague stood at 58 for the week. Earlier on, at the end of September 1610, James had fallen ill enough for the queen to go to him at Greenwich and bring him back to Hampton Court. He had nothing resembling plague, but he was still too weak on October 11 for his doctors to allow him full freedom of action.

20. *Hatfield*, 21:230. James had left the city on July 25 for his progress (*SPV*, 12:24).

Finally, James seems to have come to London to honor the November 1 celebration of All Saints' Day and to open Parliament, primarily because he needed that body to vote large sums of money for the crown as soon as possible (*SPV*, 12:56, 73).

Whatever the case at court, in any event, public plays were probably still prohibited during this autumn of 1610. Although the Venetian ambassador on November 15 would consider the plague to be so far diminished as to be all but extinct because only 22 deaths had been reported for the week, plague death figures jumped by twenty to 42 for the seven days following and were still no lower than 39 for the week after that, only sinking far down to 15 in the report of December 6.

Playhouses had been closed since July. Did they open after December 6? Correre remarked on January 28, 1611, that "the city is almost quite free of plague, contrary to general expectation, for the great damp of the winter led people to look for much sickness."[21] Were the city and the privy council concerned enough, therefore, to close playhouses in advance, or did they allow playing in December 1610 and wait for Lent, which would inhibit playing anyhow? Whatever the case, the playhouses must have opened without hindrance after Easter, March 24, 1611, and remained open throughout the whole year, plague now ceasing to be a problem for the remainder of Shakespeare's career. Thus ended a span of time extending from July 1608 through November 1610 which included at least twenty-four months in which the public playhouses had been closed because of plague.

All performances of new Shakespeare plays in this period could have taken place only at court, with a few exceptions: the public theaters were probably open for most of the period between February and June 1610, with closures for Lent and possibly at the end of May for the assassination of Henry IV. Whether the court performances from 1608 to 1610 included any new plays by Shakespeare is the concern of the sections III and IV, as is the possible emergence of new plays from 1611 to 1613, when plague was no longer a factor in the public theaters. The cessation of these crippling sieges that had inhibited performance opportunities so profoundly was ironically coincident with the end of Shakespeare's professional career.

21. *SPV*, 12:132. This ready association of dampness with chances for plague is significant to the general point made in Chapter 3 about the (relative) accuracy of some contemporary observations and the role of humidity in propagating the activities of the rat flea bearing bubonic plague.

II

Have we not forgotten an important change in the activities of the King's Servants that might alter the scenario just sketched? What of the move to the private playhouse at the Blackfriars? Might not this playhouse, opened in a liberty inside London, have offered some kind of refuge in these plague years?

It has long been known that on February 4, 1596, James Burbage, father of Richard Burbage and entrepreneur whose theatrical experiments define the early history of Shakespeare's company, purchased space in the old Blackfriars building in the city of London.[22] Nine months later, the upper-class residents of the area surrounding the old Blackfriars monastery petitioned the privy council to stop Burbage, complaining that "the said Burbage is now altering and meaneth very shortly to convert and turn the same into a common playhouse." Evidently the privy council supported this petition, for they "forbad the use of the said house for plays."[23]

Despite this frustration, Richard Burbage and his brother Cuthbert (their father now being dead) continued to extend their Blackfriars holdings by the purchase of an interest in more property there, an interest whose fruition would have to wait upon the death of one of the other owners (*MSC*, 2.1:70–76). Nevertheless, the Burbage brothers continued their purchasing program, buying more space in the Blackfriars structure in 1601, 1610, and 1614. There seems to have been some long-range (Burbage) plan here that did not necessarily involve drama, despite what Chambers and, later, Schoenbaum have inferred.[24] Surely the Burbage brothers must have assumed that any future public theatrical enterprise might be opposed by the residents as they had opposed it in 1596—and many of the residents were quite powerful. Henry, first Lord Hunsdon, lord chamberlain, for example, had been one of the 1596 petitioners against the playhouse, despite the fact that he was the titular sponsor of the Lord Chamberlain's Servants, the company of which the Burbages and Shakespeare were members.

Further, the Burbages had revealed a lack of personal theatrical

---

22. See James O. Halliwell-Phillipps, *Outlines of the Life of Shakespeare*, 2 vols. (London, 1889), 1:299–304.

23. See *MSC*, 1.1:90, and Chambers, *Elizabethan Stage*, 2:507–509.

24. Chambers, *Elizabethan Stage*, 2:508–512, and S. Schoenbaum, *William Shakespeare: A Documentary Life* (New York: Oxford University Press, 1975), p. 213.

ambitions for this area when, in 1600, they leased their aborted
acting space in the Blackfriars building as a theater for a children's
company—the Children of the Chapel Royal, to be renamed in 1604
the Children of the Queen's Revels—presumably more acceptable
to the residents. This lease to the children's group was for twenty-
one years, a standard term showing no great confidence on the part
of the Burbages in the Blackfriars area's future availability to an
adult company of common players. This lack of confidence seems
to have been emphasized four years later when, in 1604, those who
had leased the space from the Burbages for the children's company—
Henry Evans and others—approached the Burbages for an early ter-
mination of their lease. The Burbages did nothing about this offer.
Their inaction, unless they were bargaining hard, suggests their continuing sense of the inviable nature of the location for the dramatic
purposes they themselves had envisioned before they were stopped
back in 1596. Indeed, after 1596 had come the privy council orders
of 1600 and 1601 stipulating the allowed number of playhouses in
the city. As recently as 1606, the Red Bull enterprise in hand by
Martin Slater and Aaron Holland trying to form a new company at
a new playhouse had been summarily halted, Cecil acting for the
privy council.[25]

Four more years later, in 1608, the Burbages received new over-
tures by the owners of the Children of the Queen's Revels. Their
troubles, encountered during the previous Lent of 1608, had led to
serious problems. In July 1608, plague kept the Blackfriars closed,
but, if there had not been plague, there was the continued prohibition
of the young players alluded to by the offended French ambassador
La Boderie when the boys were closed down on March 29, 1608. For
such reasons, presumably, the leaseholders made another overture
to the Burbages and were this time successful, negotiating a surrender of their lease. In the same summer of this surrender, new leases
of the Blackfriars space were executed on August 9. They involved
a new syndicate, made up of William Shakespeare and four of his
fellows among the King's Servants, who became the new
leaseholders.[26]

What was the purpose in all this? The desire by Shakespeare and

25. Cecil Papers 197/91[e], in the collection at Hatfield House, *not* 199 91(2) as
per calendar in *Hatfield*, 17:234.
26. See Chambers, *Elizabethan Stage*, 2:53–54, 213–214.

his fellows to acquire an exclusive and more expensive playhouse outside of the jurisdiction of the city has been the favorite scholarly answer, but this explanation may oversimplify.[27] Why did the Burbages now want to cooperate in lifting the lease from the children's company?

The Burbages had some reasons for *not* responding earlier. There were many other ways for them to dispose of the property. In fact, the usual method would be to turn their space in the old Blackfriars building into apartments for wealthy and privileged persons—such as those who had signed the petition in 1596—whose in-town houses were to be found throughout this Blackfriars area of the city. Furthermore, there was no reason to believe that the residents of this area would now be any more sympathetic to a new public theater in their neighborhood than they had been twelve years earlier. Nor was it worth trying to establish a playhouse in an area such as the Blackfriars because it was a liberty, exempt from city jurisdiction and thus safer for acting. Indeed, if any such protection was indeed possible for actors playing in Blackfriars because the area was still connected with the crown, this protection was soon to disappear, a fact of which Burbage and his fellows cannot have been ignorant during the 1608 August in which they made up the new lease. In barely a month, on September 30, 1608, a new charter would formally extend the jurisdiction of the city of London to include Blackfriars. The district would no longer offer protection from the city authorities.[28]

In any case, the question of whether a Blackfriars acting place could afford protection to the King's Servants from plague closings would be clearly settled early in the fall. Whitefriars, an area legally and historically comparable to Blackfriars, was yielded to the city by the crown at the same time as was Blackfriars. At this time, as previously observed, the public theaters remained closed by plague: on August 11, 1608, when the new Blackfriars syndicate was formed, the weekly bill of mortality showed 70 deaths from plague. Several months later, on October 19, plague was still raging and Shakespeare's troupe was thus (significantly) playing in Coventry instead of at the Globe. Now, in October, some arrests were made. Those jailed were theater people who had acquired space in the Whitefriars in March 1608.

27. See Schoenbaum, *William Shakespeare, A Documentary Life*, pp. 213–214.
28. See Chambers, *Elizabethan Stage*, 2:480, 511.

item. William Pollard and Rice Gwynn were by this Court committed to the jail of Newgate there to remain during the pleasure of this Court, for that they yesterday last suffered a stage play to be publicly acted in the Whitefriars during the time of the present infection contrary to his Majesty's late proclamation. (*MSC*, 2.3:318–319)

Clearly these former liberties of Whitefriars and Blackfriars were not to be refuges for actors trying to play in plague time. Nor were Shakespeare and his fellows, now far away in Coventry, trying to use Blackfriars in this manner. They obviously understood the situation, even if Pollard and Gwynn did not.

If the private theaters were not opened to combat plague closings, they may have been opened to combat weather. The winter experienced by London in 1607–8 may provide some explanation. Le Roy Ladurie's well-known study of the "little ice age" in Europe has perhaps encouraged overenthusiastic claims about the period in which Shakespeare lived. Commenting on H. H. Lamb's *Climate History and the Modern World* (1982), Le Roy Ladurie observed that "around 1600, the Alpine glaciers crushed the most exposed hamlets around Chamonix, marking the start of the new seventeenth-century cold spells" which were to continue until around 1850. The worst of these spells would occur in the 1690s and thus do not affect Shakespeare's lifetime.[29] But weather was emerging as something of a problem in the winter of 1607–8, before the summer in which the Blackfriars changed hands. Thick ice, as previously observed, had covered the Thames in December and January, and the idea of a winter playing house may have come to seem attractive to Shakespeare and his fellows. Certainly the anonymous author of *Historia Histrionica* would note that "before the wars there were in being all these playhouses at the same time. The Blackfriars and Globe on the Bankside: a winter and summer house belonging to the same company called the 'King's Servants'."[30] This distinction in seasons did not seem to have been necessary for Shakespeare and his fellows between 1593 and 1608.

Aside from plague or weather, there may simply have been some assurances of political support if residents complained about a playhouse in their midst. Now, in 1608, no objections seem to have been

29. See E. Le Roy Ladurie, *Times of Feast, Times of Famine*, trans. Barbara Bray, paperback edition (New York: Doubleday, 1988) with a new afterword, pp. 312–313.
30. James Wright, *Historia Histrionica* (London, 1699).

forthcoming, or, if there were any, they were ineffective. Theater at the Blackfriars becomes a well-known fact of the early Stuart era.

Estimating a time when performances started at the Blackfriars is therefore of some importance here, for the presence of an extra and possibly different theatrical outlet has obvious relevance to any argument about Shakespeare's production. But there is no definite indication of when Shakespeare's company began here. The payments by the court to the King's Servants for private practice during plague are the first suggestions of activity, but such activity was not necessarily at Blackfriars or before paying audiences. Nor does information from the title pages of plays performed by the King's Servants and published in the four years following 1608 offer enlightenment on an opening date for the Blackfriars. Title pages of plays published in the period often did indicate provenance, as is well known, but I find no indication of Blackfriars (title page) provenance for a play by the King's Servants until the 1625 quarto of Beaumont and Fletcher's *Scornful Lady.*

This hardly means that the King's Servants did not perform sooner at their new Blackfriars location; an extract from the depositions of John Hemmings and Richard Burbage, members of the new Blackfriars syndicate, responding to Edward Kirkham's litigation about the Blackfriars playing area, often guides the biographer of Shakespeare here. The deposition, dated November 2, 1612, states:

> And the said John Hemmings for himself further answereth and saith that he, this defendant, hath for the space of four years last past or thereabouts, [1608–12?] had and received and as yet doth receive a certain share or portion of such profits as did, or doth arise by such plays and interludes as were and are played in the said playhouse by virtue of a demise [conveyance by lease] of some part of the said playhouse granted unto him by the said other defendant, Richard Burbage, sythence [since] the surrender of the foresaid lease surrendered by the said Henry Evans, as aforesaid.[31]

Against this statement—or at least contributing to its ambiguity—is the plague restraint. No matter the date of ownership, after the summer 1608 execution of the new Blackfriars lease no playhouses would be allowed to open until at least January 1610. Further, in 1610 a foreign prince went to see *Othello* not at the more expensive Blackfriars but at the popular Globe. Thus the first known occasion

31. See Fleay, *Chronicle History,* p. 238.

(at least to the present writer) of a play at the new Blackfriars theater was January 10, 1611, for which a contemporary document records this note: "10s. January 10 for going unto a play at Blackfriars."[32] But a new play by Shakespeare, *Winter's Tale*, was to be performed at the larger playhouse in spring 1611 and seen by Simon Forman.

The relevance of the Blackfriars to Shakespeare's own production requires more investigation than there is space for here. Nonetheless, this study is unaffected by the actual opening of the new private playhouse. After the new syndicate acquired its lease, Shakespeare seems to have been denied the new Blackfriars space as often as he was denied the Globe.

III

Whatever the case with the Blackfriars playing place, the pattern of composition for William Shakespeare in this first Stuart decade seems to have remained consistent with his earlier Stuart practice. He produced plays when there was a prospect of their being performed; and when there was, Shakespeare's creative activity seems to have surged. *Pericles*, which can be dated within at least gross limits, illustrates and reinforces this point.

The play was apparently seen by the Venetian ambassador to England, Zorzi Giustinian, who went "with the French ambassador and his wife to a play called *Pericles*."[33] Scholars have usually put a performance of the play between January 5, 1606, and November 23, 1608, because, it is said, Giustinian was ambassador in England at that time. Furthermore, the French ambassador was Antoine LeFevre de La Boderie, ambassador-in-ordinary. Those dates of his stay coinciding with Giustinian's own time in England offer an intersection point for one performance, at least. A minor difficulty in the tradition is that Thornton Graves and, following him, E. K. Chambers, as well as the editor of the New Arden *Pericles*, all begin La Boderie's stay in England May 16, 1606, and this is incorrect. Zorzi Giustinian, the source of this information, dated his reports to Venice in the continental (new) style. Thus, if his May 18 letter noted that La Boderie arrived in England two days previously, this

32. See Lionel Cranfill's cashbook in "Sackville MSS," *Cranfield Papers*, 2 vols., ed. A. P. Newton (London, HMSO: 1940–66), 1:232.

33. See E. K. Chambers, *William Shakespeare*, 2 vols. (Oxford: Clarendon Press, 1930), 2:335, for the relevant documents.

arrival date was not May 16, 1606, but (English) May 6. By the same token, Giustinian did not leave England November 23, 1608, as he himself reported in his dated letter to the doge of Venice, but, by English reckoning, November 13.

Even given these minor adjustments, it is difficult to determine how soon after La Boderie's arrival in England he could have seen *Pericles* with Giustinian. In this spring, the theaters were open through the last week in June. From July to December 1606, as previously noted, the city playhouses were closed and probably still dark until early April 1607. Even then, a week of playing was halted as a result of a request to the lord chamberlain on April 12 to prohibit plays. From that time on, there was no public playing through December 1607 with the onset of extremely cold weather.

To continue reviewing familiar material, the playhouses were probably still closed through Lent and all of March 1608, but then open until mid-July. Then they were closed again up through the date on which Giustinian left England in the following November. To summarize, then, Giustinian and La Boderie could have seen *Pericles* together at three different times: May and June 1606, one week in April 1607, or April through mid-July 1608.

Pericles was entered in the stationers' register on May 20, 1608, and the entry seems to me ultimately misleading in connection with a date of first performance because commentary on the entry becomes confused with the performance history of *Antony and Cleopatra*. The two plays, as is well known, were entered together:

20 May [1608]

Edw.Blount. Entered for his copy under the hands of Sir George Buck, Knight, and Master Warden Seton, a book called *The Book of Pericles Prince of Tyre*. *Edw. Blunt* Entered also for his copy by the like authority a book called *Antony and Cleopatra*.[34]

Since many commentators, as well as I, have pushed the date of a first performance of *Antony and Cleopatra* back to 1606 (most critics, citing Daniel, guess at a two-year timespan that includes 1606), it is frequently assumed that *Pericles*, occupying the same entry, might also have been performed as many as two years earlier than the 1608 stationers' register date. But there are indications that

---

34. See W. W. Greg, *A Bibliography of the English Printed Drama to the Restoration*, 4 vols. (London: Bibliographical Society, 1939–62), 1:24.

Pericles was actually a much more recent play than *Antony and Cleopatra*—that it may have first been produced only shortly before the stationers' entry that describes it.

In this connection, it is important to consider that *Pericles* was extremely popular—perhaps even one of Shakespeare's greatest hits—no matter how bland it may seem to many modern palates. Two ambassadors went to see it, the title of the play even being recalled in the text that describes their playhouse visit. Further, a doggerel poem, *Pimlyco*, cited by A. H. Smyth as an allusion to the play, is more than simply referential.[35] Entered in the stationers' register April 15, 1609, the poem humorously celebrates a large beerhall in Hogsden (Hoxton), a district north of London and west of the Kingsland Road and north of Old Street Road which had apparently become very popular.[36] It was especially frequented in 1609 because, according to the dramatist Thomas Dekker, Pimlyco was one of the few places during plague-time open for some kind of entertainment:

> Oh pitiful Poetry, what a lamentable prenticeship hast thou served and (which is the greater spite) canst not yet be made free! No, no, there is no good doings in these days but amongst lawyers, amongst vintners, in bawdy-houses, and at Pimlico. There is all the music (that is, of any reckoning), there all the meetings, there all the mirth, and there all the money.[37]

The poem *Pimlyco*, published as a quarto with the date 1609 on the title page, celebrates this same beer hall, with the poet humorously exaggerating Pimlyco's wild popularity as a place of resort:

> Amazed I stood, to see a crowd
> Of civil throats stretched out so loud.
> As at a new play, all the rooms
> Did swarm with gentles mixed with grooms
> So that I truly thought all these
> Came to see *Shore* or *Pericles*.[38]

35. See Chambers, *William Shakespeare*, 2:217.

36. For Pimlyco and Hogsden, see the references collected by E. H. Sugden, *A Topographical Dictionary to the Works of Shakespeare and His Fellow Dramatists* (Manchester: Manchester University Press, 1925), pp. 251–52, 412.

37. See *Work for Armorers* in Dekker, *Non-Dramatic Works*, 4:97.

38. See *Pimlyco* (London, 1609) STC 19936. *Jane Shore* is mentioned as a new play in Beaumont and Fletcher's *Knight of the Burning Pestle*, which, however, is itself difficult to date. *Knight* was first printed in 1613.

In other words, the crowds and the mixing of classes made the event seem like the opening of a new play such as *Jane Shore* or *Pericles*.

To essay a date for the first production of *Pericles* in order to determine something about the continuity or discontinuity of Shakespeare's production after 1606, one can try to work backward from these verses, assuming a Jacobean reader's familiarity with the play in 1609. In this same year (whether earlier or later than *Pimlyco* it is impossible to determine), appeared both the first and the second quartos of *Pericles*, entitled "The Late and Much Admired Play Called Pericles Prince of Tyre . . . As It Hath Been Divers and Sundry Times Acted by His Majesty's Servants at the Globe on the Bankside. By William Shakespeare."

Three significant chronological points are suggested by the wording of this title. First, the early modern English adjective "late" commonly meant "recent." If, in *Pimlyco*, *Shore* and *Pericles* are presented as examples of popular new plays, the title pages of the *Pericles* quartos affirm this relative newness at some time in the year 1609. The second point implicit in the quarto title pages (reinforced by the *Pimlyco* remark) is that *Pericles* made a big impression—was "much admired." Further, there were two quartos in one year, and a third in 1611. Finally, the 1609 quarto title pages indicate that *Pericles* was acted at the Globe. Thus the play must have been performed prior to 1609 (a plague year), and consequently the title refers—as does *Pimlyco*—to the play's popular reception at a time when the Globe was open. A glance at Figure 1 suggests, however, that the most recent opportunity for such a Globe performance was no earlier than the first two weeks of July 1608, before plague resumed its sway in London. In sum, all these texts suggest that in 1609 *Pericles* was a very popular play shown at the public theater—recently.

Two earlier documents expand on this scenario. One is the well-known prose work of George Wilkins printed in 1608 and entitled "The Painful Adventures of Pericles Prince of Tyre. Being the True History of the Play of Pericles as it Was lately Presented by the Worthy and Ancient Poet John Gower." The book has a short "Argument" that concludes by stating that the play *Pericles* was "excellently presented" by "His Majesty's Servants" and "at the Globe" (sig. A3). The relevance of this short novel based on an amalgam of Gower's and of Thomas Twine's redactions of the old Latin tale of Apollonius of Tyre (the former in the *Confessio Amantis* [*STC*

12144] and the latter in *Painful Adventures* [*STC* 709]), and on Shakespeare too, has, I think, been misperceived by critics dealing with the problem of *Pericles*.[39] If Wilkin's text is not a line-by-line or scene-by-scene, or even episode-by-episode redaction of Shakespeare's play (as it is not), this need not necessarily raise great puzzles, nor are any great matters accomplished by painstakingly listing and disparaging the deviations, making the book seem a strange offering because it does not produce what it seems to advertise, a version of the play. The text is best considered for itself, and as a document offering pertinent information about the date and circumstances of the Shakespeare play.[40]

Painful Adventures indicates, to put it simply, that the author, in 1608, purports to be offering a "history" of the popular play *Pericles* shown at the Globe. But in presenting this history the author, even though using the Shakespearean names "Pericles" and "Marina" (neither is in Gower or in Twine; only in Shakespeare) as well as some Shakespearean episodes, pulls in other material from the traditional and available printed Twine and Gower tales about Pericles/Apollonius of Tyre.

That Wilkins had actually seen Shakespeare's play as he claims in his introduction, whatever his conflations, is, however, clear—from a series of trivialities. Shakespeare and Wilkins both present a tournament scene that appears in no other version of the story; it has never been pointed out how accurately Wilkins mirrors Shakespeare's presentation here. Very briefly, there is a parade of six tournament knights (the last being Pericles), each of whom has three identifying attributes: a nationality, an emblem on his shield, and a motto on the shield explaining the emblem. Assuming that Shakespeare's play is his source, we can note that Wilkins (sigs. C4ᵛ-D), while wobbly about the nationalities, couples emblems and mottos precisely as they are coupled in the *Pericles* quartos in each case, even though the latter was published only after Wilkins's own book came out. The only divergences are that Wilkins has slightly varied the order in which the knights appear (for Shakespeare's 1, 2, 3, 4, 5, 6, Wilkins has 1, 3, 2, 5, 4, 6). Further, Wilkins in all cases confuses the announced nationalities of the knights—but in two cases where the play quarto does not give nationalities at all, Wilkins adds them.

---

39. For a review of source studies here, see *Pericles*, ed. Hoeniger, pp. xiii-xix.

40. For discussion of Wilkins, see Wilkins, *The Painful Adventures*, ed. Kenneth Muir (Liverpool: The University of Liverpool Press, 1953), pp. iii-xv and *Pericles*, ed. Hoeniger, pp. lix-lxii.

In other words, Wilkins remembered what he *saw* painted on shields, where the emblems and the mottos were displayed, but the nationalities of the various knights, announced by an actor on stage, as well as the order of their appearance he misremembered, but remembered better than the quarto! Neither slip excludes him from having seen the play, for otherwise he is quite accurate.

But given his accuracies, why did Wilkins proceed to combine his correct memories—visual devices, the names of the two leading characters—with extraneous sequences from *older* printed versions of the original Apollonius story—Twine's and Gower's? Here is a narrative I propose for the situation.

After the theaters were closed by plague in July 1608, *Pericles*, already in production, could now no longer be seen at the Globe. But it had been so popular that it was now, in plague time, still worthwhile for someone to fashion a conflation—a kind of potpourri report—of this hit for those who had not been able to see the play or who could be persuaded to want a souvenir of it. Because the script would hardly have been available to Wilkins, he had to make do with his own memory of the production at the Globe supplemented by available printed versions of the tale. His purpose, as seems clear from both his title page and introduction, was not to hide any dependence on the play *Pericles, Prince of Tyre* but to sell books by associating his offering as closely as possible with the memory of the highly popular Globe performance of the play. "The True History of the Play of Pericles as it Was lately Presented by the Worthy and Ancient Poet John Gower" is the subtitle of Wilkin's work, and since Gower himself had been dead for several centuries, "lately" must have applied to the choric figure Gower in Shakespeare's play.

In 1609, further, no one (except perhaps those at court for the holidays) could see *Pericles* at all because of the plague. There was therefore money to be made by writing a book purporting to be all about this unseeable and vastly popular drama. The point seems to have been grasped only a little later by the acting company, or by whatever other agency allowed the playscript to be published in the quartos while plague still raged.

Given the validity of this scenario, the record of London playhouse availability (see Figure 1) suggests this chronological problem. If Wilkins saw *Pericles* at the Globe prior to the second half of 1608, he could first have seen it either in spring 1608, or before that during a brief interval in April 1607, or almost a year before that in 1606—

or, of course, earlier. But the farther one moves backward in time to an earlier date for *Pericles*, the dimmer becomes the relevance of recentness as suggested by "late" and "lately" in Wilkins's own description and in the quarto titles of 1609. In fact, from the viewpoint of the 1609 observer who thinks of *Pericles* as recent, one must posit it as a very popular play first presented at the Globe in April or May 1608, entered for some reason in the stationers' register almost immediately, on May 20, 1608, but then not available to the public at the Globe for seventeen months after mid-July. In this respect, the situation with *Pericles* is another reminder of how one ignores the problem of plague in this period not only to the detriment of chronology but also to the possible distortion of relationships between dramatic and nondramatic texts. Wilkins's work, for example, may not be the only reporting of a play to a reader-audience prevented from going to the playhouse by plague.

To recapitulate briefly, the performance of *Pericles* was itself made, uniquely in this period, the subject of a book by Wilkins in the same year the play opened but after the playhouses were shut by the authorities. Then, with the playhouses still closed, the playhouse script was printed in quarto twice in 1609 with a title page alluding to its recent popularity, an allusion seconded by the comment in *Pimlyco*. Finally, in additional support of this scenario, the play was seen at an uncertain date, but definitely between May 6, 1606, and November 13, 1608, whenever the playhouses were open, by the Venetian ambassador, the French ambassador and his wife, and the secretary from Florence (another indication of the play's popularity). Because this group presumably had numerous opportunities to be together in England, the traditional dating of *Pericles* has tended to split the difference and to place *Pericles* in 1607, or perhaps as early as 1606. But the record of theater closings suggests that the leeway is not that wide. The two ambassadors were friendly by June 1606, but plague had already begun. It was to continue throughout most of 1607, closing the theaters. They reopened in the spring of 1608, when the ambassadors were still in England socializing together, and it is then, presumably, that they saw *Pericles*.

Pericles may also have been close in time to Shakespeare's *Cymbeline*, but this possibility cannot be addressed without a consideration of Shakespeare's *Winter's Tale* and *Tempest* as well, for the circumstances affecting the first performances of these three plays are related. They are the subject of the following section.

IV

In his well-known "Book of Plays," Simon Forman chronicles the period from April 20 to May 15, 1611: seven folio sheets describe his experience. He saw four productions at the Globe, three of them Shakespearean: *Macbeth* on April 20, *Winter's Tale* on May 15, and *Cymbeline* at some unspecified time.[41] Forman's text cannot be taken alone as an indicator of the tempo of Shakespearean production; it must be considered together with records of court performances in the two Christmas seasons of 1610–11 and 1611–12. These latter suggest that *Cymbeline* was probably presented at court in the holidays before the Forman period, that it was performed at the Globe between March and June 1610, before the theaters were again closed by plague, and finally that it was separated from *Winter's Tale* and *Tempest*, which were probably first produced in the spring of 1611.

My discussion of these plays derives from the lucky amplitude of court performance records surviving for the interval April 1611–April 1613, which offer information relevant to the earliest production dates for Shakespeare's three "final comedies." This information is most useful in connection with the enunciation of two performance principles that seem to have obtained with the city companies in the first Stuart decade. The first principle is that before presenting a play at court the city companies ordinarily established its success in the public theater. Probably (or most certainly) some members of the aristocracy would have seen a new play being shown in the city at the Globe before it came to court, but this fact is irrelevant to the newness of the play at court. For the relevant audience at court, whoever the courtiers that might attend the play, was an audience of at most five: the monarch and his family, none of whom would ever go to the Globe.

This principle of the "proved play" is illustrated by the occasion

41. Because Forman wrote "1610" for the year in which he described his experiences as a playgoer, scholars have had to point out that next to the date "the 20 of April" Forman affixed his shortland symbol for "Saturday." Saturday fell on April 20 only in 1611, but Forman's absentminded retention of the former year in dating is understandable enough even in April when one recalls that for many persons Lady Day on March 25 was the beginning of the new year. For Forman, see Chambers, *William Shakespeare*, 2:337–341, and R. W. Hunt and J. Dover Wilson "The Authenticity of Simon Forman's *Bocke of Plaies*," in *RES* 23 (1947), 193–200.

of the performance at court of *Winter's Tale* in 1611. Simon Forman,
as previously mentioned, saw the play at the Globe in April 1611.
Then, Shakespeare and his fellows were paid for performing *Winter's
Tale* at court on November 5, 1611. This date in 1611 happened to
be particularly important; it had recently been officially sanctioned
by Parliament as a special commemorative anniversary of the Gunpowder Plot, to be celebrated forever after with thanksgiving. Something of the significance of the occasion is conveyed in the account
of the Venetian ambassador, who was invited to the palace for the
first celebration of this anniversary in 1611.

> On Tuesday [November 5] as a singular favor I spent the whole after-
> noon with their Majesties, the Princes, and the Princess. I found all
> the Lords and Ladies of the court assembled to congratulate their
> Majesties on this solemn anniversary of the day on which, six years
> ago, their lives were miraculously saved as from the Gunpowder Plot.
> ... The King and Prince tilted at the ring, and so did many gentlemen
> of quality. While the fête lasted, which was till sundown, I was at a
> window along with the Queen, who showed me great attention. (*SPV*,
> 12:238)

Shortly thereafter, the Venetian ambassador took his leave separately of king, queen, princes, and princess and departed. But that
evening the king (and presumably the royal family and the court)
watched *Winter's Tale*, and from the point of view of the actors (and
of the master of the revels) there was probably no more crucial
occasion for a fresh and well-executed play. Thus the fact that the
one selected by the company had been performed at the Globe seven
months previously is quite significant for establishing in what sense
a play would be "new" for the court. It would, in effect, be new to
the monarch—but also audience tested.

The second performance principle is that Shakespeare and his
fellows (or the master of the revels) avoided repeating plays before
the king over two consecutive years. *Winter's Tale* may again serve
as exemplar. Already shown to James in November 1611, it was
presented in the following year to Princess Elizabeth and the County
Palatine, but not to the king himself.

Both principles are important for any consideration of the dates
of Shakespeare's final comedies, because the greatest amount of
information about these plays comes from unusually abundant records of performance. These records, which serve as the basis of my
discussion, are summarized in Table I—a list of four occasions be-

tween 1611 and 1613 when titles of Shakespearean and other plays were recorded. It is useful, at the outset, to preface this table with several remarks. First, performances during the Christmas of 1612–13 were complicated by unusual matters of state. These winter holidays were to feature the marriage of Princess Elizabeth to the Elector Palatine, and in celebration of this occasion many plays were planned. But Henry Prince of Wales fell sick on October 27, 1612, and was regarded as gravely ill by November 1. The All Saints' festivities and the Gunpowder Plot anniversary (with their attendant play performances) were put off indefinitely (*SPV*, 12:464; *Chamberlain*, 1:384). To everyone's horror, the prince died on November 6. Public plays were suppressed in the city for five weeks and all celebration, reveling, and wedding festivities were postponed.[42] But King James seems to have felt compelled to maintain a truncated version of the Christmas holiday. He saw seven plays beginning with a children's company performance of *Cupid's Revenge* on New Year's Day (the queen saw no plays, staying in seclusion).[43]

The wedding, for obvious matters of state and with the County Palatine and his nobility waiting now in England unable to depart, simply had to be gone through with, despite this disaster. The nuptial festivities resumed at Shrovetide, the royal couple being married on Shrove Sunday (February 14). Plays were presented at court for several weeks in Lent by way of celebration, the paradox of Lent presumably illustrating the "dirge in marriage" and "mirth in funeral" motif invented by Hamlet's uncle for far different reasons: hence, in any event, the atypical playdates for 1613.

The apportioning of the play titles in Table I can be seen as an indication of the rising status of those who had hitherto been merely children in the royal family. By 1611, both Henry, prince of Wales, and his sister Elizabeth were obviously of an age to command plays themselves without the king being present. Thus an important differentia in this table are plays commanded by the king as opposed to other members of the royal family.

---

42. See *MSC*, 1.1:88. Plays were probably not again allowed until December 7, when the prince was buried, but playhouses may have remained closed until the court formally ended mourning on February 5 (*SPV*, 12:493).

43. Since the time was hardly an occasion of joy, these performances are an interesting indication of the role of plays at court as part of a formalized and ritualistic celebration probably expected of the monarch at this time of year rather than as examples of James's personal recreative enjoyment. For the record of plays this season, see *MSC*, 6:54–58.

In this connection it is important to echo David Cook (*MSC*, 6:xxv) on the subject of differing court payments. Reimbursement for professional dramatic activity at court since the early days of Queen Elizabeth was not exactly £10 per play. Rather, actors were habitually awarded £6.13.4 per play, a sum rendered less odd if understood as twenty nobles or ten marks (*MSC*, 6.13:210a, 35:84a). The monarch's own gratuity, or "reward," as it was called in court records, was in addition to this sum and early in Elizabeth's reign began to be standardized at £3.6.8 (five marks).[44] It is this reward that becomes a significant indication of the nature of the royal audience for a play; its presence always signals the attendance of the monarch at a performance.

This practice of royal rewards is of some importance to the early Stuart era, when as many as five royal persons might be concerned with court performances. Thus, when only Queen Anna or the royal offspring were in attendance, payment of plays—from crown funds at least—was not £10 apiece but only £6.13.4. That this distinction may even have been a privileged one may be gathered from the fact that all fifteen plays seen by Prince Charles, Princess Elizabeth, and the County Palatine at the wedding festivities, despite Elizabeth's momentary importance as the center of festivities for which rewards might not be inappropriate at all, were still paid only at this rate of £6.13.4 apiece because the king was not present. A warrant dated May 20, 1613, paying the King's Servants for fourteen plays before Prince Charles and the royal wedding couple was not, say, 14 x £10 for a total of £140 but only £93.6.8 (£6.13.4 per play). Thus the sum paid per play is an important indication of the king's attendance or absence. It is misleading to indicate simply that in a given year the King's Servants presented some seventeen plays at court; the audience must be specified, and in most cases James would have seen only a portion of the plays listed.

Because of the relative ubiquity of *Winter's Tale* in these records, it is possible to make some observations about the first performances of Shakespeare's final comedies. For example, it seems safe to suggest that neither *Winter's Tale* nor *Tempest* had been seen at court in 1610–11 (for which there is no record of play titles), and that both plays were first performed in public, *Winter's Tale* being seen by

---

44. For a Jacobean award of "twenty nobles for every play and by way of his Majesty's reward five marks" to Shakespeare's company in the holiday season of 1605–6, see *MSC*, 6:44.

Table I

Forman May 1611	Holidays 1611–12 Before king	Holidays 1612–13 Before king	Wedding 1613 king absent
Macbeth			
Cymbeline			
Winter's Tale	*Winter's Tale*		*Winter's Tale*
	Tempest		*Tempest*
	King and No King		*King and No King*
	Twins' Tragedy		*Twins' Tragedy*
	Nobleman		*Nobleman*
	*Maid's Tragedy**		*Maid's Tragedy**
		*Cardenio**	
		1 Henry IV	*1 Henry IV**
		Much Ado	*Much Ado*
		Captain	
		Alchemist	
		Bad Beginning	
			Othello
			Julius Caesar
			Knot of Fools
			*Philaster**
			Merry Devil of Edmonton

Source: For Forman's "Book of Plays," see Chambers, *William Shakespeare*, 2:337–341. For plays performed by the King's Servants during the 1611–12 and 1612–13 holidays and the 1613 wedding, see *MSC*, 6:55–57 and *MSC*, 13:47–49—the chamber and revels accounts, respectively.

*Asterisks refer to problematic plays as follows. *Maid's Tragedy* seems to be The Proud Mayds Tragedie that Revels Accounts and Chamber Accounts attribute to the Lady Elizabeth's players acting before the king on Shrove Tuesday; but according to the Chamber Accounts (titles not mentioned in Revels Accounts) it is the King's Servants who in the 1612–13 season offer *The Maid's Tragedy* to the wedding party (king absent). As to *1 Henry IV*, the Chamber Accounts list *Sir John Falstaff* as a play presented by the King's Servants before the wedding party; but at Christmas time, when the company performed plays before the king himself, the Chamber Accounts refer to one play as *The Hotspur*. It being the same season, I conclude that both titles refer to a revival of *1 Henry IV* first shown to the king and then to the wedding party. *Cardenio* was first shown before the king and then played before the ambassador from Savoy on June 8 (*MSC*, 6:55). It has been attributed to Shakespeare and Fletcher (Chambers, *William Shakespeare*, 1:539–542), but whether or not correctly so it falls into the pattern of a new play or new revival, being shown first to the king in 1612–13 and later to an ambassador in May. *Philaster* seems to have been played twice before the wedding party, listed the second time as *Love Lies Ableeding*.

Forman in spring 1611 and *Tempest* perhaps first appearing in spring or autumn 1611.

When then, was *Cymbeline* first performed? Table I suggests that the Palatine wedding created an unusual work situation for Shakespeare and his fellows. As many as fifteen performances were required of the company in addition to the six holiday plays presented before the king himself for the Christmas of 1612–13. The company seems to have dealt with the problem of supplying so many plays by repeating before the County Palatine all six productions from the holiday set of the year previous (1611–12). The Elector Palatine had not been in England then and thus had not seen any of the 1611–12 plays.

Shakespeare's company seems also to have felt free to repeat to the County Palatine three of the new plays or productions first shown before the king in the current (1612–13) season, including what one assumes were new revivals of *1 Henry IV* and *Much Ado about Nothing*.[45] But the wedding group did not see *Captain, Alchemist,* or *Bad Beginning;* when the actors were paid for performing before this lesser royalty, these new plays had yet to be shown to the king.[46] The performance dates are uncertain, but James (and the wedding group) may have seen the new plays during the wedding celebrations of early Lent.[47]

So great was the demand for wedding plays that Shakespeare and his company seem to have revived still other pieces. *Julius Caesar* and *Othello* appear on the lists, the latter already revived at the Globe in the spring of 1610. It is, then, in the context of these revivals that the use (or nonuse) of *Cymbeline* by the company at this time becomes significant.

Simon Forman saw *Cymbeline*, as well as *Macbeth*, at the Globe during the late spring of 1611. Yet *Cymbeline* does not appear in the 1611–12 holiday season at court; of the plays Forman recorded, only *Winter's Tale* appeared. Nor does *Cymbeline* appear at court in the following year, during the season of the Palatine-Elizabeth wedding. But again, *Winter's Tale*, and now *Tempest*, are repeated, if not for the king then for the wedding couple.[48] This persistent

45. Indeed the whole list of plays is interesting in its suggestion that revivals of old Shakespeare dramas resemble modern ways of working. The revivals were clearly new productions and thus treated as new plays—introduced into the repertory and used until stale.

46. By the same token, the Children of the Chapel presented *Cupid's Revenge* on January 1, 1613, to James, and only afterward, on January 9, to the wedding group.

47. Because the king saw *Cupid's Revenge* on January 1, one assumes that he was attempting to conduct business as usual despite Prince Henry's death (see *MSC*, 6:57). The king had not received ambassadors until perhaps a week after December 26 (*SPV*, 12:471–472.); then he probably saw plays in January until he left for Royston on the eleventh (*Chamberlain*, 1:407), returning on February 14, Shrove Sunday, for the wedding festivities.

48. The wedding couple also viewed such old Shakespearean plays as *Othello* and *Julius Caesar*, and non-Shakespearean repeats from the *Tempest* season such as Beau-

omission of *Cymbeline* from the court repertoire in favor of revivals suggests that it had already been shown at court, and rather recently, perhaps in the holiday season of 1610–11. Like *Pericles* (and *Macbeth*), also persistently absent from Table I, *Cymbeline* was too newly old to be viable even for the Princess Elizabeth's wedding; new because it was still in production at the Globe in the spring of 1611, but old in that it had already been seen by the court. Both of these "final comedies"—*Pericles* and *Cymbeline*—were then a first wave, *Winter's Tale* and *Tempest* being the second.[49]

A brief summary of this narrative for *Pericles, Cymbeline, Winter's Tale,* and *Tempest* is as follows. Several contemporary documents combine to suggest that *Pericles* was probably performed at the Globe in 1608, the same year as its register entry, during the break in plague from April through mid-July. After *Pericles,* the extended reclosing of the playhouses lasted approximately eighteen months, through January 1610. A hiatus in plague of five months, February through June, then allowed for the reopening of the theaters (excluding Lent and the possibility of two weeks in late May because of the assassination of Henry IV). Then plague dominated the summer and autumn of 1610. Simon Forman saw *Cymbeline* in spring 1611, but because the play does not appear with *Winter's Tale* and *Tempest* in the 1611–12 holiday list (new plays for the king), nor in the 1612–13 holiday list (which includes several repeats for the wedding couple), it had probably already been viewed by royal audiences. There is therefore a strong possibility that *Cymbeline* was presented at court in 1610–11 and tried out at the Globe during the February–June 1610 hiatus of the previous spring.

Forman saw *Winter's Tale* at the Globe in spring 1611, after the reopening of the theaters. *Winter's Tale* and *Tempest* both appear in the holiday list of plays to be shown before the king in 1611–12, suggesting that they were new plays that year. Forman did not view *Tempest* at the Globe, but it is possible that the play was performed

---

mont and Fletcher's *King and No King,* Tourneur's *Nobleman,* and the anonymous *Twins' Tragedy.* Sir George Buck referred to *King and No King* as "Allowed to be Acted in 1611," according to Sir Henry Herbert (see Chambers, *Elizabeth Stage,* 3:225); Tourneur's play was entered in the stationers' register February 15, 1612, along with *Twins' Tragedy.* Such entries are not, of course, chronologically definitive.

49. The same logic may apply to *Macbeth,* giving substance to a traditional dating of the play long before the Forman performance. The Scottish play does not appear in any of these holiday seasons and may paradoxically have been too recent to be revived.

there in the spring. In any event, the King's Servants and their leading dramatist responded with alacrity to the lifting of performance prohibitions. Even so, the "final comedies" are split, chronologically, in two equal parts separated by plague.

The last Stuart play by Shakespeare for which there is a contemporary record is *Henry VIII*, called new when it was first acted at the Globe in June 1613 but actually played several times previously.[50] Scholars have urged the appropriateness of the play to the wedding festivities of Elizabeth and Frederick, and some have pushed back the date of its first performance to February 1613, notwithstanding the play's absence from the holiday lists.[51]

Although the extent of Shakespeare's claim on *Henry VIII* is still a matter of vigorous debate.[52] the more relevant problem here is the possible gap that separates the play's first known performance from

50. Sir Henry Wotton to Sir Edmund Bacon on July 2: "The Kings Players had a new play called *All Is True* representing some principal pieces of the reign of Henry VIII." *Life and Letters of Sir Henry Wotton*, 2 vols., ed. Logan Pearsall Smith (London, 1907), 2.32. See also Maija Jansson Cole, "A New Account of the Burning of the Globe," *Shakespeare Quarterly* 32 (1981), 352.

51. For example, in his edition of the play, R. A. Foakes speculates that what Chambers calls Shakespeare's odd "reversion to the epic chronicle" at the end of his career may be attributed to the political appropriateness of a play celebrating Protestantism at Elizabeth's marriage and perhaps linking Elizabeth I with the princess. In dealing with its absence from the holiday lists, he says: "The play may not have been acted at court, or it may possibly have been that play which raised expectation on 16 February, but because of the greater attractions of a masque, was not performed." *King Henry VIII*, Arden edition., ed. R. A. Foakes (London: Methuen, 1966), pp. xxx-xxxiv.

52. Shakespeare's hand has also been urged in *Two Noble Kinsmen*, for both his and Fletcher's names appear on the title page of the 1634 quarto, which also refers to a performance at Blackfriars. The Shakespeare–Fletcher alliance on the quarto title page together with the frequently cited borrowing in III.v. from Beaumont's *Masque of the Inner Temple and Gray's Inn*, presented at Whitehall in February 1613, seem to many scholars to position this play at about the same time as *Henry VIII*, but there are some difficulties here. The Beaumont masque does not transmit the antimasque text for comparison to that presented in *Two Noble Kinsmen*, only stage directions that name at least three additional actors. Nor have commentators made it clear whether King James was so fond of the antimasque as to want to see it again incorporated in *Two Noble Kinsmen* (or vice versa) in the same year—if *Two Noble Kinsmen* was presented at court. In his 1970 edition of *Two Noble Kinsmen* (University of Nebraska Regents Series), Richard Proudfoot (p. xii) assigns the probable date of first performance to winter 1613–14 (at Blackfriars, the Globe being destroyed) and believes the earliest likely date to be summer 1613. Allusions in the text as a source for the date are, however, highly speculative, and the earliest text appeared in 1634. Proudfoot's summary of the authorship controversy is judicious, as is that of Waith in *Two Noble Kinsmen*, ed. E. M. Waith (Oxford: Clarendon Press, 1989), pp. 4–26.

the putative first performances of·*Winter's Tale* and *Tempest*—a plague-free gap in which one might expect Shakespeare to have increased his production. If it was indeed ready for the wedding, *Henry VIII* was probably written after the Christmas season of 1611–12, although not performed at court at that time. This possibility would lend credence to the argument that Shakespeare composed in spates of plays, for *Henry VIII* would then be close in time to *Winter's Tale* and *Tempest*.

Pursuing the matter of plays written in Shakespeare's final period, *Cardenio* has been attributed to Shakespeare. Whether or not he wrote it, the play was performed before King James during the Christmas season of 1612–13, and *Timon of Athens* and *Coriolanus* may also have filled this gap of Shakespeare's time between 1611 and 1613. But it is significant that neither of the latter two plays appears on the 1611–12 and 1612–13 holiday lists. One might thus assume that *Timon* and *Coriolanus*, if written toward the latter part of Shakespeare's career, were first performed *prior* to Christmas 1611 or *after* the wedding festivities in 1613, which at least allows for the possibility that they cluster with other of Shakespeare's plays. Under the circumstances, however, it is idle to pursue this possibility. At the same time, it may be equally presumptuous to assume a gap in Shakespeare's production at this time since there exist so few pieces with which to put together the puzzle of his last years as a professional dramatist.

The scarcity of documentary records, central to this problem, is compounded by the issue of Shakespeare's so-called retirement. There is some reason to think he may have been living in Stratford in 1611 (Shakespeare was 47),[53] and, if so, he would obviously have been less involved with the theater. But it is also known that he kept his ties with London during the next several years and invested in property in Blackfriars. Indeed, whatever Shakespearean plays were or were not performed between 1611 and 1613 at court and at the Blackfriars theater, the conflagration at the Globe is fiery witness to Shakespeare's continued presence—however erratic—on the Globe stage.

Finally, the impact of the fire on the King's Servants has not, I think, been sufficiently appreciated. It obviously called a halt to business, constituting another major economic setback compounded

---

53. Shakespeare's cousin Thomas Greene vacated New Place by May or June 1611; see Chambers, *William Shakespeare*, 2:96–99.

by the fact that company sharers had to pay out £1400 for building an entirely new theater.[54] And it would seem that the Blackfriars acquisition was not a financial solution even to the immediate problem, because in the aftermath of the disaster, a matter of great interest in the context of the company's concept of the use of Blackfriars, the company went on tour. They are to be found in Strafford, Folkestone, Oxford, and Shrewsbury during the latter part of 1613.[55] The Globe itself was not usable for a calendar year, reopening only on June 30, 1614. The major disruption occasioned by the fire may have been the career of William Shakespeare; one hears of no new Shakespearean productions after 1613.

V

I have suggested that Shakespeare did not write plays if he had no stage readily available for public performance, and that biographers might usefully construct a narrative about his development as a dramatist which waives imperative symmetries to deal with the disorders in the poet's environment. The conundrum of Shakespeare's final years in itself does nothing to dim the plausibility of this particular narrative merely because it is a conundrum. If it is a question whether Shakespeare's relationship to the theater changed after 1611, it is not necessary to retire him so as to resolve the problem. If it has come to be traditionally assumed that Shakespeare stopped writing plays several years before his death (which he presumably did not expect), it is still not known whether he stopped abruptly or tapered off, or indeed why he would want to do either.

In the present narrative, I offer no version of Shakespeare's last years, but I do argue that prior to 1611, the year of *Tempest*, his creative behavior shows a pattern. His professional activity was intimately tied to the incidence of plague and to other matters that influenced performance opportunities at court and at the Globe, and these factors affected his production of new plays—their rate and number. He wrote quickly and prolifically in the Stuart period when the theater was available to him. But because so many factors made the stage unavailable between 1603 and 1611, Shakespeare produced

54. See Herbert Berry, *Shakespeare's Playhouses* (New York: AMS Press, 1987), pp. 183–193.
55. Chambers, *Elizabethan Stage*, 2:217–218.

fewer plays than he might have. His creativity may, in fact, have been idle for long periods. Shakespeare's choice of common drama over poetry in effect had become for him a creative risk. In the Stuart period, the conditions of his profession almost overwhelmed what was otherwise an already astonishing production. That this statement may seem odd is perhaps the ultimate tribute to Shakespeare's creativity, which did not perish but merely falter.

It has, then, been my purpose to challenge traditional and privileged historical pictures of an early modern English playwright at work. Obviously, no recreation of the past is the only one possible, nor can any historical narrative achieve complete rediscovery. In the end, this study has approached the historical person, Shakespeare, the early modern English playwright, from a vantage point that does not insist on symmetry and considers appropriate to historical narrative some attention to the often chaotic interplay of societal forces with the psychic responses of members of that society. These phenomena emerge as primary elements challenging critics who wish to describe with new methods and in a new way those literary figures who tower against the traditions of Western culture.

The works of William Shakespeare reflect and echo the stresses and interimagistic refractions of his culture. As such, they will always be deeply fertile and endlessly challenging texts. In the difficult and still immature study of historical personality, however, the *author* of these texts is an equally significant and compelling phenomenon. His psychodynamics, his interaction with his culture, and the role of his creative life in the economy of his own psychological equilibrium are issues that must be dealt with, for they are difficult challenges to any biographical efforts. This book offers one approach to these challenges. It presents a structurist model of a historical Shakespeare attempting the incredible acts of his creations in a society where his art was not yet an intellectual tradition. It was an art that did not bloom and flourish naturally in the spring of an English cultural Renaissance, but an art that had to be wrested from and forged in the crucible of daunting social disruption, danger, and indifference.[56]

56. I use the term "structurist" here in the sense assumed by Christopher Lloyd in "Realism and Structurism in Historical Theory," *History and Theory* 28 (1989), 296–325, esp. 324.

Appendix 1

Playing in Lent: 1580–1613

Between 1580 and 1611 plays were probably forbidden by the authorities from Ash Wednesday to Easter. There are, however, signs that enforcement varied in intensity. This appendix presents, first, indications of the Lenten closing of playhouses during Shakespeare's professional lifetime, and, second, ambiguous texts and evidence of one instance in which Lent does not seem to have been observed at all. On the whole, the documents suggest a Lenten cessation of playing in the public playhouses during Shakespeare's Stuart career.

Evidence for Lenten Stoppage

1578: Ash Wednesday, February 12; Easter, March 30

Jan. 3, 1578. When it allowed a company of Italian actors to perform in London, the privy council of England specified that "one Dronsiano, an Italian, a comedian, and his company, may play within the city and the liberties of the same between this and the first week in Lent" (*Acts*, 10:144).

1579: Ash Wednesday, March 4; Easter, April 19

March 13, 1579. The privy council of England conveyed a command "to the Lord Mayor of London to take order within the City and in all other places within his jurisdiction that there be no players suffered to play during this time of Lent, until it be after the Easter week; and also to advertise their Lordships whose players they be, and in what places they have played since the beginning of this Lent, and that this order may be observed hereafter yearly in the Lent time." The same order was given to the justices of the peace in Middlesex (*Acts*, 11:73–74).

1584: Ash Wednesday, March 4; Easter, April 19
   Dec 1, 1583. Sir Francis Walsingham, secretary to the privy council of England, wrote the lord mayor of London, who seems to have been showing excessive enthusiasm in his restraint of plays: "To explain more plainly their pleasures herein to your lordship, who [the privy council] considering in their grave wisdoms that without frequent exercise of such plays as are to be presented before her Majesty, her servants cannot conveniently satisfy her recreation and their own duties, were therefore pleased to direct their letters unto you, that upon the week-days and work-days at convenient times your Lordship would give order that they might be licensed between this and Shrovetide to exercise their plays and interludes, Sundays only excepted, and such other days wherein sermons and lectures are commonly used" (*MSC*, 1.1:67).

1594: Ash Wednesday, February 13; Easter, March 31
   February 6, 1594. This was the last day the Earl of Sussex's Servants paid Philip Henslowe a portion of the playhouse revenues until April 1 (*Diary*, pp. 20–21). But since Sussex's Servants joined the Queen's Servants when playing resumed in April, the internal affairs of both companies may have caused the temporary stoppage which occurred well before Ash Wednesday.

1595: Ash Wednesday, March 5; Easter, April 20
   March 14, 1595. Henslowe's *Diary* (p.28) shows this as the last day of play until Easter Monday.

1596: Ash Wednesday, February 25; Easter, April 11
   February 27, 1596. Henslowe's *Diary* (p. 35) shows this to be the last day of play. Henslowe notes that February 22–23 were "Shrove Monday" and "shrof tewsday," and then he notes payments received for the rest of the week through February 27. After this, the notation of receipts breaks off until "ester mundey," April 12, when acting resumed.

1600: Ash Wednesday, February 6; Easter, March 23.
   June 22, 1600. The privy council issued the well-known edict

(inspired by complaints against the projected new playhouse by the Lord Admiral's Servants) that regulated the conditions of play performance in London. The second part of this order not often quoted: "Secondly, forasmuch as these stage-plays by the multitude of houses and company of players have been too frequent, not serving for recreation but inviting and calling the people daily from their trade and work to misspend their time, it is likewise ordered that the two several companies of players assigned unto the two houses allowed may play each of them in their several houses twice a week and no oftener, and especially that they shall refrain to play on the Sabbath Day, upon pain of imprisonment and further penalty, and that they shall forbear altogether in the time of Lent, and likewise at such time and times as any extraordinary sickness or infection of disease shall appear to be in or about the City" (*Acts*, 30:397).

1601: Ash Wednesday, February 25; Easter, April 12
March 11, 1601. The privy council sent a letter to the lord mayor of London "requiring him not to fail to take order the plays within the city and the liberties, especially at Paul's and in the Blackfriars, may be suppressed during this time of Lent" (*Acts*, 31:218).

December 31, 1601. Renewal of the edict noted for June 22, 1600 (*Acts*, 32:466–467).

1602: Ash Wednesday, February 17; Easter, April 4
March 12, 1602. Henslowe's *Diary*, two entries (p. 212): "Lent the 12th of March 1602 unto Thomas Blackwood when he rid into the country with his company to play: in ready money the sum of 10s"; "Lent unto John Lowen the 12 of March 1602 when he went into the country with the company to play: in ready money the sum of 5s." Blackwood and Lowen were then members of Worcester's Servants, who were playing in London.

1604: Ash Wednesday, February 22; Easter, April 8
April 9, 1604. Privy council order to the lord mayor of London: "Whereas the King's Majesty's Players have given . . . good service in their quality of playing, and for as much likewise as they are at all times to be employed in that service, whensoever they shall be commanded, we think it therefore fit, the time of Lent being now past, that your lordship do permit and suffer the three companies of players to the King, Queen, and Prince publicly to exercise their plays in their several and usual houses for that purpose."[1]

1. *Henslowe Papers*, ed. W. W. Greg (London: A. H. Bullen, 1907), p. 61.

1608: Ash Wednesday, February 10; Easter, March 27

October 1607–February 13, 1608. The College Revels of St. John's, Oxford, are recorded with allusions to unsuccessful arguments against the presentation of a tragedy at the college "because it was near Lent and consequently a season unfit for plays." Nevertheless, the tragedy, *Periander*, was presented; the Epilogue interrupts to remark: "But we forget time's limits; Now 'tis Lent."[2]

October 4, 1608. Entered on this date in the stationers' register was Thomas Middleton's *A Mad World My Masters*, published later in this year. E. K. Chambers notes the line in 1.1: "'Tis Lent in your cheeks; the flag's down."[3]

1609: Ash Wednesday, March 1; Easter, April 16

April 27, 1609. "Given to a company of players, my Lord Vaux's Men in reward not playing, because it was Lent & therefore not fitting: 10s."[4] This event did not occur in London.

1615: Ash Wednesday, February 22; Easter, April 9

March 29, 1615. A summons to members of the King's Servants, who "have presumed notwithstanding the commandment of the Lord Chamberlain signified unto them by the Master of the Revels to play this prohibited time of Lent. . . . Charge them . . . in the mean time that neither they, nor the rest of their Company presume to present any plays or interludes, as they will answer the contrary at their perils" (privy council register, *MSC*, 1.4/5:372).

From the "Character of a Common Player": "When adversities come, they come together: for Lent and Shrove Tuesday be not far asunder, then he is dejected daily and weekly."[5].

In a dialogue published in 1699, one of the speakers responds to the statement that all players have, by law, been traditionally suppressed in England. The other speaker, Truman, replies: "He that told you so strained a point of truth. I never met with any law wholly to suppress them. Sometimes indeed they have been prohibited for

---

2. *The Christmas Prince* ed. F. S. Boas (Oxford: *Malone Society* Reprints, 1907–), 47:228, 285.

3. E. K. Chambers, *The Elizabethan Stage*, 4 vols. (Oxford: Clarendon Press, 1923), 1:316, n. 1.

4. J. T. Murray, *English Dramatic Companies, 1558–1642*, 2 vols. (London: Russell & Russell, 1910), 2:255.

5. John Stephens, *Satirical Essays* (London, 1615), Sigs. R2ᵛ. R4.

a season, as in time of Lent, general mourning, or public calamities, or upon other occasions, when the government saw fit."[6]

Mixed Indications

1593: Ash Wednesday, February 28; Easter, April 15
April 12, 1593. The minutes of the London court of aldermen urges "the present [immediate] suppressing of bear-baiting, bowling alleys, and such like profane exercises," but a marginal gloss indicates "Elders of the Council. Bear-baiting and plays."[7] Possibly this was anticipatory of the end of Lent; otherwise the note seems to imply that playing has proceeded during Lent.

1597: Ash Wednesday, February 9; Easter, March 27
February 12, 1597. In his *Diary*, Philip Henslowe noted Shrove Monday and Shrove Tuesday and continued to record payments from players until the following Saturday, February 12. Payments then stopped until March 3, when Henslowe prefaced a new series of payments with "beginning in Lent / March 1597" (p. 56). Twelve payments were recorded between March 3 and March 22, the Tuesday before Easter, after which payments ceased until "Easter Monday" (March 28).

1599: Ash Wednesday, February 21; Easter, April 8
February 24, 1599. Since the previous July 29, Henslowe had begun receiving from the Lord Admiral's Servants proceeds from the galleries (*Diary*, pp. 94–95). These payments were made approximately once a week through February 24, 1599, the Saturday after Ash Wednesday. No subsequent payments are to be found until Monday, March 26 (two weeks before Easter), when the payments begin again weekly.

1600: Ash Wednesday, February 6; Easter, March 23
February 6, 1600. This day was Ash Wednesday. Two Henslowe entries are relevant: first, "Lent unto the company the 6 of February 1599 [1600] for to buy a drum when to go into the country"; second, entries beginning on February 13 have the marginal notation "since

---

6. For this and other references after 1615, see G. E. Bentley, "Lenten Performances in the Jacobean and Caroline Theaters," in *Essays on Shakespeare and Elizabethan Drama*, ed. Richard Hosley (Columbia: University of Missouri Press, 1962), pp. 351–359.
7. Chambers, *Elizabethan Stage*, 4:314.

we left playing" (*Diary*, pp. 130–131). Elsewhere in the *Diary*, Henslowe has recorded gallery receipts at weekly intervals from October 6, 1599 until February 10, 1600, after which there is a hiatus until March 9, six weeks before Easter. On March 9, Henslowe begins receiving payments again (p. 120).

Appendix 2

Plague Figures for Shakespeare's Stuart Period: 1603–1610

Basis of Statistics

Because the London playhouses were closed by order of either the city council or the privy council of England when the weekly bubonic plague deaths in London rose to a certain level, the basis for any discussions about theater closures are the death figures themselves. Where do these figures come from and how reliable are they? In this appendix I first discuss the classes of data and then list figures available from the accession of James to 1610—Shakespeare's Stuart period. An important proviso to be born in mind is that the figures below tabulate what were *thought* to be cases of plague in the period. Whether specific cases—or even epidemics—of the disease actually occurred, from the viewpoint of modern medicine, is not relevant here.[1]

Plague figures can be found in four classes of document variously applicable to different time periods. For the period January to December 1603, we have the *annual bill of mortality. Weekly bills of*

1. For this latter issue, consult J. F. D. Shrewsbury, *A History of Bubonic Plague in the British Isles* (Cambridge: Cambridge University Press, 1970), and *The Plague Reconsidered*, ed. Paul Slack (Local Population Studies with the S.S.R.C Cambridge Group for the History of Population and Social Structure: Matlock, Derbyshire, 1977), and Paul Slack, *The Impact of Plague in Tudor and Stuart England* (London: Routledge and Kegan Paul, 1985), pp. 69–78.

mortality are available for July 1603 to June 1604. For the period
July 1604 to December 1605, we must rely on a handful of briefs of
weekly bills of mortality and on various other *miscellaneous documents*. Briefs of weekly bills of mortality for the period January
1606 to December 1610 are substantially augmented by the records
of John Bell's *London Remembrancer*.

Weekly bills of mortality. The character and authenticity of these
records have been discussed by F. P. Wilson in his 1963 edition of
The Plague in Shakespeare's London.[2] This paperback reprint of the
original 1927 study provides an important supplement to Wilson's
original Appendix 1: a preface calling attention to the almost complete run of weekly bills of mortality for London from July 1603 to
June 1604 held by the Houghton and the British libraries. This series
of bills is supplemented, Wilson notes, by twenty-nine more weekly
London bills that have surfaced elsewhere.

There is no complete collection of weekly bills of mortality from
1603 to 1616. The earliest weekly bill surviving for this period is
the one issued on Thursday, July 21, 1603. We have the complete
weekly runs from then to April 12, 1604. Four additional weekly
bills (for May and June 1604) complete the totality of such bills
listed by Pantzer in the revised *Short Title Catalogue* for the period
of Shakespeare's life after June 21, 1604.[3]

There also survive for the same period five weekly briefs. These
are blank printed forms to be filled out every week in ink by the
clerk of the hall. They exist, filled out, for February 23, 1609, and
August 31, 1609 (*STC* 16743.4–16743.5), and, according to Wilson
(pp. 196–99), for November 12, 1607. I have found two more briefs,
for July 12, 1604, and March 29, 1605.

The weekly bills of mortality were compiled from Thursday to
Thursday. When some writer of the times discusses the weekly
plague death figure, the number of deaths noted thus usually derives
from the latest published report or bill following the Thursday com-
pilation. The bill itself might appear in print one or two days after
Thursday. Hence, a Wednesday (June 16) remark that "there were
nine deaths this week" refers to a figure compiled and reported no

2. F. P. Wilson, *The Plague in Shakespeare's London* (Oxford: Oxford University
Press, 1962), app. 1.
3. For all these weekly bills, see *STC* 16743.4–16743.11. In the British Library,
there is also a weekly bill in manuscript dated August 17, 1609; see Wilson, *Plague
in Shakespeare's London*, p. 192, n. 6.

later than the previous Thursday (June 10), a figure itself only tabulating the seven days preceding (June 3–9).

Annual bills of mortality. The only surviving example of this second class of record from Shakespeare's lifetime shows the total deaths for the year 1603 in London, summarized weekly and by parish. Annual bills may have been only occasional, for *STC* lists them only in 1603, 1625, and 1629–36 (*STC* 16739–16743). Such lists may have been compiled only for years of very widespread plague, such as 1603 and 1625.

Miscellaneous documents. Because the weekly and annual bills of mortality can tell us in sum only about 1603 and part of 1604, plague death figures for the remainder of 1604 and for 1605–1610 must be furnished by other documents. This third class is a mélange: various comments from diaries and letters of the period reporting the "plague bill." By the nature of the archival situation, such allusions can continue to surface indefinitely. The allusions are especially useful, lacking plague bills, in conjunction with Bell's *London Remembrancer*.

London Remembrancer. Most valuable are the statistics to be found in this 1665 London work by John Bell, a document sufficiently problematic to require discussion (Murray, Bentley, and others simply accept it; Wilson remained wary). For the years 1605–1610 there survive few weekly London bills of mortality, either because of the destruction of the parish clerk's hall in the great fire of London in 1666 or because John Graunt, a statistical historian, took the records home and never returned them. But plague death figures from these missing bills had already, seemingly, been preserved by John Bell, who was clerk to the company of parish clerks before the London fire of 1666.[4] Bell preserved the figures from the now-destroyed bills of mortality in his *London's Remembrancer*, and John Graunt, in his *Natural and Political Observations* (London, 1662), lists yearly plague death figures for 1605–10. Because all these figures survive only as part of an argument among seventeenth-century actuarial statisticians about the general history of mortality

4. A brief account of Bell may be found in *The Economic Writings of Sir William Petty*, 2 vols, ed. Charles Henry Hull (Cambridge: Cambridge University Press, 1899), 1:lxxx–lxxxi.

in London over the years, and because they are second-hand reports from vanished documents, the data remain suspect and require verification.

Since John Bell renders the fullest set of figures, I have used his. It is important that their accuracy be established, so I compare them here to plague death figures occasionally available among the other classes of documents which Bell had probably not seen—especially the Venetian state papers deposited in various locations in Italy. In each comparison I date and describe the source, tabulate the plague death figure mentioned, and then compare it with the figure for the same date listed by John Bell. Because the correspondence between these two bodies of figures proves extremely high, I conclude that Bell's plague death statistics are as accurate transcriptions of the relevant London records for the Shakespeare years as his own human errors in copying might allow. I suggest, therefore, that these figures may be used with some assurance in determining weekly plague death rates between 1605 and 1610 in London.

April 17, 1606. Dudley Carleton to John Chamberlain (*Carleton,* p. 78): "The sickness is well abated to twelve this last week." 12
Bell: 12

July 23, 1606. Zorzi Giustinian to doge of Venice (*SPV,* 10:384): "Deaths from plague are on the increase; last week there were 50; this week it is feared that the figure will be higher."   50
Bell: 50

July 31, 1606. Zorzi Giustinian to doge of Venice (*SPV,* 10:385): "The plague has carried off this week twenty more than it did last week."   ? + 20
Bell: July 24, 1606   46
        July 31, 1606   [46 + 20]   66

October 5, 1606. John Chamberlain to Dudley Carleton (*Chamberlain,* 1:234): "this last week's increase makes us all startle."
                                                                                      (increase)
Bell: September 25, 1606   87
        October 2, 1606   141
Compare the increase of 54 here with R. White's remark of October 4, 1606: "The sickness increased in London this week fifty-six."[5]

5. Edmund Lodge, *Illustrations of British History,* 3 vols. (London, 1838), 3:192.

October 16, 1606. The earl of Shrewsbury to the earl of Salisbury (*Hatfield*, 18:325): "You have done me a great favor to advertise me of the decrease of those that died of the plague the last week [in London]." (decrease)

Bell:	October 2, 1606	141
	October 9, 1606	106

July 15, 1608. John Chamberlain to Dudley Carleton (*Chamberlain*, 1:262): "Our bill is shrewdly risen this week to 102 whereof 26 of the plague." 26

Bell: 26

October 21, 1608. John Chamberlain to Dudley Carleton (*Chamberlain*, 1:264): "Our weekly bill little abated, not past 11 in all; the whole number [of burials in London] being 247; of the sickness, 124." 124

Bell: 124

October 28, 1608. John Chamberlain to Dudley Carleton (*Chamberlain*, 1:267): "Our bill was this week 240 in all; of the sickness, 102." 102

Bell: 102

November 11, 1608. John Chamberlain to Dudley Carleton: "Our bill is abated (thanks be to God) this week forty-seven in the whole summer."[6] 47

Bell:	buried of all causes (11/03)	236
	buried of all causes (11/10)	189
	difference	47

February 3, 1609. Marc Antonio Correre to doge of Venice (*SPV*, 11:232): "[The plague]...carries off about sixty a week."

ca. 60 per week

Bell: figures for three successive weeks ending in above date (January 19–February 2) 81, 67, 56

February 23, 1609. Brief (*STC* 16743.4): 46*
[*added incorrectly; should be 39]

Bell: 46

March 3, 1609. John Chamberlain to Dudley Carleton (*Cham-*

---

6. Thomas Birch, *The Court and Times of James I*, 2 vols. (London, 1849), 1:82.

berlain 1:288): "Our bill was this week 33 of the sickness, and 173
in all."   33
Bell: (in all: 173)   32

March 9, 1609. Marc Antonio Correre to doge of Venice (*SPV*,
11:246): "cold weather since the middle of February has diminished
deaths from plague by more than half."
Bell: February 9   90
        February 16   62
        March 9   43

April 21, 1609. Dudley Carleton to John Chamberlain (*Carleton*,
p. 111): "There died fewer by 7 of the plague this week than the
last."   ? − 7
Bell: April 13   93
        April 20   86
        difference   7

August 31, 1609. Brief (*STC* 16743.5):   177
Bell: 177

November 15, 1610. Marc Antonio Correre to doge of Venice (*SPV*,
12:80): "This week's bulletin gives only twenty-two deaths." 22
Bell: 22

December 3, 1610. Marc Antonio Correre to doge of Venice (*SPV*,
12:100): "The list of deaths this week does not exceed twelve in 121
parishes."   12
Bell: 12

Weekly Plague Figures

The death figures reported in the following tables refer to the previous seven days' span. For example, the 1603 listing for 4/21 gives
number of dead from plague reported on Thursday, April 21, 1603,
compiled from all parishes. Primary sources are listed with each
year date; exceptions to the primary sources are footnoted.

Report date	Plague deaths		Report date	Plague deaths
1603 (*STC* 16740.5)			3/15	10
4/7/03	4		3/22	17
4/14	4		3/29	16
4/21	8		4/5	17
4/28	10		4/12	20[a]
5/5	11		4/19	10[a]
5/12	18		4/26	19[a]
5/19	22		5/3	20[a]
5/26	32		5/10	20[a]
6/2	30		5/17	24[a]
6/9	43		5/24	34[a]
6/16	59		5/31	14
6/23	72		6/7	11
6/30	158		6/14	16
7/7	263		6/21	9
7/14	424		6/28	6[a]
7/21	917		7/5	10[a]
(out parish count			7/12	8[b]
included ff.)			7/19	13[a]
7/28	1,196		7/26	25[a]
8/4	1,932		8/2	
8/11	1,745		8/9	9[a]
8/18	2,713		8/16	13[a]
8/25	2,539		8/23	13[a]
9/1	3,035		8/30	20[a]
9/8	2,724		9/6	20[a]
9/15	2,818		9/13	16[a]
9/22	2,195		9/20	14[a]
9/29	1,732		9/27	15[a]
10/6	1,641		10/4	14[a]
10/13	1,146		10/11	
10/20	642		10/18	6 }
10/27	508		in "fortnight"[a]	
11/3	594			
11/10	442		1605	
11/17	251		3/29	21[a]
11/24	105		10/3	30[d]
12/1	102		10/10	22[a]
12/8	55		10/24	22[d]
12/15	96		12/26	5[e]
12/27	74		1606 (*London's Remembrancer*)	
1604 (*STC* 16743.10–11)			1/2	6
1/26	15		1/9	4
2/2	27		1/16	3
2/9	27		1/23	6
2/16	16		1/30	3
2/23	12		2/6	5
3/1	16		2/13	7
3/8	15		2/20	12

Report date	Plague deaths	Report date	Plague deaths
(Appendix cont.)		1/15	16
2/27	9	1/22	14
3/6	7	1/29	28
3/13	9	2/5	33
3/20	14	2/12	20
3/27	17	2/19	17
4/3	13	2/26	14
4/10	27	3/5	20
4/17	12	3/12	30
4/24	11	3/19	33
5/1	17	3/26	22
5/8	13	4/2	13
5/15	13	4/9	23
5/22	14	4/16	27
5/29	9	4/23	26
6/5	16	4/30	43
6/12	19	5/7	17
6/19	15	5/14	15
6/26	24	5/21	23
7/3	25	5/28	13
7/10	33	6/4	11
7/17	50	6/11	10
7/24	46	6/18	14
7/31	66	6/25	21
8/7	67	7/2	27
8/14	75	7/9	33
8/21	85	7/16	37
8/28	85	7/23	51
9/4	116	7/30	43
9/11	105	8/6	77
9/18	92	8/13	69
9/25	87	8/20	76
10/2	141	8/27	71
10/9	106	9/3	105
10/16	117	9/10	121
10/23	109	9/17	124
10/30	101	9/24	177
11/6	68	10/1	150
11/13	41	10/8	113
11/20	28	10/15	110
11/27	22	10/22	82
12/4	45	10/29	68
12/11	38	11/5	66
12/18	28	11/12	55[f]
12/25	38	11/19	46
		11/26	21
1607 (London's Remembrancer)		12/3	19
1/1	38	12/10	28
1/8	26	12/17	7

Report date	Plague deaths	Report date	Plague deaths
(Appendix *cont.*)		11/17	69
12/24	9	11/24	70
12/31	4	12/1	90
		12/8	68
1608 (*London's Remembrancer*)		12/15	75
1/7	3	12/22	53
1/14	4	12/29	39
1/21	3		
1/28	2	1609 (*London's Remembrancer*)	
2/4	4	1/5	56
2/11	0	1/12	60
2/18	6	1/19	81
2/25	1	1/26	67
3/3	7	2/2	56
3/10	3	2/9	90
3/17	2	2/16	62
3/24	5	2/23	46[g]
3/31	4	3/2	32
4/7	1	3/9	43
4/14	4	3/16	33
4/21	6	3/23	68
4/28	4	3/30	89
5/5	7	4/6	73
5/12	6	4/13	93
5/19	7	4/20	86
5/26	11	4/27	99
6/2	10	5/4	92
6/9	14	5/11	89
6/16	10	5/18	93
6/23	13	5/25	66
6/30	16	6/1	52
7/7	16	6/8	65
7/14	26	6/15	36
7/21	24	6/22	43
7/28	50	6/29	47
8/4	45	7/6	60
8/11	70	7/13	57
8/18	79	7/20	58
8/25	73	7/2	91
9/1	123	8/3	100
9/8	136	8/10	126
9/15	107	8/17	101[h]
9/22	143	8/24	150
9/29	147	8/31	177[g]
10/6	103	9/7	141
10/13	131	9/14	158
10/20	124	9/21	210
10/27	102	9/28	144
11/3	109	10/5	154
11/1	71	10/12	177

Report date	Plague deaths	Report date	Plague deaths
(Appendix *cont.*)		5/17	18
10/19	131	5/24	11
10/26	55	5/31	13
11/2	84	6/7	9
11/9	69	6/14	14
11/16	67	6/21	26
11/23	59	6/28	25
11/30	51	7/5	38
12/7	28	7/12	45
12/14	23	7/19	45
12/21	23	7/26	40
12/28	39	8/2	47
1610 (*London's Remembrancer*)		8/9	50
1/4	32	8/16	73
1/1	19	8/23	60
1/18	31	8/30	99
1/25	17	9/6	96
2/1	21	9/13	89
2/8	11	9/20	86
2/15	18	9/27	72
2/22	10	1/4	63
3/1	7	10/11	79
3/8	6	10/18	59
3/15	17	10/25	49
3/22	8	11/1	58
3/29	7	11/8	40
4/5	8	11/15	22
4/12	13	11/22	42
4/19	15	11/29	39
4/26	14	12/6	15
5/3	21	12/13	12
5/10	19	12/20	26

[a] *SPV*, 10.

[b] "Sackville MSS," in *Cranfield Papers*, 2 vols., ed. A. P. Newton (London, HMSO: 1940–66), 1:64.

[c] "Sackville MSS," 1:104. This plague bill lists 9 deaths in London, 9 deaths outside of London, and 3 in the outer liberties, but incorrectly totals "19." Bell also lists 19 here.

[d] *Chamberlain*, 1:209, 212.

[e] John Bell, *London's Remembrancer*.

[f] From a brief; see Wilson, *Plague in Shakespeare's London*, pp. 198–199.

[g] From briefs; *STC* 16743.4–5.

[h] Plague bill in manuscript; see Wilson, *Plague in Shakespeare's London*, p. 192, n. 6.

Appendix 3

The Playing Season at the London Theaters

Between 1590 and 1616, players who acted in London had frequently to resort to touring the provinces when conditions made it impossible for them to perform in the city. But it cannot therefore be assumed that the London players had a regular playing season—that, for example, they acted from September to June and then ordinarily broke for the summer; nor do theater historians such as E. K. Chambers make this assumption. Yet, because such a claim has been made by the editors of the Oxford Shakespeare, the matter is worth some discussion.[1] If players were accustomed to break in the summer months to tour, then they generated far more provincial records of performance than have been reported; otherwise, the players simply ceased acting in the summer—both being unlikely circumstances. At the same time, many scholars have not seemed to adopt a position on provincial touring consistent with the assumption that ordinarily the players did *not* break for the summer. Such scholars often allude to instances of provincial touring by London companies without indicating curiosity about the circumstances that brought the players to tour in the first place. A search ought to be made for the cause of every provincial tour identified in the activities of any London company. Otherwise, the unstated assumption is that provincial touring simply happened as the mood dictated.

1. Stanley Wells et al., *William Shakespeare: A Textual Companion* (Oxford: Clarendon Press, 1987), p. 90.

It is possible that generalizations (spoken or unspoken) on the subject of the drama year in the city have been based on evidence from the first decade of the seventeenth century, when plague often closed the playhouses in summer months, and these closings may have served to warp our notion of the normal structure of the dramatic year. Any argument for or against regular provincial tours must be drawn from some series of "normal" years embracing a span of Elizabethan and Stuart drama to the death of Shakespeare. The period that offers itself as possibly normal is that which began with the opening of the playhouses after the plague of 1592–93 and lasted for nine years until the death of Queen Elizabeth in 1603. Accordingly, I here offer a survey of this nine-year period.

Was provincial touring a regular, planned activity, or rather an ad hoc reaction to circumstances? If London actors indeed expected to play—when undisturbed by events—a twelve-month year, then evidence of a particular city company in the provinces implies not a regular tour (in summer or winter) but some situation in London making it difficult or impossible for players to carry on there. Why, for example, did the King's Servants play in New Romney on April 21, 1612, and the Queen's Servants in Lydd on April 23, one week after Easter (*MSC*, 7:111, 141. Fiscal year for Lydd is July 22; for Romney, Lady Day)? It is possible that the reference to the Queen's Servants is to another company by the same name if some of the men named in the patent for the Queen's Servants made up companies of their own for provincial playing as Chambers suggests.[2] However, the coincidence in time of the provincial activities of the King's and the Queen's Servants is also suggestive. Or, again, why, after the destruction of the Globe in June 1613, did the King's Servants go on provincial tour? One who holds the view that the city companies regularly toured in the summer, might aver that the company simply began its touring season early since there was no theater. On the other hand, there was indeed a theater, the Blackfriars playing place. Why was this not used for the remainder of 1613? Or do the "1612–1613" records for Folkestone, Oxford, Stafford, and Shrewsbury, where the company might have toured after the fire, refer to the autumn of 1612, since the reporting years of Folkstone, Oxford, and Stafford began in September, November, and October, respectively? If they do, what happened in London in 1612?

2. E. K. Chambers, *The Elizabethan Stage*, 4 vols. (Oxford: Clarendon Press, 1923), 2:234–235.

Available information on the subject of summer playing in London in the 1590s is summarized below, then followed by brief discussions of the problematic seasons in 1595, 1596, and 1597. Much of the material is inevitably drawn from Henslowe's *Diary* in the form of receipts for specific plays on specific days, indication of the same kind of theatrical borrowings, lendings, and other expenditures in London in summer as obtained in the nonsummer months (transactions often requiring or specifying the presence of players in London at the time), or other miscellaneous events. I arbitrarily end the summer on September 29, the Feast of St. Michael, although it should be remembered that the law term of Michaelmas invariably began on the octave of the feast—October 6—because Michaelmas itself absorbed lawyers and their clients, who had to remain in the country until they finished the accountings and rent collectings deadlined around this day in their own villages and towns.

June 3–September 30, 1594. Performances took place in London (*Diary*, pp. 21–24).

June 3–26, August 25–September, 1595. Performances took place in London (*Diary*, pp. 7, 9, 30. A rule across p. 30 separates June 26 from August 25). The Lord Admiral's Servants visited Bath and Maidstone.[3]

June 1–July 18, 1596. Performances took place in London (*Diary*, pp. 47–48). Hunsdon dies July 22. Play restraint from plague, July 22 *Acts*, 26:38). Lord Admiral's Players in Coventry presumably in the summer.[4] A letter from Thomas Nashe to William Cotton in September alludes to the lack of dramatic activity.[5]

June 1–July 28, 1597. Performances took place in London (*Diary*, pp. 58–60). Chamberlain's Servants in Faversham summer 1597 (*MSC*, 7:64). A restraint was occasioned by *Isle of Dogs* performance from August 10 (*Diary*, p. 240).

June 3-September 29, 1598. Performances took place in London (*Diary*, pp. 68–69, 94).

June 1–September 28, 1599. Performances took place in London (*Diary*, pp. 121–124).

3. Chambers, *Elizabethan Stage*, 2:141.
4. *Records of Early English Drama: Coventry*, ed. R. W. Ingram (Toronto: University of Toronto Press, 1981), pp. 344–346.
5. Chambers, *Elizabethan Stage*, 4:319.

June 3–September 12, 1600. Performances took place in London (*Diary*, pp. 135–137).

June 30–September 5, 1601. Performances took place in London (*Diary*, pp. 196–197). Thomas Downton (Admiral's), Robert Shaw (Admiral's), and Richard Jones (Admiral's) were in the city making among them eight to ten weekly payments of debts to Henslowe between June 30 and September 5.

June 12–September 10, 1602. Performances took place in London (*Diary*, pp. 202–205).

Three summers—1595, 1596, 1597—show breaks in London playing, consecutive years that might well encourage the notion of routine summer cessation from city playing. Indeed, references to the visits of city companies to provincial towns are recorded for two of these summers, the Lord Admiral's Servants being in Dunwich August 19–26, 1596 (*MSC*, 11:156 for 1595, 1596). Nevertheless, the summer breaks for these years had specific, unroutine causes.

In the summer of 1597, to move backward, the performance of *Isle of Dogs* seems to have occasioned a restraint from July 28 to October 11. Illustrative is an entry in Henslowe for August 6, 1597 (*Diary*, p. 239) in which Richard Jones is said to bind himself to play "in my house only known by the name of the Rose and in no other house about London public, and if restraint be granted, then to go for the time into the country and after to return again to London. If he break this *assumpsit*, then to forfeit unto me for the same a hundred marks." The assumption here is that summer acting is the rule, not the exception.

In the summer of 1596, a plague restraint little noticed by scholars was effected July 22; this restraint lasted at least through September (*Acts*, 26:38) and perhaps to October 27, when according to Henslowe the Admiral's Servants resumed play (*Diary*, p. 54).

The summer of 1595 seems the only marked exception to the rule that in normal times playing went on routinely in London during the summer; hitherto, no indications of play suppression have been observed for that year. Yet, as noted above, Henslowe seems to have indicated the end of play June 26, separating this date with a ruled line from August 25, when he again recorded receipts. In fact, this gap accords with the time of a serious civil disturbance, information about which has been generally unavailable in the expected sources; in addition to the loss of privy council records for the first decade of the 1600s, a volume of the acts of the privy council for the 1590s, a segment comprehending August 26, 1593–October 1595, has also long been missing (a later privy council appendix attempting to summarize this period does not cover the summer of 1595; (*Acts*, 25:vii-xii). But the *Remembrancia* (2:97) refer to disorders in Southwark on June 23, 1595 and a proclamation of July 4 bans unlawful assembly and imposes a curfew.[6] The sequence of events is best indicated by the following selection from Stow and Howes *Annals*. At that time, there was apparently a great scarcity of food in London, driving prices up.

Some apprentices and other young people about the city of London being pinched of their victuals more than they had been accustomed, took from the market-people in Southwark butter for their money, paying for the same but three pence the pound, whereas the owners would have had five pence. For the which disorder the said young men on the twenty-seven of June, were punished by whipping, setting on the pillory, and long imprisonment. . . . The 29 of June, being Sunday in the afternoon, a number of unruly youths on the Tower Hill, being blamed by the warders of Tower Street Ward, threw at them stones and drave them back into Tower Street, being heartened thereunto by sounding of a trumpet, but the trumpeter, having been a soldier, and many other of the company were taken by the sheriffs of London and sent to prison. About seven of the clock the same night Sir John Spencer, Lord Mayor, rode to the Tower Hill attended by his officers and others to see the Hill cleared of all tumultuous persons where, about the middle of the Hill, some warders of the Tower and lieutenants' men being there, told the mayor that the sword ought not in that place to be borne up, and therefore two or three of them catching hold of the sword, some bickering there was, and the sword-bearer with other[s] hurt and wounded; but the Lord Mayor, by his wise and discreet pacification, as also by proclamation in Her Majesty's name, in short time cleared the hill of all trouble, and rode back, the sword-bearer bearing up the sword before him.

The Queen's Majesty, being informed of these and sundry other disorders committed in and about her city of London by unlawful assemblies, and some attempting to rescue out of the hands of public officers such as had been lawfully arrested, whereby the peace had been violated and broken, Her Majesty, for reformation thereof, by proclamation dated the 4th of July, straitly charged all her officers, both in the city and places near adjoining in the counties of Middlesex, Kent, Surrey, and Essex, that had authority to preserve the peace and

to punish offenders, more diligently to the best of their powers see to
the suppression of all offenders against the peace, upon pain to be not
only removed from their offices, but to be also punished as persons
maintaining or comforting such offenders. And because the late unlawful assemblies and routes were compounded of sundry sorts of base
people, some apprentices and some others wandering idle persons of
condition, rogues and vagabonds ... her Majesty, for better direction
to her officers of justice and inquisition to be made, notified her pleasure to her Council to prescribe orders to be published and straightly
observed, and for the purpose a Provost Marshall with sufficient authority to apprehend all such as should not be readily reformed and
corrected by the ordinary officers of justice.... The orders prescribed
were the same day also by proclamation published. (*Annals*, sigs. 355ᵛ–
356).

On July 22, five of the unruly youths from Tower Hill were condemned of high treason and on July 24 were hanged, drawn, and
quartered on Tower Hill. It is very likely that these events closed
the playhouses during the summer. In fact, this disturbance may
have been the background for the September 13, 1595, petition by
the lord mayor and aldermen of London to the privy council (*MSC*,
1:76–78) to put down plays—for this petition complains that, since
the provost marshal's commission was revoked, the disorderly
young people had returned to the Theater and the Bankside. The
privy council's own response may possibly be seen when, according
to Stow, on the following February 5, 1596, "two marshals" were
appointed in the city of London "for the apprehending of vagrant
and other disordered persons" (*Annals*, sig. 356).

Appendix 4

The Difficulty of Dating Shakespeare's Plays through Internal Evidence

So-called internal evidence is constantly evinced in assessments such as that made in the New Arden *Coriolanus* regarding the date of this tragedy. Citing a metrical table in Chambers's *William Shakespeare*,[1] the New Arden editor observed: "Metrical tests, for what they are worth, agree on indicating a comparatively late date, between *Antony and Cleopatra* and *Pericles*. The incidence of feminine endings and pause-variations is comparable with that in *Cymbeline* and *The Tempest*."[2]

More recently, the editors of the Oxford Old Spelling Shakespeare argue for a date of *Macbeth* as follows: "The metrical test and the colloquialism-in-verse test both place *Macbeth* after *Lear* and *Timon* but before *Antony*. Oras's pause tests also place it after *Lear* but before *Antony....* The stylistic tests are also resolutely consistent in giving *Macbeth* priority over *Antony....* On the other hand it is possible that the stylistic figures for *Macbeth* are being slightly warped by the hand of an adapter; if so, *Macbeth* could be placed somewhat later."[3]

1. E. K. Chambers, *William Shakespeare*, 2 vols. (Oxford: Clarendon Press, 1931), 2:400.

2. *Coriolanus*, Arden edition, ed. Philip Brockbank (London: Methuen, 1976), p. 28.

3. Stanley Wells et al., *William Shakespeare: A Textual Companion* (Oxford: Clarendon Press, 1987), pp. 128–130.

Because the theoretical problems raised by such positivist methods as isolating and tabulating presumed Shakespearean stylistic traits are too far-reaching to elaborate on in this brief space, in this appendix I only note difficulties encountered via the resultant mathematics, problems that merely broach questions of consistency.[4]
Early in the century an influential body of such statistics was presented by E. K. Chambers in the appendices of *William Shakespeare*. Chambers discussed some of the problems inherent in such tables, but he went on to reproduce and correct a number of them, including Fleay's, and constructed several more himself. Here is one of these frequently used (Chambers) tables excerpted for twelve Shakespearean plays. (Chambers defined a split line of poetry as an iambic pentameter line divided among two or more speakers.)

	(1) Full lines (5 + 6 foot)	(2) Split	(3) Unsplit	(4) Unsplit with pauses	(5) (4) (4) as % of (3)
Julius Caesar	2,161 [2,261?]	129	2,132	437	20
Hamlet	2,290	194	2,096	552	26
Measure	1,460	148	1,312	398	30
Othello	2,362	268	2,094	694	33
King Lear	2,043	243	1,800	691	38
Macbeth	1,595	246	1,349	494	37
Antony	2,589	470	2,119	935	44
Coriolanus	2,413	394	2,019	749	37
Cymbeline	2,537	393	2,144	1,027	48
Winter's Tale	2,049	330	1,719	699	41
Tempest	1,378	227	1,151	481	42
Pericles	648	84	564	209	37

Explaining column (4) as representing full verse lines where occurs "the use of a period, semicolon, interrogation mark or exclamation mark in the *Eversley* text,"[5] Chambers then makes a formalist assumption: that, as he remarked elsewhere,[6] a significant metrical statistic for dating Shakespeare's plays is the frequency of such pause-broken full lines in any given Shakespearean play. Chambers

4. For discussion of frequency interpretation, see Richard W. Miller, *Fact and Method* (Princeton: Princeton University Press, 1987), chap. 6, "The New Positivism."
5. Chambers, *William Shakespeare*, 2:408.
6. Ibid., 1:255–269.

thus constructs his column (5) to express this pause-break-relative frequency. These figures (assuming their accuracy) then become *chronologically* significant items, and so their tabular arrangement is roughly chronological. Rising percentages indicate the passage of time in Shakespeare's life, and temporal arrangements of the plays become inevitable. The "metrical character" of *Antony and Cleopatra* "forbids" one, as Chambers put it, to place the Roman tragedy before *Macbeth* or *Lear;* in the series of numbers produced by Chambers's column (5), one derives the *numerical* order (1) *Macbeth* (37%), (2) *King Lear* (38%), and (3) *Antony* (44%). But if these ascending percentages are to be consistent chronological criteria, they must ultimately lead to an arrangement of Shakespeare's last ten plays that differs from what Chambers allows elsewhere. Column (5), by itself, for instance, generates merely by ascending percentages the following series:

1.	*Measure*	30%		6.	*King Lear*	38%
2.	*Othello*	33%		7.	*Winter's Tale*	41%
3.	*Coriolanus*	37%		8.	*Tempest*	42%
4.	*Pericles*	37%		9.	*Antony*	44%
5.	*Macbeth*	37%		10.	*Cymbeline*	48%

These figures fail to reflect, for instance, that *Antony and Cleopatra* appears in the same 1608 stationers' register entry as *Pericles* while *Tempest* is not reported until 1611, but Chambers himself does not adhere to their putative chronological indexing. Elsewhere (*William Shakespeare*, 1:479–480), writing of the date of *Coriolanus*, Chambers observes that "the evidence of style and meter puts *Coriolanus* between *Antony and Cleopatra* and *Pericles*."

On the other hand, it seems that, adopting Chambers's own criteria, one may reasonably pronounce one Shakespearean play as earlier than another if its percentage is as much as seven points *higher* than a following play: *Antony and Cleopatra* is supposed to be earlier than *Coriolanus*. Elsewhere, Chambers's chronological order stipulates the sequence *Cymbeline, Winter's Tale, Tempest*. But according to the metric percentage points, this reflects the sequence 48%, 41%, 42%. Similarly, Chambers's chronological order of *Antony and Cleopatra–Coriolanus–Pericles* reflects the sequence 44%, 37%, 37%.[7] But this logic would also make possible a sequence

7. Ibid., 1:484–489; 1:476–480, 518–528.

such as *Antony* (44%), *Lear* (38%), *Macbeth* (37%), since the ratios are similar.

The difficulty of the metrical approach may be further illustrated by evolving a different set of percentages, comparing column (2) of Chambers's table with column (1). One could ask what proportion of verse lines in a Shakespearean play are broken so as to be divided between speakers who are talking to each other (Chambers's split lines). This is to offer hypothetically that the practice in a writer to have his dramatic characters seem to interrupt or respond to each other by picking up the latter part of an iambic pentameter line initiated by the first speaker is a stylistic fact. Therefore, any tendency to do this increasingly—or decreasingly—might be stylistically, and perhaps even chronologically, significant, since such a tendency could perhaps change over time. The proposition is no less (or more) reasonable than others recently raised. So, to illustrate, *Julius Caesar*, which has 2,161 full lines (at least according to Chambers, who wrote before Spevack's concordances were produced), has 129 split lines, or 5.9%. Seeking comparable percentages for the Stuart dramas listed below by performing the same calculation, and assuming that ascending percentages represent a passage of time, one obtains:

1.	*Measure*	10%	6.	*Pericles*	15%
2.	*King Lear*	11%	7.	*Tempest*	16%
3.	*Othello*	11%	8.	*Winter's Tale*	16%
4.	*Cymbeline*	15%	9.	*Coriolanus*	16%
5.	*Macbeth*	15%	10.	*Antony*	18%

By this table, *Antony and Cleopatra* is Shakespeare's last play! But if numerical figures are based on verifiable phenomena, they do not necessarily indicate passage of time. I adverted to such difficulties in Chambers at length in an earlier work,[8] but the editors of the Oxford Old Spelling Shakespeare, discussing the problem of the canon and chronology of Shakespeare's plays a number of years later, subscribed to the validity of such language tests. Raising doubts about overdependence on statistics from the era of Chambers, they nevertheless opted for the greater reliability of "linguistic" evidence, especially colloquialisms. For these they presented a new table, in-

8. L. Barroll, "The Chronology of Shakespeare's Jacobean Plays and the Dating of *Antony and Cleopatra*," in *Essays on Shakespeare*, ed. Gordon Ross Smith (University Park: Pennsylvania State University Press, 1965).

dicating that such linguistic evidence could "give us a little more information about Shakespeare's style."[9] One column of that table is listed below; it indicates the ratio of colloquialisms to number of words in each of several Shakespearean plays. The ratio in each play was arrived at by the dubious practice of totaling a number of different elisions *deemed* colloquialisms and then dividing this total by the number of lines in the play. *Measure for Measure*, for example, contains a weighted total of 68 colloquialisms in 13,077 words (0.00520), expressed as the ratio 5.20; *Hamlet* has a weighted total of 11 colloquialisms in 21,433 words 0.000513), expressed as the ratio 5.18 [sic].

Troilus	1.84	*Pericles* (S)	4.95
Measure	5.20	*Coriolanus*	15.82
Othello	7.06	*Winter's Tale*	14.67
Timon (S)	8.57	*Cymbeline*	11.58
King Lear (Q)	5.62	*Tempest*	10.30
Macbeth	10.17	*Henry VIII* (S)	11.20
Antony	11.02	*Two Noble Kinsmen* (S)	15.80

Source: Adapted from Stanley Wells et al., *William Shakespeare: A Textual Companion* (Oxford: The Clarendon Press, 1987), p. 105, Table 9. Copyright 1987, by permission of the Oxford University Press.

Granting for the moment the dubious validity of these figures as descriptions of objectively definable phenomena (from a positivist viewpoint) and assuming that they have chronological significance, then the order of Shakespeare's Stuart plays according to ascending numbers in the list would be *Pericles, Measure for Measure, King Lear, Othello, Timon, Tempest, Macbeth, Antony and Cleopatra, Cymbeline, Winter's Tale, Henry VIII, Two Noble Kinsmen,* and *Coriolanus.* Yet *Othello* was first recorded in 1604, as was *Measure for Measure;* the table has both following *Pericles,* first recorded in 1608, and it has *Othello* following *King Lear,* too, first recorded in 1606.

Another test favored by Wells et al. is one for midline pauses—not their frequency but (per Oras) their relative distribution within the verse line. This "most reliable figure," the number of pauses to be found per 100 lines, Wells et al. use for Shakespeare's Stuart plays as listed below.[10]

9. Wells et al., *Shakespeare Companion,* pp. 93–109.
10. Ibid., p. 108.

Troilus	54.6	Pericles (S)	31.4
Measure	42.2	Coriolanus	29.8
Othello	49.2	Winter's Tale	31.2
Timon	39.1	Cymbeline	30.0
King Lear (QF)	39.1	Tempest	33.6
Macbeth	35.3	Henry VIII (S)	25.2
Antony	29.6	Two Noble Kinsmen	25.8

Source: Adapted from Stanley Wells et al., *William Shakespeare: A Textual Companion* (Oxford: The Clarendon Press, 1987), p. 108, Table 10. Copyright 1987, by permission of the Oxford University Press.

Here, because the passage of time is to be expressed by descending figures, the chronological order of plays would be *Othello, Measure for Measure, Timon, King Lear, Macbeth, Tempest, Pericles, Winter's Tale, Cymbeline, Coriolanus, Antony and Cleopatra, Two Noble Kinsmen,* and *Henry VIII.* According to this list, then, *Antony* and *Pericles,* twin entries in 1608, are separated by three plays, one of which (*Cymbeline*) was seen in 1611, both twins also being preceded by *Tempest,* recorded in the autumn of 1611.

With such figures as background, furthermore, Wells et al. offer the following chronological assessment of Q *Lear.* "Both the metrical test and the pause test" put *Lear* "between *Othello* and *Macbeth,* either just before or just after *Timon.*"[11] But the colloquialism test by the same editors (see above) seems to put both Q and F *Lear* before *Othello,* and several plays before *Macbeth.*

Again, discussing the date of *Coriolanus,* Wells et. al. note that "stylistic tests uniformly place the play after" Q *Lear, Macbeth,* and *Antony.*[12] But in the midline pause test *Antony* actually follows *Coriolanus*—by 0.2 points, to be sure, a trivial figure from one viewpoint. But that viewpoint is not a numerical one. In the colloquialism test, *Coriolanus* also follows *Winter's Tale, Cymbeline,* and *Tempest.*

Ultimately, any characteristics of a play that can be enumerated (including, say, the number of speaking parts) can be arranged in numerical order that in turn can be assigned to represent the forward or backward passage of time. Further, the mathematics of calculating percentages inevitably reveals percentages, but any table of such percentages, as a whole, is only as revelatory as what the items constituting the percentages themselves allow. If one uses tests whose results are expressed in numbers, quantitative measures must

11. Ibid., p. 128.
12. Ibid., p. 131.

be rigidly adhered to within the scientific universe created. Numbers are either significant or not significant in such discourse. They are significant, for example, when percentages describe the concentration of gas in a closed room necessary to bring on death in humans. If, on the other hand, numbers are used to be merely indicative or corroborative of other (nonenumerable) factors, then the panoply of numbers and percentages becomes a form of rhetoric, a dialectical mode of persuasion rather than a precise indication of phenomena. "Internal evidence" remains most often an oxymoron. To rely on it in calculating the chronology of dramatic texts is to evade important epistemological issues.

Appendix 5

The Date of *Coriolanus*

Most attempts to establish the date of *Coriolanus* by contemporary allusion refer to one of three events: a great freeze (a reference in *Coriolanus* to "the coal of fire upon the ice"), a dearth of corn (grain), or a rebellion. Such topical allusions in conjunction with metrical tests have served some editors to place *Coriolanus* in 1606.[1] Each of these topical allusions raises difficulties. Allusions to a great freeze are to be found during the span of Shakespeare's life from a time earlier than 1608. The Thames had been frozen over in 1564 and also in 1598; as John Stow describes December of that year: "Great frosts, the Thames nigh overfrozen at London bridge, but thawed about one week before Christmas, and began again to freeze on St. John's Day [Dec. 27], and a great snow on the 28th, so that the Thames was again nigh frozen as before, but on New Year's day it thawed" (*Annals*, sig. 3V3). The Thames froze again in December and January of 1607–8; thick ice kept the ship *Husband* from discharging cargo in London.[2] Thus ice allusions could date *Coriolanus* in 1598 or 1607–8.

The topic of food shortages and famine is rather more complicated.

1. See *Coriolanus*, Arden edition, ed. Philip Brockbank (London: Methuen, 1976), pp. 24–29, for a resumé of these matters.
2. Thomas Birch, *The Court and Times of James I*, 2 vols. (London, 1849), 1:70, and *SPV* 11:82.

London rioted as early as 1595 because of food shortages (see Appendix 3). In 1606, a suggested year of dearth, there are many indications that the English grain harvest was *abundant*. But several years later, Zorzi Giustinian wrote on June 22, 1608: "Such is the scarcity of provisions for some time past now that the King is in doubt whether he should make his usual Progress or not. The people of Northampton [one of the areas of the Midlands insurrection], which was the county destined for the Progress, have informed him of their inability to support the charges, and so will all the other counties that he might think of visiting. The want of grain is particularly felt, and although a large quantity has been imported from Danzig and those parts, which is most unusual, yet this country does not seem to feel the relief" (*SPV*, 11:146). Then, about a year later, on August 23, 1609, in the midst of the year-long London plague, Marc' Antonio Correre wrote: "The weather has been so bad lately that it has been impossible to gather the crop. The corn [grain] is suffering and rotting in the fields, just as the drought in the early season caused a poor hay-crop which is of great importance in this country, because of the number of animals fed on it. All this, joined to the looseness of the money market and the great concourse of people at Court, causes a dearth of everything" (*SPV*, 11:326).

Well beyond 1609, however, in 1611, an interesting event was noted. Between May 15 and May 30 it rained a little, "after a very long drought which has never been known before in this kingdom, which threatened famine and a notable rise in the price of bread." At that time, King James had already halted his cross-country progress as he thought that "in such a burnt up land he could not journey with all the court, save to the great damage of his subjects" (*SPV*, 12:161–162). And though it did rain a little, the growing season was now so far advanced that the benefit to the country was deemed slight and food shortages were expected to last into the following year, when drought would also be in Scotland where fires were raging on many of the forested hilltops (*SPV*, 12:410). Still, encouraged by this little rain, the king had almost decided to resume his progress, but on June 27 he again put it off for several months. Even then, he would cut the length of the progress to a third of its usual duration. As it was said of the situation, "the delay is caused by the recent drought, and the lack of all provisions in this year of penury. Corn, oats, and hay have doubled in prices" (*SPV*, 12:176). First mentioned on April 11, 1611, and then again on April 24, this 1610–11 event was a true drought. To attempt to date *Coriolanus* via topical allusion to drought is therefore seriously to consider the years 1610–11.

On the matter of political unrest, commentators emphasize the Midlands insurrections. These risings against enclosure in Northamptonshire and Leicestershire were known by June 3, 1607 (two days before Shakespeare's daughter was married in Stratford-upon-Avon). By June 16, the city guard in London had been reinforced and the uprising itself had been put down with some bloodshed. By June 25, the revolt was said to be a thing of the past as the king issued a commission to look into grievances. On June 28, a proclamation was published in London for the suppressing of riotous assemblies against enclosures and for the reformation of grievances. Plague, we recall, would set in by the following week. In August, the formal hearings on the enclosure riots began, plague still keeping the theaters closed. Finally, on August 6, the rebellion area was reported by the earl of Rutland to Cecil as "now very quiet" (*SPV*, 11:5–6, 8; *Hatfield*, 19:208, 8; *Annals*, sig. 4E6ᵛ). Thus, using this insurrection as indicator, one might place *Coriolanus* some time after June 1607, during the first interval that plague permitted playing. This would have been the Christmas holidays at court, 1607–8, and, for the Globe, the spring of 1608, after which the play could not be shown because of plague (except at court) for more than a year.

For all three classes of topical allusion, the possible dates of first performance range from the freezing of 1598 to the freezing of 1607–8 or 1608–9 to the Midlands insurrection of 1607 to the drought of 1609–11. One topical allusion thus undermines the persuasiveness of another, which once again throws the entire theory of topical allusions into doubt.

Because *Coriolanus* does not appear in the 1611–12 or 1612–13 lists of plays performed at court, it either lay in the future or was too recent for revival. Although nothing in the way of topical allusions can really pinpoint the date of the first performance of *Coriolanus*, many drought references, if accepted as allusions, are not inconsistent with the tragedy appearing contemporaneously with *Cymbeline* (see Chapter 5).

Index

Index entries for authors and editors of books cited are to first citations only.

Acting: prohibitions because of plague, 97–100, 103–104, 131, 145–146, 158, 179–186, 189–190; social status of, 8–12

Acting companies:
Children of the Chapel Royal, 35, 188, 204
Children of the King's Revels, 100
Children of Paul's, 47
Children of the Queen's Revels, 35, 188
Earl of Hertford's Servants, 47
King's (Lord Chamberlain's) Servants, in Bath, 107–109; and Blackfriars theater, 187–192; and court patronage, 23–49; and king of Denmark, 148–149; and Lenten suspension, 211–216; at Mortlake, 112–113; and plague rewards, 114, 180–183; and playing season, 227–232; and royal patent, 32–45; at Somerset House, 50–59; at Wilton, 59–69, 111–113
King's Servants (Scottish), 67
Prince's (Lord Admiral's) Servants, 34, 42, 44–48, 54–55, 109, 146, 155, 182, 213
Queen Anna's (Worcester's) Servants, 44–48, 109, 147, 158, 182
Queen Elizabeth's Servants, 212
Sussex's Servants, 212
Lord Vaux's Servants, 214

Actors: Italian, 211
Akrigg, G. P. V., 27
The Alchemist, 203
Alexander, Robert, 107
All Fool's, 124
All Saints' Day, 28, 119, 164, 186, 201
All Souls' Day, 28
Alleyn, Edward, 2, 34, 55, 110, 149
Alleyn, Joan, 110
Ambassadors to England, 50, 60, 63, 67, 143; Aremberg, Count of, 52–57, 64; Cavalli, Marin, 36; Constable of Castille, 49–50, 57, 122; Correre, M. A., 181–185; Duodo, Piero, 60–62; Giustinian, Zorzi, 192–193, 220; La Boderie, Antoine de, 188, 192–193; Molino, Nicolo, 30, 61–62, 114–127; Rosny, Marquis of, 50; Scaramelli,

Ambassadors to England (cont.)
   Girolamo Carlo, 103
Anna of Denmark, Queen of England,
   28, 36, 45–51, 53–56, 63, 113, 127–
   128, 148, 179–184, 202
Aremberg, Count of (Charles de Ligne),
   52–53, 57, 64
Arundel, 14th Earl of (Thomas How-
   ard), 179
Augustine, St., 137
Austria, Archduke of (Albert), 52

Bacon, Sir Edmund, 206
A Bad Beginning Maketh a Good End-
   ing, 203
Bald, R. C., 39
Balmford, James, 111
Barnes, Barnabe, 165–170
Barrett, W. P., 90
Barry, Lording, 100
Bath, 107–109, 111
Bean, J. M. W., 91
Bear-baiting, 2, 176, 215
Beaumont, Francis, 206; and John
   Fletcher, 191, 194
Bedford, Countess of (Lucy Harington
   Russell), 179
Bell, John, 219
Bentley, G. E., 46, 100, 215
Bergeron, D. M., 5, 35
Berry, Herbert, 9, 208
Biraben, Jean Noel, 76
Birch, Thomas, 160, 180, 181, 238
"Black Death." See Plague
Blackfriars, 187–190
Blackwood, Thomas, 213
Boas, F. S., 214
Bogdan, Stephen, 183
Bradley, E. T., 29
Bradley, L., 73
Bradwell, Stephen, 80
Brahe, Tycho: and eclipses, 156
Brandon, Samuel, 161–162
Braudel, F., 24
Bristol, 110
Brockbank, Philip, 233
Brooke, George, 64
Bruce, John, 101
Burbage, Cuthbert, 127, 175, 187–189
Burbage, James, 187
Burbage, Richard, 39–41, 112, 114, 126,
   127, 175, 187, 191
Bye Plot, 59, 63–64, 126

Calderwood, David, 36
The Captain, 202–204

Caraman, Philip, 138
Cardenio, 177, 203, 207
Carey, Sir Robert, 36
Carleton, Dudley, 27, 48, 120, 128, 144,
   179, 220–222
Carter, J., 107
Case, R. H., 160
Castile, Constable of. See Ambassadors
   to England
Cavalli, Marin. See Ambassadors to
   England
Cecil, Robert. See Salisbury, Earl of
Chabod, F., 24
Chaloner, Sir Thomas, 62
Chamberlain, Sir John, 30, 39, 72, 120,
   131, 140, 144, 147, 159, 160, 180,
   204, 220–222
Chambers, E. K., 11, 33
Chancellor, E. B., 52
Chapman, George, 38, 124
Charles, Duke of York, 202
Chester, 111
Christian IV, King of Denmark, 134,
   145, 169
The Christmas Prince, 214
Cipolla, C. M., 91
Clapham, Henoch, 96
Clark, William, 64–65
Clarkson, L., 85
Cleopatra, 160
Cobham, Henry Brooke, Baron, 36, 64,
   65, 126
Coke, Sir Edward, 138
Cole, M. J., 206
Condell, Henry, 38, 112
Cook, David, 202
Cope, Sir Walter, 126, 127, 171
Copley, Sir Anthony, 64
Correre, M. A. See Ambassadors to
   England
Cotton, William, 229
Court, royal: bed chamber at, 56;
   Christmas performances at, 47, 55,
   59, 68, 113,; 119–124, 155, 169, 180,
   199–207; Lord Chamberlain at, 33–
   34; privy chamber at, 56; revels at,
   27–28; at Wilton, 106
Coventry, 109, 190, 230
Craik, T. W., 9
Cranfill, L., 192
Creighton, C., 74
Cripplegate, 111
Cuddy, Neil, 33
Cunningham, Henry, 140–141
Cupid's Revenge, 201, 204

Daniel, Samuel, 160–165, 170, 193
Dasent, J. R., 17
Dee, John, 112
Dekker, Thomas: *Dead Term*, 174; *Meeting of Gallants*, 91; *Work for Armorers*, 176, 194
The Devil's Charter, 166–168
Dollimore, Jonathan, 3
Donne, John, 38
Douglas, Sir George, 183
Dover, 107, 146
Downton, Thomas, 230
Dronsiano (Italian actor), 211
Drought, in England, 240–242
Droysen, J. G., 6
Dunwich, 230
Duodo, Piero. *See* Ambassadors to England
Durham, 138; Bishopric of, 136
Durham House, 52

Easter, 104, 120, 133, 157
Eclipses, 135, 155–156
Edmonds, Sir Thomas, 113
Egerton, Sir Thomas, 32
Eisenstadt, S. N., 23
Elizabeth, Princess (of Bohemia), 200, 201–204
Elizabeth I, Queen of England, 26, 36, 101
England's Farewell, 148
Eros, 163
Erskine, Sir Thomas (Viscount Fenton), 36
Essex, Earl of (Robert Devereux), 34–37, 41
Evans, Henry, 188
Every Man in His Humor, 125
Every Man Out of His Humor, 125

Faversham, 229
Ferne, Sir John, 136
Ficino, Marsilio, 94
Fleay, F. G., 175, 191
Fletcher, John, 203; and Francis Beaumont, 191, 194
Fletcher, Lawrence, 37
Foakes, R. A., 102, 206
Folkestone, 208, 228
Forman, Simon, 144, 199–200, 203–205; and *Macbeth, Winter's Tale, Cymbeline*, 199
Foulis, Sir David, 144
Fraser, R., 2

Frederick V, Palatine of the Rhine, 200–202
Freehafer, John, 177
Furnivall, F. J., 49

Galloway, David, 107
Garnet, Henry, 133–141, 144; *Book of Equivocation*, 138; execution, 141; trial, 140–141, 147, 171
Garnier, Robert, 161–162
Garter, Order of: recipients, 40
Gawdy, Sir Philip, 38, 132
Giuseppi, M. S., 30
Giustinian, Zorzi. *See* Ambassadors to England
Globe Theatre. *See* Theaters
Goeurot, Jean, 76
Goldberg, J., 5
Gottfried, R. S., 73
Gorman, J. L., 6
Gower, John, 195
Gowry Plot: anniversary, 149
Graunt, John, 77
Green, M. A. E., 30
Greenblatt, Stephen, 3
Greene, Thomas (actor), 53, 54,
Greene, Thomas (Shakespeare's cousin), 207
Greenwich Palace, 51, 104, 148–149, 180
Greg, W. W., 39, 98
Grey of Wilton, Lord Thomas, 64–65
Grosart, A. B., 174
Gunpowder Plot, 132, 149, 185, 200
Guy, John, 24
Gwynn, Rice, 190

Hagley (Worcestershire), 132
Halliwell-Phillipps, J. O., 107, 187
Hampton Court, 26–27, 36, 41, 113–117, 147–148, 179–185
Harris, Marvin, 3
Harvey, Gabriel, 118
Hatcher, John, 91
Hay, Lady Honora Denny, 140
Heinemann, Margot, 5
Hemmings, John, 38, 54, 112, 181–183, 191
Henry, Prince of Wales, 25, 28, 45, 62, 136, 174, 201
Henry IV, King of France, 184
Henslowe, Philip, 2, 102–103, 149, 213–216, 229–230
Herring, Francis, 91, 111
Hertford, 131

Heywood, Thomas, 46–47
Hibbard, G. R., 107
Hillebrand, H. N., 175
Hirst, L. F., 84
History. *See* New Historicism
Hoeniger, F. D., 177
Hogsdon, 194
Holland, Aaron, 188
Holstein, Duke of, 127–128
Hosley, R., 215
How to Learn a Woman to Woo, 124
Howes, Edmund, 36
The Hotspur (1 Henry IV?), 203
Howard, J. E., 3
Howard of Waldon, Thomas, Lord. *See* Suffolk, Earl of.
Hughes, P. L., 34
Hull, C. H., 219
Hunsdon, 2d Lord (George Carey), 33, 34, 36
Hunsdon, 1st Lord (Henry Carey), 187
Hunt, R. W., 199
Husband (merchant ship), 240

Ingram, R. W., 109
Ipswich, 147
The Isle of Dogs, 229
Ivychurch, 147

Jack, R. D. S., 5
Jackson, W. A., 164
James I and VI, King of England and Scotland, 23, 25, 27–31, 35–39, 45, 51, 57–58, 63, 114, 146, 180, 185, 201; accession-day of, 108; on acting and actors, 25; on arts and letters, 58; assassination rumors, 139, 141–143; coronation of, 105; coronation procession of, 49; and lion club, 58; and rewards to players, 201; in Scotland, 101; on "solace," 29; and Venice, 60–61, 141–142. *See also* Greenwich; Hampton Court; Richmond; Whitehall
James, William (Dean of Durham Cathedral), 136–138
Jane Shore (Edward IV?), 194–195
Jeayes, I. H., 132
John of Bourdeaux, 79
Jones, H. V., 62
Jones, Inigo, 38
Jones, Richard, 230
Jonson, Ben, 19, 38, 125, 203

Kellway, Simon, 81
Kent, 107, 110
Kepler, Johannes: and eclipses, 156
Keysar, Robert, 174
A King and No King, 203
Kingsford, C. L., 34
Kingsland Road, 195
Kirkham, Edward, 175
The Knight of the Burning Pestle, 194
Knollys, Sir William, 37
The Knot of Fools, 203

La Boderie, Antoine de. *See* Ambassadors to England
LaCapra, Dominick, 26
Lady Day (March 25), 164
Lake, Sir Thomas, 58, 145, 185
Lamb, H. H., 190
Larkin, J. F., 34
Laughton, J. K., 34
Law, Ernest, 49, 53
Lee, Maurice, Jr., 27
Lee, Sir Sidney, 34
Leech, Clifford, 9
Leicester, 109
Lemon, Robert, 30
Lennox, 2d Duke of (Lodovic Stuart), 40–41
Lent, 129, 169, 201; playhouse closings in, 71, 209, 211–216
Le Roy Ladurie, E., 190
Lévi-Strauss, Claude, 6
Lewkenor, Sir Lewis, 51, 61
L'Isle, 1st Viscount (Robert Sidney), 180
Littleton, Humphrey, 133
Littleton, Stephen, 132
Lloyd, Christopher, 22, 209
Locus, definition of, 2
Lodge, Edmund, 30, 106, 160
Lodge, Thomas, 79
London
    Bartholomew Fair, 181, 185
    bear-baiting in, 174
    Bills of Mortality, 217
    Corporation of, 97
    Court of Aldermen, 215
    disturbance in (1595), 230
    freeze in, 159, 160, 178, 190, 193, 238
    Lord Mayor of, 145, 157, 231
    plague: 172–176, 217–226; "briefs" for, 218; deaths (1603–10), 217–226; orders in, 90–91, 97, 179, 230
    provost marshal, 146
    theater closings in, 14–15, 174
    theater playing season in, 227–232

Love Lies Ableeding (*Philaster*?), 203
Lydd, 228

McIlwain, C. H., 114
A Mad World My Masters, 214
Maidstone, 229
The Maid's Tragedy, 203
Main Plot, 59, 63. *See also* Bye Plot
Manningham, John, 36
Mar, Earl of (James Erskine), 145
Markham, Sir Griffin, 64–65
Mary, Princess, 130
Masque of the Inner Temple, 206
Mathew, David, 5
Meres, Francis, 12
The Merry Devil of Edmonton, 203
"Metrical tests," 119, 134, 227–239
Michaelmas term, 64, 106, 110, 131,
  146, 229
Middleton, Thomas, 24, 100, 214
Midlands insurrection: and *Coriolanus*,
  240–242
Miller, R. W., 18, 234
Moldavia, Pretender to (Stephen Bog-
  dan), 183
Molino, Nicolo. *See* Ambassadors to
  England
Montgomery, Earl of (Philip Herbert),
  38
Montrose, L. A., 3
Morris, C., 73
Mortlake, 112
Moseley, Humphrey, 177
Mountjoy, Christopher, 111
Muir, Kenneth, 140–141, 196
Mullett, C. F., 73
Munck, Levinus, 62, 106
Murray, D., 79
Murray, J. T., 107, 122

Nashe, Thomas, 229
Neville, Alexander, 164
Newce, Captain William: and "assassination plot," 142–143
Newgate Prison, 147
New Historicism: and biography, 1–6,
  20, 22; and the covering law, 18; and
  cultural poetics, 3–6; and historical
  writing, 1–20; and "internal evidence," 233–239; and the Renaissance "state," 23–24; and
  structuralism, 209; and "topical allusions," 134–150, 237
New Romney, 228
Newton, A. P., 56, 192

Nichols, John, 46
The Nobleman, 203
Northampton, Earl of (Henry Howard),
  35, 61, 140
Northamptonshire, 108, 111
Northumberland, 9th Earl of (Henry
  Percy), 101
Norwich, 110
Nosworthy, J. M., 133
Nottingham, Earl of (Charles Howard),
  35, 51, 115, 140
Nungezer, Edwin, 112

Oath of Allegiance (1606), 142
Old Street Road, 194
Orgel, Stephen, 35
Oxford, 59, 131, 208, 228

Pantzer, K., 218
Parliament: delayed, 158; prorogued,
  113, 114, 129–130
Paul, H. N., 148–149
Paul V, Pope, 141
Peck, L. L., 39
Pembroke, Countess of (Mary Sidney
  Herbert), 38, 163, 164
Pembroke, 3d Earl of (William Herbert),
  38–41, 106
Percy, Thomas, 137
Percy, Charles, 36
Periander, 214
Petty, Sir William, 219
Philaster, 203
Philip II of Spain, 50
Phillipps, Augustine, 54, 112
Pimlyco, 194–195
Pingré, A. G., 156
Plague
  bubonic, 77
  contagion theory of, 95
  cloth in, 85, 91
  epidemiology, 72–100; bacillus, 78,
    82; domestic animals, 92; fleas,
    84–85, 91, 186; rats, 85
  London authorities and, 90–91, 97
  "miasma" theory of, 93
  outbreaks of, 73–74, 103–104
  payments to King's Servants during,
    114, 181–183
  "pestilence" as, 80
  playhouse closings during, 97, 104,
    131, 144, 171, 179, 197
  pneumonic, 81–82
  Royal College of Physicians and, 91
  Scottish authorities and, 104, 146

Plague (*cont.*)
   septicemic, 78
   signs of ("tokens," etc.), 80
Plutarch of Chaeronea, 161–163
Pollard, William, 190
Pollitzer, R., 76
Pott, Thomas, 42
Preston, Amias, 42
Privy Council, 36, 71–72, 101, 115, 120,
   121, 211–213, 231–232; Privy Coun-
   cil Register (items destroyed), 72, 130
Proclamations, 34, 104, 105, 146, 181,
   232
*The Proud Maid's Tragedy. See The
   Maid's Tragedy*
Proudfoot, Richard, 206

Rabb, T. K., 4
Ralegh, Sir Walter, 36, 52, 65
Revels, Master of, 33
Rhamnus, 163
Richmond Palace, 112, 144
Rickert, R. T., 102
Ricoeur, Paul, 6
Roberts, James, 118
"Robin Goodefellow" (play), 120
Rochester, 148
Rosny, Marquis of (Maximilien de Be-
   thune). *See* Ambassadors to England
Rotberg, R. L., 4
Royal court. *See* Court, royal
Royston, 58, 127, 182, 184, 204
Rutland, Countess of (Elizabeth Sidney
   Manners), 39
Rutland, 5th Earl of (Roger Manners),
   37
Rye, W. B., 184

St. James's Day (1603), 105
St. Stephen's Day, 154, 164
Salisbury, 59, 106, 110
Salisbury, Earl of (Robert Cecil), 30, 34–
   36, 41, 102–104, 113, 126–128, 137,
   143, 185
Sawyer, Edmund, 30, 180
Scaramelli, Girolamo Carlo. *See* Am-
   bassadors to England
Schoenbaum, S., 2, 35
The Scornful Lady, 191
Shakespeare, William
   canon in 1604, 123–124
   and "common plays," 8–13
   court patronage of, 23–49
   dating of his plays, 117–119; *Antony*

and Cleopatra, 160–168; *Macbeth*,
   133–143; *Pericles*, 192–198
final comedies, 172–186
new historicism and, 1–20
New Place, 3, 207
plays: *All's Well that Ends Well*, 123,
   203; *Antony and Cleopatra*, 16, 21,
   80, 123, 135, 151–156, 170, 193–
   194, 233; *As You Like It*, 124; *The
   Comedy of Errors*, 125; *Coriolanus*,
   123, 177, 233–235, 238–243;
   Cymbeline, 123, 177, 198, 203,
   233; *Hamlet*, 118, 135, 138, 170;
   Henry IV, Part 1, 203; *Henry V*,
   125; *Henry VIII*, 123, 177, 206,
   237; *Julius Caesar*, 16, 203; *King
   Lear*, 21, 118–119, 123, 134–135,
   150–156, 178, 233; *Love's Labor's
   Lost*, 125; *Macbeth*, 16, 21, 119,
   123, 133–134, 147–151, 156, 170,
   203, 205, 233; *Measure for Measure*, 16, 21, 119–123, 171, 235;
   The Merchant of Venice, 125; *The
   Merry Wives of Windsor*, 125; *A
   Midsummer Night's Dream*, 120,
   124; *Much Ado about Nothing*,
   124, 203; *Othello*, 16, 21, 120, 123,
   171, 184, 194, 203, 235–238; *Pericles*, 118–119, 123, 156, 177, 192–
   195, 235; *The Tempest*, 123, 172,
   177, 202–203, 208, 233, 235–238;
   Timon of Athens, 123, 177, 207,
   233; *Troilus and Cressida*, 118–
   120, 124; *Twelfth Night*, 16, 118,
   124; *The Two Noble Kinsmen*
   (with John Fletcher), 123, 177, 206,
   237; *The Winter's Tale*, 123, 155,
   177, 192, 199–200, 202–203
Poems: *Lucrece*, 16–19, 37; *Sonnets*,
   12; *Venus and Adonis*, 16–19, 37
rate of composition, 169–171
"retirement," 207
"stylistic analyses" of, 227–239
Shaw, July, 133
Shaw, Robert, 230
Shaw, W. A., 34
Sheffield, Edmund, Baron, 136
Shrewsbury, 109, 228
Shrewsbury, 8th Earl of (Edward Tal-
   bot), 102
Shrewsbury, J. F. D., 73
Sidney, Sir Philip, 38, 41, 164
Sinfield, Alan, 5
Sir John Falstaff (*1 Henry IV*?), 203
Skeyne, Gilbert, 77

Slack, Paul, 73, 217
Slater, Martin, 188
Smith, G. R., 236
Smyth, A. H., 194
Somerset, Thomas, 36
Somerset House, 52
Sorlien, R. P., 36
Southampton, 3rd Earl of (Henry Wriothesley), 37–41, 126–128
Southwark, 111
The Spanish Maze, 125
Spencer, John (Lord Mayor of London), 231
Staffordshire, 133
Starkey, David, 33
Stationers' Register, 118
Stephens, John, 214
Stephens, Leslie, 34
Stopes, Charlotte C., 37, 127
Stow, John: and Edmund Howes, 36
Strafford, 207
Strand, 127
Streitberger, W. R., 124
Stuart, Arabella, 140, 183, 184
Suffolk, Countess of (Catherine Knyvett Howard), 140
Suffolk, Earl of (Thomas Howard, Lord Chamberlain), 33–34
Sugden, E. H., 194
Surrey, 111

Taylor, John, the Water Poet, 29
Tennenhouse, Leonard, 5
Theaters
  Blackfriars, 187–192
  conditions of, 17–20
  Fortune, 55, 122
  Globe, 33, 184, 190, 195; fire destroys, 207; Simon Forman at, 204–205
  Red Bull, 188
  Whitefriars, 190
Theobalds, 102, 179, 181
Tower Hill, 231–232

Tresham, Sir Thomas, 108
Twigg, Graham, 81
Twine, Thomas, 195
The Twins' Tragedy, 203

Van Zwanenberg, David, 93
Venice, 60, 141
Veyne, Paul, 6

Waith, E. M., 206
Wallace, C. W., 175
Walsingham, Audrey, 140
Walsingham, Sir Francis, 212
Watson, William, 64–65
Wells, Stanley, 18,
Westminster, 129, 131
Whitechapel, 103
Whitefriars, 189–190
Whitehall Palace, 54, 117, 124, 147, 151, 159, 181, 182
Wickham, G. W., 5
Wilbraham, Roger, 102
Wilkins, George, 195
Williams, Raymond, 3
Wilson, F. P., 71
Wilson, J. D., 199
Wilton, 32, 59, 60, 65, 110–114, 124
Winchester, 59, 64, 106, 110
Windet, John (printer), 164–165
Windsor, 148; castle, 146
Winter, Robert, 132
Winwood, Sir Ralph, 30, 140, 180
Wittgenstein, Ludwig, 7
Woodall, John, 80
Worcester, 4th Earl of (Edward Somerset), 45–47, 113, 115, 140
Wotton of Maherly, Edward, Lord, 50–51
Wotton, Sir Henry, 206
Wright, James, 190
Württemburg, Prince Lewis Frederick of, 184, 191
Wu Lien-Teh, 76

York, Archbishop of, 136

Library of Congress Cataloging-in-Publication Data

Barroll, J. Leeds (John Leeds), 1928–
    Politics, plague, and Shakespeare's theater: the Stuart years /
Leeds Barroll.
      p. cm.
    Includes bibliographical references and index.
    ISBN 0-8014-2479-8 (cloth)
    1. Shakespeare, William, 1564–1616—Stage history—To 1625.
    2. Shakespeare, William, 1564–1616—Political and social views.
    3. Theater—Social aspects—England—History—17th century.
    4. Plague—Social aspects—England—History—17th century.
    5. Political plays, English—History and criticism. 6. Great
Britain—Politics and government—1603–1625. I. Title.
PR3097.B37 1991
822 3'3—dc20   91-55238